A LONG JOURNEY

An Autobiography

by

Frieda Brewster

Grosvenor House
Publishing Limited

All rights reserved
Copyright © Frieda Brewster, 2025

The right of Frieda Brewster to be identified as the author of this work has been asserted in accordance with Section 78 of the Copyright, Designs and Patents Act 1988

The book cover is copyright to Frieda Brewster

This book is published by
Grosvenor House Publishing Ltd
Link House
140 The Broadway, Tolworth, Surrey, KT6 7HT.
www.grosvenorhousepublishing.co.uk

This book is sold subject to the conditions that it shall not, by way of trade or otherwise, be lent, resold, hired out or otherwise circulated without the author's or publisher's prior consent in any form of binding or cover other than that in which it is published and without a similar condition including this condition being imposed on the subsequent purchaser.

A CIP record for this book
is available from the British Library

Paperback ISBN 978-1-83615-157-9
Hardback ISBN 978-1-83615-158-6
eBook ISBN 978-1-83615-159-3

For Pat and Margaret

ACKNOWLEDGEMENTS

My thanks to Margaret Rose, Carol Burns, my colleagues at the City Literary Institute (London) and my family for their criticism and encouragement.

CONTENTS

INTRODUCTION		vii
THE NEW WORLD		1
1	Hunky Hill	1
2	Mama Versus the Priest	8
3	World War I – Russian Revolution	16
4	The Palmer Raids	27
5	Mount Troy School and Socialist Sunday School	32
6	Latimer and Allegheny High Schools	42
7	Sacco and Vanzetti	54
8	Anniversary of 'Radnicka Straza' (Workingmen's Guard)	58
9	Back to Beginnings – Sex, Love and Birth Control	66
10	The New Brick House	83
11	University – The Liberal Club	87
12	Gastonia Comes to Pittsburgh – A 'Keystone Cop's Arrest'	102
13	The Wall Street Crash – Marriage	110
14	New York – Lawrence Textile Strike	125
15	West Virginia Strike	137
16	Farewell to the States	148

THE OLD WORLD — 155

17 Arrival – Life Among the Miners — 155
18 Moscow – The Luxe Hotel – Depression — 163
19 Comintern Courier – Paris – Berlin – Vienna – Shanghai — 172
20 Goodbye to Moscow – Dublin — 210
21 King Street – 'Olga Petrova the Beautiful Spy' – Cable Street – Birth of my Son — 221
22 International Brigade — 228
23 A Welcome Visit — 235
24 War — 239
25 Manchester – Birth of my Daughter — 246
26 Back Home to Pittsburgh – The F.B.I. — 262
27 A New Life — 273
28 Horrifying Revelations – A Watershed — 279

EPILOGUE — 287

AFTERWORD — 293

APPENDIX — 300

LIBERAL CLUB PRESS CUTTINGS — 300

FAMILY PHOTOGRAPHS – CROATIA — 306

INTRODUCTION

In 1911, before the First World War, I was born in Pittsburgh in the United States to Yugoslav immigrant socialist parents. This book is the story of my life from the early days of this century through the turbulent years which were to change not only that country but the world.

It is not a 'history' as such but an attempt has been made to show the historical background of the events in which I took part. Rarely more than a spear-holder or foot-soldier, I was not one of the 'important' people in this socialist and later communist movement of which I write.

Because of my mother's influence and encouragement, unusual for those times, I strove, not always successfully, to become an 'independent' woman. This emerges again and again in my story.

My path led from Pittsburgh to New York, to London, to Moscow and as a courier for the Comintern to Paris and other European capitals but primarily Nazi Berlin. I was then sent to Chiang-Kai-Shek China at the time of the Long March.

Back in London I took part in the struggle against Mosley and worked in the International Brigade offices.

The rest of my days were less eventful. The trauma of 1956 when Stalin's crimes were revealed and the Hungarian uprising took place, was a turning point.

In the late sixties and early seventies I welcomed whole-heartedly the emergence of the feminist movement, an answer to what I had sought all my life. It helped me to realise that the socialist society in which I still believe must be democratic with people themselves taking the decisions which affect them. But I have also accepted that nowhere does my kind of socialism yet exist. How, when and in what shape it will emerge, if ever, lies in the future.

I agree with Ernst Fischer who writes in 'An Opposing Man' that "what is remembered is hardly ever a situation as a whole but rather my experience of it".

THE NEW WORLD

Chapter 1
Hunky Hill

Under the big black cross, I knelt beside Frances. Palms together, her eyes on the life sized Jesus, she prayed. I clasped my hands in a circle above my head and as I slowly lowered my arms said aloud, "Workers of the world unite. You have nothing to lose but your chains and the world to gain." She gave me a hard look as I imitated the signs she made in front of her face.

We rose, ran out of the cemetery entrance and down the hill. "Your prayer wasn't proper," she shouted. "But I said 'amen' like you." I yelled back.

"You should have talked to God. You'd know if you went to church."

"I was as good as you." Angrily I entered our front door, made straight for the kitchen.

"Why don't we go to the Catholic church in Millvale?" Mama, her black hair in a loose knot above her oval face with its high cheekbones and large brown eyes looked down at me.

"Frances?" she asked. I nodded, told her what had happened. "I did just like in Socialist Sunday School." Mama's eyes danced.

"And what did Frances say?" "Jesus Christ forgive her sins and fathers and sons. She made signs and I copied her."

"What did you say then?"

"In the name of the father, the mother, the son and the daughter."

Mama laughed aloud but at my look became serious. "You're so young, Frieda, and if I try to explain, will you understand?"

My mouth tightened; lips turned down to hold back the tears. I hated being the youngest. She recognised the signs, sat down in the old rocker and lifted me onto her lap.

"Most of our neighbours don't think like we do. They believe everything that happens is because that's how their God wants it. So even if it's a very bad thing ....

"Like when Mr Borich fell in the mixing machine and was drowned?" I interrupted.

She shuddered. "Something like that. They say it was God's will."

"And what do we say?"

"That the machine should have had a guard, a little fence around it so no one could fall in." Mama shook her head, "And his poor wife left with four small children."

I ignored that. "Why wasn't there a fence?"

Because Mr Borich's boss didn't want to spend the money on it."

"So, it was his fault, not like Frances believes. I'm going to tell her why we don't go to the Catholic Church." I slipped down and ran to the door.

My startled mother began to protest, "Frances is older ...." then laughed as I turned and waved.

This was the beginning of my attempt to understand why, even though on the Hill we were all children of Croatian immigrant parents, my family was different.

When I read Golda Meir's autobiography many years later, I realised it had been easier for her to know why she was different. She writes:

> 'I must have been very young, maybe only three and a half or four. We lived on the first floor of a house in Kiev and I can still quite distinctly remember hearing about a pogrom that was to descend on us .... I knew it was something to do with being Jewish ....
>
> I can remember how I stood on the stairs that led to the second floor where another Jewish family lived, holding hands with their little daughter and watching our fathers trying to barricade the entrance with wooden boards ......

Above all, I remember being aware that this was happening to me because I was Jewish, which made me different from most of the other children in the yard.'

To be in a family dominated by socialist ideals was harder for a small child to comprehend or to explain.

We arrived on Hunky Hill, Mount Troy in the early summer of 1916. For more than ten years my parents had lived in rented rooms on the north side of Pittsburgh, earlier known as Allegheny. Cramped, squalid though they were, it was in such places that my mother gave birth to three children, cooked, cleaned, washed for the family, my Uncle Peter and socialist comrades who were our boarders.

Mama longed for a house with a garden away from the grime and noise of the city. Into a blue jar went every penny, nickel and dime she could spare. When the winter weather stopped papa's work this money had to be used but then she'd start again.

The family and boarders moved several times. When East Ohio Street, where I was born, became very crowded we left for

*Kindergarten photograph age four or five:
Me second row from front, seventh from left*

similar rooms in Spring Garden. In this narrow valley mist and fog lingered. The sun shone weakly through haze created by the smoke of my factory chimneys.

My parents talked again of buying a house outside the city because the war in Europe brought steady work and better earnings for my father. But it was Topol, one of our boarders since before my birth and a valued friend, who hastened the move.

One day at noon he walked into the kitchen where mama was ironing. "You're not at work? What's wrong?"

"Sit down Maria. There is something you must know." My mother told us how anxious she'd been as she waited.

"The Doctor tells me I have tuberculosis. I must go to a warmer climate. You must keep the children away from me till I leave."

"I couldn't speak, I just held his hand. He was an educated man and I had learned so much from him. I remember how sad his face was as he looked down at me. Within three days he had left."

Worried about us, especially me who had been his favourite, mama insisted we leave the gloomy valley. Her children needed fresh air and sunshine. Papa had to be convinced for it meant a large mortgage but, in the end, they bought an old farmhouse above Millvale. With a happy face she told us one morning, "We are moving into our own house, high up on a hill away from street cars, sidewalks and smoke."

☙

Bubbling with excitement, on moving day we ran up and down the stairs with boxes, brooms, buckets, beds, chairs, tables, the old sofa, everything was loaded onto the wagon. Wedged between mama and the moving man, I clung tight as we went from wide, straight streets uphill after hill. The two huge horses strained, hoofs rang, sparks flew on the cobbled surface. Finally, from a cinder road the wagon turned up the last hill, a wide unmade track of ruts and furrows.

We stopped at the top on a level strip of land, not very long and no wider than a broad street. The sweating horses rested; heads bent. Tony daringly jumped from the back of the wagon.

The Truhar Farmhouse on Mount Troy, 1920

"We're on a mountain," he cried.

The moving man laughed as he climbed off, lifted me down and helped my mother descend.

"Thank you so much, it was very hard for you and the horses. You are a very good driver."

He seemed pleased. "This is Pittsburgh, lady, all up and down. But that last bit sure was rough. Is there water for the horses?"

Mama found a bucket, called Tony. "That little shed has a well with a pump." She handed him a key. The horses drank deep.

"Our new home," mama said. I looked wide-eyed at what seemed a massive building, an old white clapboard farmhouse with many windows, planted firmly on flat land to the left of the uphill road. Beyond it was a broad path which wound up to a cemetery at whose entrance, clearly visible, stood a large black, wooden cross.

To the right four smaller houses were in a row. Behind them the ground fell steeply to a valley called Millvale.

Sandwiches and tomatoes from a white shoe box were handed around, most to the moving man. Then the real work began. Tony was a big help as mama and the young man carried furniture into the house. Paula carried chairs and even I managed brooms and stray saucepans.

At last everything was inside. Mama paid the driver and gave him an extra dollar. "He was a good man, didn't grumble." We waved as the wagon rolled down the track.

Mama had explained why papa couldn't be with us, "He'd have lost a day's pay."

In the house she sat down. "I'll rest a bit. Go and explore but be careful."

We ran through large rooms, up and down stairs, then out of the back door. A tall linden tree stood in the spacious yard. It was in leaf, decorated with clusters of yellow flowers. Beyond loomed a barn bigger than the house itself. Inside we discovered two haylofts. The privy, a three and a half-holer, tacked onto the side of the barn made us laugh.

Mama called us. "Come, I'll show you the garden." Across the lane which led to the cemetery a large rectangular space sloped gently downwards. There were pear and apple trees, fruit bushes, roses in the overgrown garden with its large areas of knee-high grass.

"Can we go in there?" Mama nodded, laughed as she watched us run through this green fragrance, call out at each new discovery.

Yet we were not isolated in some rural haven. Below the far side, where the other houses stood, ran the Allegheny River, with steel mills on the opposite banks. Slightly off shore was Walker's Island, the garbage dump for this part of Pittsburgh, while huddled in the valley were the factories where some of the men and young girls from the Hill worked. At times when the wind was in our direction, we got the stench of garbage and tanneries as well as factory smoke.

But there was magic too for at night when flames and sparks rose from open hearth furnaces they were reflected in the softly flowing water and conjured up images from which tales could be woven. Only twenty yards away, on our side, we found fields, wild flowers, birds and butterflies. Behind our barn wooded hills stretched down towards Millvale opening a magnificent view across the valley.

*Family outside House on the Hill: Maria Truhar (my mother)
back row right, Sebastian Truhar (my father)
second row second left, me next to my father,
Tony (my brother) bottom right
Paula (my sister) bottom left.*

So we started a new life where we could play in safety and sunshine. Behind the content of my parents was also worry and the need for a regular income. My father now got a job at Heppenstalls, a steel mill in Lawrenceville, where his pay did not depend on the weather. He went into furnaces while they were still hot to replace the bricks, suffocating work which took its toll.

Chapter 2

Mama Versus the Priest

"Out of my house." Through the open front door my mother's voice reached the ears of those in the funeral procession which had halted just outside. The children of the Hill, ever ready to follow the hearse, stood and waited. I left them and ran outside.

"But I am the priest," roared the grey haired man who stood in our hall, his mud spattered cloak sweeping the floor.

If you hadn't burst in as though you owned the place, if you'd asked, I might have listened and let you in. But no priest orders me around."

"I always change into my vestments here. Out of my way woman." He pushed mama roughly aside, strode into our dining room followed by a boy carrying a satchel.

I'd never seen mama so angry. She rushed into the kitchen, returned with the large broom and threw open the dining room door. "Now get out or I'll sweep you out."

The amazed priest stood speechless but as she advanced the boy snapped shut the case and made his escape. Snatching up his cloak the priest followed. "You're a wicked woman and you'll burn in hell for this."

Mama put down the broom and stood on the porch, hands on hips. I stood beside her, imitated her posture.

"There's plenty of hell in this world, who don't you do something about that."

"And she actually laughed" was repeated in awed voices again and again as the news spread like wildfire on the Hill. The devout Mr Broz crossed himself each time he saw one of our family.

My brother and sister didn't care as their friends weren't from the Hill. But my gang, all near my age, deserted me. Silence gave way to abuse as I defended my mother, declared "I don't believe in God either and I wasn't even christened." That remark cost me dear. Though life soon returned to normal, if ever afterwards I quarrelled with one of them they retaliated by calling me 'unchristened calf' as though that settled everything.

It wasn't till many years later when mama spoke of the old days and this episode was mentioned that I asked, "Tell me, why did you do that?"

"Well Frieda we were once Catholics just like the others on the Hill. Papa even served at the altar. The priests were always harsh. But we were devout, went to mass. It was your Uncle Peter who changed us. He lived with us in those early days, worked in a barber shop patronised mainly by Croatian immigrants. One evening at supper he spoke of a strange incident that morning.

'Dusan was in my chair and I asked after his friend Bozo. He told me I might not see him again as a machine had taken off his hand. We all exclaimed then a quiet voice from a new customer asked – Did your friend get compensation? – Dusan didn't think so, the sister was looking after his friend.

The quiet man said – "We're getting used to it, aren't we? Nearly every day there's an accident. And they don't give a damn about us, do they? If one of us gets hurt or killed they just put another in his place. Plenty more of us keep coming from the old country.

Talking stopped, everyone was listening. Then one shouted – What the hell can we do about it? We have to work. – The newcomer said – Nothing on our own but we could get together to help each other. We've started a club and you'd all be welcome. – He gave each of us one of these.'

Peter handed the paper to me. Papa read it out – Bratsvo, brotherhood and friendship. – But nothing more was said.

Two months later Peter told us he had joined this club. Some of the members had been socialists in the old country and were full of new, wonderful ideas about how life could be made better for people like us. I didn't pay much attention; not till he told us he had left the church."

Mama paused, laughed. "Funny to remember now how I reacted. I crossed myself and prayed – Holy Mother of God, please forgive – then turned on him.

"What's happened to you – how can you – what will our mother say?"

He answered that he was a socialist now, had learned a lot from Bratsvo. 'Socialists want a different kind of world in which all can share in the good things of life.' It sounded as though he was reading from a book.

Then his face lit up and words poured from him.

'Don't be angry, Maria. You and I have had a hard life. We worked all day and often went to bed hungry. You were still a child when you went off to service. And now you wash, iron, cook, scrub, look after boarders as well as us just so you can live.'

He flung out both arms. 'And this room. Did you never ask yourself when you worked in those splendid rich houses why they lived so well and why our homes were bare?'

I looked around the large kitchen. A sink, a stove, a table, upright wooden chairs, the shabby couch which at night became Peter's bed. 'It's God's Will'.

Frightened, I drew back at the look he gave me. 'That answer was why I left the church. A socialist cannot believe that. We are not going to accept this world as it is, we are going to change it.' He spoke with such conviction, then smiled at me, and gave me some pamphlets. 'Read these, they explain better than I can. You're an intelligent woman, think of yourself, don't just accept what the priest says.'

It was hearsay. Again I crossed myself yet reached for the booklets. As you know papa always interrupts but this time he listened quietly, told Peter he'd go with him to the next meeting.

At confession I told the priest about Peter and asked for his guidance. His voice was stern. 'Your brother is a bad man. You must expel him from your household. The socialists are evil, they stir up the people and do the devil's work. We all have our place. It is his will. Before you come again see to it that his wicket man is no longer in your home.' I bowed my head to receive absolution.

For days I pondered the priest's answer. I thought back to the time when I was a skivvy in that wonderful Vinkovci house in the old country. How different it was from our one-room cottage with its earthen floor to which I returned once a month, helped my mother in the fields. One day as I weeded, I spoke aloud – Why if there's a God, has he made us so poor and those in Vinkovci so rich. – As the words were uttered I fell to my knees, crossed myself, repeated over and over again – Father, forgive me for doubting you. – Yet even in those very early years I often felt humiliated and deep down could not understand why God had so ordered the world.

One evening after work Peter came in, his arms full of roses. 'Only fifteen cents and I knew you'd like them, Maria. The woman badly needed the money.'

Mama smiled, "You know, Frieda, at that time we always lived in rooms, not a blade of grass, not a bloom anywhere near us. I was so happy I kissed Peter. Not since my wedding day had I been given flowers.

Well, that decided me. How could such a man be wicked as the priest said. He was kind, gentle, had helped me and papa in our hardest days. The priest was wrong about him and so could be wrong about other things. This knowing one's place and it being God's will. I'd had no childhood. I wanted something better for any children I might have. Papa had long since become a member of Bratsvo and now I too joined.

Later, before you were born, we also became founder members of the Croatian Socialist Party in the States. This happened in 1907, the same year as our paper Radnicka Straza (Workingman's Guard) appeared. But it took me two more years to free myself from religion."

Mama used that phrase often when she talked of the early days. The belief that socialism and religion were incompatible was held by many before World War I.

The socialists enthusiastically welcomed the new ideas proposed in this era of ferment. Darwinism, with its implied attack on fundamentalist religion, was attractive to these young Croatians who saw it as an exciting alternative to a faith in 'God's will' which they believed so hampered struggles for change and improvement. They were also aware of the power of the church when priests, primarily Catholic, entered the industrial battlefields on the side of the employers.

For example, during the 1902 miners' strike, in the Church of the Annunciation of Shenandoah, Pennsylvania, Father Filey told the miners:

"You should have the manhood to go back to work and defy the United Mineworkers of America. It is a bloodstained organisation and will be bloodstained until it ceases to exist. It was formed to promote crime and protect criminals. Everybody was happy and contented here until Mitchell and Fahy came."

Mitchell and Fahy were union organisers.

What would the young socialists, active in those early years, have made of the important role played by some priests today who are in the forefront of the struggle for justice for the poor, especially in Latin America. And here in England there are priests and bishops who champion the unemployed, the homeless, the poor.

Mama would have found this very hard to understand.

This Croatian social and cultural society which my parents joined played an important part in my early life. At the turn of the century a few young Croatian radicals banded together and acquired a warehouse on Chestnut Street on the North side of Pittsburgh, then known as Allegheny. The building was transformed into a clubhouse with storage space for the choir's piano, the mandolins of the 'Tamburitza' orchestra, the props for the dramatic society. In the large main room self-standing reading frames displayed newspapers from Croatia and also the city's daily papers.

At a weekly popular discussion evening, wide ranging debates took place about Darwinism, religion, the old country and, most important of all, how might a more just society be achieved.

By 1914 Bratsvo was a flourishing organisation which held plays, concerts, even Croatian operettas. Papa, a tenor sang duets with Knabel, a baritone. These performances were on a Saturday afternoon. People came from as far as Canton and Youngstown,

*The mandolins of the 'Tamburitza' orchestra:
Sebastian Truhar (my father) top row second left*

Ohio. Promptly at 2.30 the show began, the venue either the Teutonia Hall on Pressley Street or the Turner Hall on South Central Street, both on the North side.

During the performances on the top floor a goulash supper was being prepared by women, my mother among them, in a room below. By half-past five the hungry audience trooped down while above chairs were cleared and the hall made ready for the evening dance when most often our own Tamburitza orchestra, led by Belec, supplied the music. Refreshments and wine were on sale and it was papa who applied for the liquor licence, valid for forty-eight hours. We children were always there and often mama bedded me down on two chairs.

From the age of five I have vivid memories of Sunday picnics held in a grove above East Street. Wide advertisement in Croatian areas brought families from Lawrenceville, Etna, East Pittsburgh as well as the North side. We joined the steep half-mile climb from the streetcar stop. Papa and the committee had spent the night in the grove, guarding the liquor and lambs, erecting the stalls. Early next morning the old country barbecue of lambs on a spit over an open fire began. The 'janjetina', served with chunks of bread and green onions, was cheap and popular.

To an accordion orchestra the grown-ups stamped and twirled on the rough boards of the dance floor while we children improvised on the grass. Inevitably a call came for the 'kolo', our native dance. A circle, often led by papa, formed then spilled onto the grounds as more and more people joined.

There was always a pause for the socialist message, a collection and the sale of pamphlets and our paper.

As evening approached, small groups gathered to sing the nostalgic old country songs. Then came the long trek downhill, the street car ride home.

Sunday picnic: Sebastian Truhar (my father)
second row third from left, me on my father's lap,
Maria Truhar (my mother) second row second from right,
Tony (my brother) front row second from right,
Paula (my sister) front row first right

*Sunday picnic.
Me front row third from left*

After 1916 our dances were held at the Socialist Lyceum, a large building at 805 James Street on the North side. This had been bought jointly by American, German, Croatian, Czech and Hungarian socialists. Here my father taught me the waltz, polka and even our kolo. Refreshments were on sale and, until Prohibition, a plentiful supply of wine. During the interval, as always, a short rousing speech was made and socialist papers sold.

Perhaps the most popular such evening came in the autumn when the 'Berba', a celebration of grape picking in the old country, was held. Stout ropes festooned with vines were fastened in a criss-cross fashion just high enough to enable dancers to pluck the attached bunches of grapes. The diligent 'politzia' swooped, hauled the culprits before a 'judge' who fined them. But they did keep the grapes.

This was a side of my life which my friends on the Hill didn't share though I did my best to explain it.

Chapter 3

World War I – Russian Revolution

A bell clanged; the patrol wagon sped towards us. With a screech of tyres, it pulled up outside the building we'd left not five minutes before. Six patrolmen spilled out, dashed into Slovene Hall. "Maybe just some drunk, it's happened before," mama said. Papa wanted to go back but the lights of the last street car that night shone in the distance. Mama's guess was wrong. They'd come for us.

We'd been invited to this entertainment by a socialist cultural society based on Lawrenceville, an industrial township on the opposite side of the river. Nearly six now in June 1917, I'd been asked to recite at their concert, always followed by dancing.

Breakfast was late the next day, Sunday. Chickens had to be fed, our cow milked. As we drank coffee, talk was all of the previous evening. Papa had led the 'kolo' then retired to sing with his cronies. Mama sat with friends, watched as children took over the dance floor in the interval, sliding and gliding.

Big Matt came over for a word with my mother, who nodded. He lifted me onto his shoulders then sat down on the bar.

"What drink, Frieda?"

"Cherry cream soda, please."

The men teased me, "Wouldn't you rather be a boy? They've a lot more fun than girls."

I considered this. It had never occurred to me. "No," I answered in Croatian. "I like being a girl and anyway, look what boys are made of." Then in English I went on, "frogs and snails and puppy dog's tails". There was a shout of laughter from the men and papa and his mates at a nearby table. As he was telling this to mama, there was a loud knock on the front door.

It was the comrade who'd been Master of Ceremonies at the concert. "Lucky you left early. The police wanted the parents of the little girl who's recited."

"The patrol wagon, we saw it," exclaimed my brother.

He nodded. "It was something Frieda said against the war in one of her verses. When I told the policeman I thought free speech was allowed in this country he gave me a dirty look, said nobody was free anymore to speak against the war."

"I thought I'd better come and warn you, told them I didn't know where you lived. But if they want you, they'll find you. There must have been a goddam stool pigeon in the hall."

Papa thanked him as they drank a glass of wine together. When he'd gone, we all talked at once. "Be quiet, we must think what to do," mama said. "Papa will go to see Pavel Hanas, he will know. But first the recitation, Tony must copy the words of "I did not raise my boy to be a soldier' for papa to take.

On this return my father looked grave. "There's a new law. You can go to jail if you talk against the war. They didn't waste much time; it was only passed on June 15th."

"What will happen now?"

"Hanas said we must wait. If they come it will be for me, not Frieda. Then I must say I didn't know about it, which is true. He thinks the police won't do anything, it's such a new law."

Papa's eyes sparkled as he smiled at us, "Pavel said to me – they will know you are a socialist but don't try to argue with them. And don't lose your temper." The tension eased as we laughed. He was notorious for getting excited in arguments.

This Espionage Act which had been approved by the United States Congress and now touched us so closely made it a crime to speak or otherwise act against the war.

From the beginning the Socialist Party had opposed the 1914 War. Americans wanted to stay out. Wilson was re-elected President in the autumn of 1916 on the slogan 'He kept us out of the War'. Yet five months later Wilson took the United States into the War. This 'man of peace' as he'd been called, knew what would happen.

On the night before he delivered his war message to Congress in April 2nd 1917, he spoke to Frank Cobb of the New York World and is reported to have said:

> Once lead these people into war and they'll forget there was such a thing as tolerance. To fight you must be brutal and ruthless, and the spirit of ruthless brutality will enter into every fibre of our national life, infecting Congress, the courts, the policeman on the beat, the man in the street.
>
> Conformity will be the only virtue and every man who refuses to conform will have to pay the penalty. The Constitution may not survive it; free speech and the right of assembly will go.

Now after only a few months of war ordinary people like my parents, who did not conform, were affected.

"You can't argue anymore at work. It's all Rah, Rah, Rah and Liberty Bonds," complained my father.

"So, it's a time when we have to keep quiet. There are other ways besides arguing," answered mama.

At least my parents weren't jailed though some thousand more prominent socialists who were against the war were prosecuted for anti-war activities between June 1917 and July 1918. Among these was Eugene Victor Debs, one of the greatest names in the United States socialist movement of this century.

In 1920 while in prison serving his ten year sentence for openly opposing the War, Eugene Debs polled nearly a million votes as the Socialist candidate for President. My father served as a Deb's Socialist poll watcher in that election.

American folk poet, James Whitcombe Riley had written of Debs,

> 'And there's 'Gene Debs – a man 'at stands
> Ad jest holds out in his two hands
> As warm a heart as ever beat
> Betwixt here and the Jedgement seat.'

Clarence Darrow, the famous lawyer, said of him,

'There may have lived some time, somewhere, a kindlier, gentler, a more generous man than Eugene Debs but I have never known him.'

This incorruptible American was a hero and inspiration to many immigrants like my parents. A snapshot of Debs holding me in his arms when I was three years old was carried for years by my proud father who showed it on every possible occasion.

I had all but forgotten the incident in Lawrenceville when papa one evening told us, "The police came to the job today, asked me a lot of questions about Frieda."

Mama looked anxious but papa said, "Don't worry, Maria. They wanted to know how come she recites such poems. I told them she's been doing it since she's three and knows all kinds. So, they said, didn't you realise it was breaking the law. No,

Eugene V Debs holding me, 1914

I didn't, I told them. It was a very new law at the time and we hadn't heard of it."

"Did you keep your temper?"

Papa smiled, nodded. "I just listened. Then the man said, 'You're an American citizen. You should bring up your children to be good Americans and not teach them such things.'

"That's all then, it's over about Frieda?' Mama was greatly relieved.

"Yes, only they said they'd keep an eye on us in the future.

When a few weeks later papa brought home a batch of anti-war leaflets, I went with him after dark to Troy Hill and thought it great fun as we pushed them through letter slots or into mail boxes. But mama worried until we got back.

On an Autumn day in 1917 when I returned from school my mother hugged me. "Just think, Frieda, plain ordinary people like me and papa have taken things into their own hands." That is how she saw the Russian revolution. Normally a reserved woman, she was near tears as she lifted me high then sat me on her lap. Her face radiant, she tried to explain. At the time I was six, did not understand but felt happy because she was so happy.

The foreign born socialists greeted the revolution with fervour, saw in it the 'dawn of socialism', a promise for their own future. The press did not see it that way. As Russia pulled out of the War their attacks became even more fierce. But the left and a section of the liberal opinion continued to give support.

One evening at supper papa told us, "Our foreman is mad as hell, says the Russians are traitors. But that Italian argues with him."

"The one with six children?"

He nodded. "You should hear him. – Meester foreman, you never been poor. In Italy we live bad, no work, always hungry. Come to America, find work, still sometimes hungry. Same for Ruskies, want to live better so make revolution. –"

We laughed with my father but mama remained serious. "You papa should keep your mouth shut. Remember they're watching you. The police have warned you once already."

He refused to meet her eyes, looked down. "I don't say much."

"You should say nothing when that foreman's around. And tell Giovanni to think of his wife and children. What will happen to them if he's fired, or even arrested."

"We can't always be quiet. Debs has called it 'the star of hope for all the world'. Maria, there's a socialist country in Europe."

Wide-eyed, we children sat silent, looked from one parent to the other. New words, 'bolshevik', 'soviet', came into conversations as did the names Lenin and Trotsky. I snuggled against mama as she sat at the end of the men's table at a Bratsvo social. No signing now, only talk of the revolution. 'It's only the beginning.' 'Soon all Europe will be socialist.' 'The peasants will join in too.' 'It was the slogan – peace, bread and land – which won over the Tsars' army.'

Mama nodded at this. "What are they talking about," I asked.

"Frieda when I was little like you there were six of us living in one room. My father was dead. We were often hungry and what he wanted was more land to grow things on and more bread to eat. When I was eleven, your brother's age, I was sent to work in a town because there wasn't enough to eat at home."

"You won't send Tony away, will you? I wouldn't like that."

She smiled, kissed me. "No, of course not. You'll understand better when you are older."

It is true I was too young to grasp what had taken place. Yet I felt this revolution they so often mentioned was more important to my parents than anything which had happened before and so I was for it.

I worried when mama and papa started to argue about Bratsvo and asked Tony what it meant.

"Pop says they should sell up because the money is needed to prepare for revolution here. Mom thinks he's crazy, there's no chance of that in America. And even if there was, it's not immigrants like us but Americans like John Reed who should do it."

"Who's right?"

"I think mom. She reads more and understands better. Pop often repeats what she's read and told him when he talks to other people. I've noticed that."

But there were others who thought like papa and a special meeting of Pittsburgh Croatian socialists was called with only one item on the agenda: "That Bratsvo should disband and its assets sold so the money could be used to help the coming revolution in America.' After a heated debate the motion was lost and Bratsvo reprieved.

Papa grumbled and muttered for days but I was glad because I associated Bratsvo with picnics, dances and fun, like Socialist Sunday school.

As time went on the papers daily predicted an early end of the revolution. All socialist papers including our Radnicka Straza had been banned in 1917 and facts were hard to come by. But the news that five thousand American soldiers had joined the intervention forces against the Bolsheviks and were on Soviet soil prompted an outcry, not only from the left but from others who believed that the Russians had the same right the American colonists had exercised to choose their own kind of government.

A 'Hands Off Russia' campaign began and again I helped papa distribute leaflets on Troy Hill. We also began to collect funds for the child victims of the famine in Russia caused mainly by the blockade, the 'cordon sanitaire' imposed by other nations, which prevented food and supplies reaching the Soviet Union.

Our Sunday school teachers gave us tins, told us we were 'Famine Scouts' now. "Collect what you can. Tell people it's for starving children and bring the tins back next Sunday."

Though mama protested that I was too little, for I looked younger than my age, I insisted on going to Millvale. I knocked on doors, said "Little children like yours and like me are dying of hunger so please put something in the tin." Was it my size, the picture of the emaciated child on the wrapping or just plain generosity? For most people gave something.

Similar activities throughout the country led to the formation of the Friends of Russia which my parents joined. They firmly believed that there was now one land in the world run by people like themselves and gave it their wholehearted support.

Life proved more complicated. What subsequently happened in Russia was a far cry from the hopes and desires of those early Pittsburgh socialists. But this does not lessen the tremendous impact the Russian revolution had on them at that time. Nor could I then know it was to have a profound influence on my later life.

The revolution caused a shock wave in the American Socialist Party. The leadership especially was opposed to the Bolsheviks while most of the Federations of foreign born and John Reed's Americans strongly supported the Soviets. To my parents this split seemed distant, nothing to do with their activities. But the day was to come when it directly affected us.

❦

One Sunday in the early spring of 1919 papa, excited and happy, burst into the kitchen where mama was preparing dinner. "Three new members, Maria. All from the same boarding house. They've been reading ZNANJE – (the new name of our paper) – for some time. When I said it's time you joined the Socialist Party Franjo answered, "Why didn't you ask sooner."

Mama turned from the stove. "So, they're coming to dinner next Sunday."

"How did you know?"

She laughed. "Papa, I've lived with you a long time. Only in future ask me first."

The following week we rushed home from Socialist Sunday School to meet our visitors. Proudly papa showed them the garden and the barn.

Enchanted by our lime tree the men sat in its shade drinking papa's wine.

"You've not seen the stables, "Tony said. With papa he led them down to the empty stalls which stretched the entire length of the barn.

"This could be a fine bowling alley. It's long enough, doesn't need much work, the barn is already there as one side." Djuro walked up and down the wide earthen path in front of the stables.

Matt nodded. "I helped make one back home. There would be less work here."

"Let's do it", shouted Tony.

Papa hesitated. "We can't do anything without consulting Maria."

They looked at him in surprise as he explained. "She's a socialist too, you know. Been in the Party since the beginning. We have to talk this over with her."

Mama listened; her expression thoughtful. "It's a good idea, a chance for you to get some fresh air away from those boarding houses. But I do not intend to cook for you so have your meals before you come."

The men regarded her with respect. She was right for after they finished making the bowling alley more young men and some single older comrades came for the bowling or just to watch the others.

When we'd had dinner after our return from Sunday school, we usually ran down to see how the bowling was going. But on this day early in June 1919, there was no sound of falling nine pins, nor the laughter and shouts as hits were scored. Instead, the men sat on the plank or leaned against the barn, one with a bowling ball still in his hand.

Pavel Hanas was holding a newspaper. "There, you see they've done it. We've been expelled from the Socialist Party, not just us, all the federations, Russians, Poles, Hungarians, Finns and more – all have been thrown out."

These young men were angry, couldn't understand this. "Who gave them the right?" "It's the damned Americans, never cared for immigrants."

More such remarks before papa intervened. "Not just us, they've got rid of Americans too. John Reed is out."

"But wasn't he there, saw the revolution, lived through it?"

"And wrote about it, a book called 'Ten Days That Shook the World'. Maybe that's why they don't like him for the right-wing leadership doesn't like the revolution either." Pavel said dryly.

Bowls and ninepins were put away and the men repaired to our yard. Mama joined them, poured wine and passed it around. I had listened to their talk, anxiously asked her, "But we'll still be socialists, won't we?"

She laughed, "We'll always be that."

Though not yet eight I felt this was something important and sat down beside my twelve year old brother.

My father spoke reflectively, "They didn't want us from the start. When Glumac came to edit the 'Straza' in 1907 he was so sure the American socialists would help us. But no, we had to do it all ourselves."

Hanas smiled. "We didn't have the vote then; we weren't citizens yet. They wanted voters."

It was all true. The language federations, as they were now called, had for years struggled on, developing their own socialist organisations without aid from the national party. In 1912 most of them became affiliated, with a translator secretary from each federation at national headquarters.

As this was explained to the young men they shook their heads, not quite understanding what was happening now. Mama interrupted, "But John Reed and Kate O'Hare won in the elections so why aren't they in charge?"

"There's an explanation of that in the paper, Maria," said Hanas. "Listen to this."

> The national election in the Socialist Party had, as usual, been held by referendum vote in the early spring of 1919. The right-wing leaders, Hillquit and Berger, were soundly defeated by the left candidates John Reed and Kate O'Hare. But Hillquit refused to publish the figures and instead there was now this wholesale expulsion of the left.

It was ironic that the leadership of the Socialist movement, which was the creation of old established American liberals but primarily early German immigrants, should now make the present day foreign born its main target.

From the turn of the century there had always been a left wing and a right wing in the Socialist Party. Understandably, those who had been part of the 'peasant migration' from central and Eastern Europe, mostly manual workers, belonged to the left. Now all of them, alongside Reed's primarily middle-class Americans, had been expelled by a right-wing leadership which refused to surrender its position. Of the 50,000 driven from the Socialist Party, forty thousand were foreign born.

These young men, for even my father was only thirty-nine, didn't quite realise that this meant the end of the Socialist Party as they had known it. The next few years were to sorely test their political convictions and beliefs as the hysteria against foreigners was again being whipped up in the wake of the Russian revolution.

What to do now? The left fought back and when the Socialist Party convention met in the Machinists Hall in Chicago on 30 August 1919, delegates from expelled branches in a dozen states appeared. When their credentials were refused John Reed and others nevertheless tried to take their seats. The platform called in the police who threw them out.

It was a summer of much talk and activity from which emerged two Communist Parties, both supporting the Communist International. Together with most foreign-born socialists, my parents became members of the Communist Party of America.

Chapter 4

The Palmer Raids

Then occurred one of those extreme actions which, from time to time, mark American political history. The newly-born Communist Parties and the trade unions became targets of attacks on a scale not previously experienced in the United States.

On 2 January 1920, on the order of Attorney General, A. Mitchell Palmer, six thousand people in the large cities were arrested and jailed.

Suddenly my parents and their friends became dangerous persons, liable to be hunted down, for they were both communist and foreign born. Some of Palmer's men were ignoring citizenship papers, long held by my parents.

Hundreds of informers had infiltrated organisations, not only of the left but also the Unions, and sent their reports to the Justice Department. In January 1920, the 'New York Times' reported, 'during the steel strike, coal strike ....secret agents moved constantly among the more radical of the agitators and collected a mass of evidence.'

It was the big Steel Strike of 1919 which had attracted so many stool-pigeons. In an attempt to halt the attack of employers on the better living standards granted during the war, the Union's call had closed nearly every steel plant in Western Pennsylvania. Immigrant labour made up the bulk of the workforce in these mills. Now the 'Red Menace' was evoked and replaced the war time hatred of the 'hun'.

The strike was a fierce and bloody encounter of which our family had a brief insight. One Saturday morning two men appeared on our front porch, their faces so bruised and swollen that I was frightened and ran for my mother.

"Matt sent us. We got beat up in the strike. He said we could come to you and rest up a bit." The man's face became distorted as he tried to smile, "If we'd gone to a hospital we'd be in jail."

Mama was all sympathy, immediately gave them a big ham and egg breakfast, arranged a place where they could be quiet and lie down. They stayed till faces and bodies were nearly healed. We never saw them again.

Not surprisingly during the Palmer raids almost all of those who had been active in the strike were arrested. Among them were many of our comrades.

Instructions came from the Party to lie low, stay away from all meetings. As usual my father did not wish to live quietly, wanted to fight back. He fumed and raged. "Why doesn't someone say something? Why don't we do something?"

To which mama replied, "There's nothing we can do. We're foreigners and would quickly be arrested." That was good common sense but did little to calm my angry father.

Protest and action did come from many quarters. Louis F. Post, Assistant Secretary of Labor, dismissed the cases of hundreds who were wrongfully held for deportation. When impeachment charges against him were referred to the House Committee on Rules, the old Jeffersonian democrat sturdily stood his ground and rebutted the charges.

In May 1920 a brochure headed 'To the American People – Report on the Illegal Practices of the United States Department of Justice' was published and distributed by twelve of the most eminent lawyers in the United States, including Felix Frankfurter, later a Justice of the Supreme Court, and Roscoe Pound, Dean of the Harvard Law School.

When papa read this pamphlet which produced evidence to show how the raids had flouted the law and constitution, he was jubilant. "It's all over, they won't dare go on."

He was wrong. Our party faced a difficult time, many of its leaders in jail. Charles E. Ruthenberg, its secretary, was given a long prison sentence. Even papa became more subdued when we heard that national communist headquarters were closed.

As the raids continued, mama worried about who might be next. "We have children to think of, papa. You must keep very quiet at work or they will arrest you." And this time he agreed.

Both the Communist Party of America and the Communist Labour Party were busy reorganising, taking steps to protect their members as far as possible from arbitrary arrest. At their 'underground' conventions later in 1920 they discovered to their dismay that they had held only about 10,000 of the 60,000 who had earlier been in their ranks. Among that ten thousand were my mother, father and uncle.

As halls and club premises closed, the Party went 'underground'. For Croatian communists in Pittsburgh our old farmhouse now became the headquarters. Meetings were most often held in the kitchen, away from the road. Neighbours were accustomed to our many visitors, comings and goings were not unusual. The house could be reached from three directions, two paths from Millvale and the long winding road from Troy Hill.

There is no doubt these gatherings were dangerous but for me they had their funny side. Mama told us firmly, "You must never mention to anyone what goes on at our meetings or who comes to them."

I wondered why for they spoke of the same things as before, relief for striking miners, distribution of leaflets. Papa wondered if it might be possible just for the choir to get together and practice but the others vetoed this. As for those who came, except for people from outlying areas, I'd known most of them all my life. And now I was supposed to refer to them as Mr A, Mr B, or by some other letter of the alphabet.

Mana was cross with me when one evening I said, "Look, Hanas is coming up the road."

"That's MB. We don't use names anymore."

I burst out laughing. "You're wrong. It's Pavel Hanas." "I told you Frieda, you must not use names. You're old enough to understand," she chided.

Of course, mama realised what might happen if our home was discovered as a meeting place for communists, a thought which had then never occurred to me.

Our house became a kind of office too, where letters, papers and minutes were kept. Mama was in charge of leaflets and pamphlets. She kept them in sacks and hid them in the hayloft. One day I helped her move them to the attic. I realised then for the first time that all this secrecy was a great worry to her and stopped making fun of the alphabet names.

During these three years of the 'underground', normal life continued. We went to school, papa to work. I played with my gang. We gardened, preserved our produce, had the annual wine making in spite of Prohibition. Relatives visited us and we them. But always we had to be on guard in what we said. The element of danger was there enough by 1922 we took part more openly in many activities which could not be called 'communist'.

Sometimes on meeting nights a visitor was in the house when I got home from school. He was the Party District Organiser, a replacement for Fred Merrick, who after having been beaten up and jailed for a short time had disappeared.

Arthur, a tall thin man with a scarred face, was a Hungarian refugee who had taken part in the Bela Kun revolutionary uprising in that country.

Once mama learned he was a university graduate she asked question after question while he drank coffee and she worked at the stove. She wanted to know more about Darwinism, the reign of Maria Theresa and the Spanish Inquisition. She was also interested in Galileo and Giordano Bruno, asked Arthur to explain their heresies. Arthur shared our evening meal and then it was papa's turn to ask questions, always political.

It was Arthur who informed the Croatian communists in Pittsburgh that the union of our Party and John Reed's was discussed and asked for their views.

"It's not such a good idea," mama was firm. "We don't want to lose our Federation or our paper which keeps us in touch with Croatian socialists and communists all over the country. Why didn't we get together in the first place?"

This was generally agreed and when in May 1921 the fusion took place the Federations of foreign-born members received considerable autonomy.

The lives of Croatian communists in Pittsburgh were further complicated when in mid-August 1922 the Communist Party convention in Michigan voted to remain 'underground'

My parents were bitterly disappointed. "It's wrong," papa said. "Look how we are helping the Free Sacco Vanzetti campaign, talking again to people."

Mama agreed. "They're not bothering our paper either, even though the name's been changed from Znanje (Knowledge) to Radnik (Worker). It's coming out regularly."

During the nationwide coal strike in 1922 we all helped to collect relief and, like many socialist and Quaker families, took in two miners' children because there was no food for them in their own homes. Victor and Joe, from Westmoreland Country, were near my age. Shy at first, they became much livelier when they realised my parents too were immigrants. And how they ate, three helpings at supper.

"Good, there'll be no left-overs. Eat, boys, eat", said mama.

Joe didn't want to go to school. "Do I have to?" he pleaded. "It's the law, mama answered. "Anyway, it's a very good school. You'll like it."

I took them to our Principal, Miss Manning. "Why are they here?" she asked. And I told her. The next day at recess she walked through the playground with an arm around each boy, her way of showing other children and some of the teachers that these boys were welcome. Miss Manning was a wonderful woman.

In 1922 also, I clashed with my teacher, Miss Ross in a way which might have been bad for my parents. Mama scolded me for being thoughtless. But Miss Ross did not pursue it.

In retrospect I believe that going 'underground' was essential immediately after the Palmer Raids but continued far longer than necessary. My parents were delighted when on 23 April 1923, the united parties emerged into the open with a new name, the Workers (Communist) Party, and began to function publicly. Comrades could once again be called by name and the books and pamphlets removed from the attic.

I entered adolescence as the socialist/communist movement entered what seemed to us a new era of activity.

Chapter 5

Mount Troy School and Socialist Sunday School

"Robert, shoulders back, don't slouch. Frieda, look up not down. All eyes on George Washington and the flag."

Each morning like a general mustering her troops Miss Ross stood up and down aisles, not content till every child stood ramrod straight, right hand raised as in a military salute.

What with previous teachers had been a perfunctory gesture now became a stern ritual as we were made to proclaim, "I pledge allegiance to God and my country. One nation, one language, one flag."

Over a third of my class though born in the United States came from immigrant families. With Miss Ross we were made to feel inferior as she spoke often of 'real' Americans. We were not allowed to forget that one of her ancestors had fought at Valley Forge.

Full of resentment I complained to mama about this daily performance. "Do it, don't make trouble for yourself," she said.

One morning I decided not to stand up. Miss Ross came over to me. "What is it Frieda? Are you ill?"

"No, I don't believe in God. We're freethinkers in our family."

Speechless, she looked down at me. The other children were very still. "Stand" came the order. Her fingers dug into my shoulder as she propelled me towards the door, closed it behind me.

Family photograph 1922: my father Sebastian, me, my mother Maria, my sister Paula and my brother Tony

I listened to the familiar words, the scrape of feet as children sat down. Teacher's pet came out holding a note. "Glad I'm not you. She's real mad."

I walked across to the drinking fountain, leaned against the wall. Miss Manning appeared, entered the room. She emerged, glanced at me. "Come to my room at recess time."

Already somewhat frightened at what I had done, I sat on the floor and to calm myself recited quietly the verses mama had taught me and the poems I'd learned at school, then in a low voice sang Socialist Sunday school songs.

Miss Manning was not angry. "It is your right if you are freethinkers not to take part in the salute. But I need a letter from your father."

Tearfully I blurted out, "They think if the teachers know I'd get into trouble." She looked at me for what seemed a long time then said firmly "not in this school".

Emboldened I went on, "She don't like any of us immigrant kids, especially Mirko. Keeps on saying we gotta act like little Americans. But we was all born here."

I thought I saw a fleeting smile as Miss Manning asked, "Is that why Mirko put a grass snake in her desk?"

"Yeah, he gets the rattan every day. It's hard for him at home too. His mom don't speak no English so he's got to go the store, look after the other kids. That's why he's not so good at school."

She stood up. "Come to me at home time. I'll give you a letter for your father. Now apologise to Miss Ross. In future you may leave the room and return when the saluting is over."

I stuttered my thanks, so relieved I could have hugged her. She smiled, nodded towards the door.

As I walked into the classroom heads were raised. Miss Ross turned from the blackboard. Despite the blue polka dot dress with its soft white collar, the wrinkled cheeks partly hidden by fading puffed out blonde hair, this slight woman was formidable as her hard blue eyes looked down at me.

"Miss Ross, I'm sorry. I did it the wrong way, should have brought a letter."

Her glance passed over me. "Get on with your work."

Papa went to see Miss Manning and returned full of enthusiasm. "She's a fine woman. I told her how we've been trying to get a decent road and city water, that I've been twice to the township office but they don't do anything."

"But what about Frieda?"

"Oh, she'll be alright. Miss Manning told me there is no religion taught in schools."

Some years later when I was in her class, she asked why papa didn't run for the School Board. "We need such people". When I told him he was very pleased.

My two years with Miss Ross were never happy though I applied myself, improved my English and learned a great deal about the American Revolutionary War. In my second year we again crossed swords. The title for our composition was 'The Best Country in the World'. In all innocence I started off with 'I believe the best country in the world is Russia where ordinary people have taken things into their own hands.'

I went on to develop my theme using all I'd heard in long evenings of talk at home. A long time had passed since our first encounter and I hoped, though she might not agree, she'd judge my work on its merits.

Yet as soon as the class settled to work, next day Miss Ross called me out. "Here is a girl who, though taken in and befriended by the American people writes, "she paused for effect, "RUSSIA is the best country in the world." She said much more as I faced my eleven-year-old classmates and seethed inwardly. But I kept my peace for this time she was wrong, I had used her title and written what I believed.

Papa was furious though mama, calm and anxious regretted this incident, hoped there'd be no trouble. For it was 1921, the Palmer raids not so distant, the KU-Klux-Klan lynching of negroes and union organisers in the South, the recent Sacco and Vanzetti frame up for a murder they did not commit, not an easy time in which to uphold socialist views.

My father went to see Miss Manning. "I told her we have a right to our opinions; it's stated in the Declaration of Independence. We are not inferior because we are immigrants. "It was Miss Ross's description of me as 'immigrant scum' which had so angered him.

"Miss Manning agreed with me, said she was sorry this should have happened in her school. "He turned to me, "You must not mention that to the other children. From the way she talked she is on the immigrant children's side. But if Miss

Ross goes to the School Board, she could make trouble. You've only a few months in her class. Just do your work and try not to annoy her."

As I turned back to my homework papa spoke seriously. "You are right, Maria, we must still be careful. I felt Miss Manning too is worried about some of the things which are happening."

It was a relief to me and I'm sure to Miss Ross when June came and our class went up to the sixth grade.

As I well knew, all teachers were not like she'd been. When on that first September day I started at Mt. Troy with Mirko, Slavo and Millie, all my age and from the Hill, it was Miss Camp, tall, unsmiling who looked down on us and the other five-year-olds. We'd be in her charge for two years. As she questioned us by name the fluent answers of those with American parents were interspersed by the broken English of immigrants' children. Many used words and phrases from the language of their parents. Some sat dumb, suffering, unable to speak.

Yet before most of us left her care we could read, write, spell, add and subtract, though the spoken English of a few remained fractured till the end of their school days. Miss Camp was not as fearsome as she appeared. I warmed towards her as patiently and kindly she dealt with us. Though firm and strict, to her we were all just children. We were fortunate to have her as our first teacher.

Spelling was very important. Each week ten new words were written on the blackboard on Monday and rubbed off on Friday when we had a 'spelling bee'. These contests had an interesting history in the United States. As early as 1750 Benjamin Franklin had proposed a public competitive game of spelling, which was seen as a way of making 'proper' speech accessible to all. In rural communities and on the western frontier, spelling was valued as a symbol of culture.

Bret Harte's 'Spelling Bee at Angel' has Truthful James saying:

> Thar's a new game down in Fris
>   That ez far ez I can see
> Beats euchre, poker and van-toon,
> They calls the Spelling Bee.

Even in my time a good speller received high praise and, on our reports, it had the grand title 'Orthography'.

In the main the other teachers treated us fairly but it was to Miss McKenna my heart went out. She had us for two years from eleven to thirteen, and brought to her teaching more explanations, satisfying answers to our questions. Poetry and literature came into our lives.

My reciting in socialist circles stood me in good stead and on Memorial days I was chosen to give Abraham Lincoln's Gettysburg Address, especially savoured his closing words, 'that government of the people, by the people and for the people shall not perish from the earth'.

We were taken by Miss Manning in our last year. Slight, grey hair in a bun, she wore blue dresses, heavy in winter, light and flowing in summer, perhaps to match the kind, blue eyes which belied her stern, upright appearance. With her we touched on many subjects, civics, biology, physiology, even the art of debating, a taste of what high school might bring.

So, in June, 1925 came the graduation ceremony on the little stage in the school auditorium. Each of us got a large Diploma with blue ribbons and a gold seal.

As I walked onto the stage Miss Manning whispered to the School Board Superintendent. In Miss Ross's class I'd angrily vowed to work hard and one day be in first place, show them what a 'hunky' could do. Now I had the satisfaction of hearing him say, as he smiled down on me, "And here is the one who's come top of the Class". The applause was polite, the faces of my parents glowed.

I opened my Diploma and discovered I had 'Satisfactorily completed the course of studies and sustained a good Moral Character'.

Even before Mt. Troy School I had gone with my brother and sister to Socialist Sunday School where we mixed with children of many nationalities. We met in a large sunny room on the top floor of the James Street Socialist Lyceum. Noise, bustle and laughter stopped as Superintendent Reinhald

Werner called us to attention. "Welcome children, into your places now."

We sat in 'Circles' according to age, each group with a teacher. Though I'd just begun to read, I pored over the pictures in the 'Cave Dwellers' and 'Tree Dwellers', written by Chicago University Professor, Katherine Dopps.

"These show how early people lived. See how they used stones to hunt other animals for food, ate wild berries and fruit, lived in caves. We don't know when or how they learned about fire, but it was important to keep fires going in the caves. Look how this boy watches over the fire."

"But we don't look like these people in the book," I objected. The white haired woman whose name I don't remember smiled kindly at me. "Tell me what is the same and what is different?"

"Fingers, hands, legs are like ours only more bent."

"Ears, nose, mouth, hair?"

"Yeah, but they're wild looking, their hair's long and they wear skins."

"They lived a very long time ago, before there were our kind of clothes. Has anyone seen somebody who looks just a little bit like these cave people?"

"Our neighbour's boy, Carlo. He hates his face 'cause his nose is squashed and his ears stick out," an Italian boy answered.

Loud laughter stopped when we saw our teacher's face. "It's not kind to laugh at other people. We can't help how we look."

She turned to a new page, the picture of a chimpanzee. "What's different here?"

"He's got hair all over."

"But look at his fingers, hands and large eyes. He's our cousin." We hooted our protest but she smiled, nodded her head.

In later classes we learned more about Darwin's theory of evolution. The teacher said firmly – "The colour of the skin might be different or the slant of the eyes. But this does not make anyone inferior. All people are part of this great brotherhood of man."

Not till 1925 when Clarence Darrow defended John T Scopes, the teacher who had been arrested in Dayton, Tennessee for violating the Anti-Evolution Law, did I understand how advanced our Sunday school teaching had been. The 'Monkey Trial' was national news and I followed intently the accounts which gave in detail courtroom battles between Darrow and William Jennings Bryan.

My brother later joined The Round Table, a discussion group for the over sixteens but still part of our Sunday school. This, I believe,
was taken by Emil Limbach who'd been to the Rand School in New York.

But it was not all books and learning. We sang several songs before the morning ended. My favourite, and my mother's was,

> We stretch our hands across the sea
>   To men of every clime
> While human hearts in harmony
> Strike a universal chime.
> Around the world we stretch our hands
> In solidarity
> With brothers stand in every land
> For human liberty.

Easter and Christmas brought parties, favours and on summer picnics we roasted potatoes and corn-on-the-cob in the embers of bonfires. At evening concerts we sang, recited, even put on little plays. Obliging teachers learned the tunes of native dances, for us our Kolo, for the Hungarians the Chardaz. The Germans always put on a yodel dance and slapped their thighs. These entertainments were fun for us and brought satisfying applause from the very mixed group of proud parents.

When the Socialist Party split in 1919 control of the Sunday School went to the Left. Our gentle wise teachers were replaced by young people who knew very little about children. Although the Round Table continued till 1927, the Socialist Sunday School had ceased to exist by 1923.

We were fortunate that during our formative years we had this social and cultural background. I look back with gratitude and pleasure to our Sunday School where I was taught many things which I could not learn in Mt. Troy school or at home. It was an oasis for children of immigrants where we were treated with equality and dignity.

❦

As I neared fourteen I decided I no longer wanted to be a 'reciter'. Since early childhood I'd appeared at meetings, concerts and in a ringing tone, with appropriate emphases declaimed socialist verse. True, these appearances had made me popular in our circles, given me tremendous confidence. But mama should understand that I was now too old for this. How to tell her? She was so proud of me, combed our newspapers to find new 'poems'. I'd have to make a round about approach.

Over coffee the next evening I asked her, "Why did I start reciting?"

My mother glanced at Tony, sprawled on the old sofa, "Because he wouldn't do it."

He laughed. "Mom was teaching me but it was you who learned the lines. You climbed on a chair, shouted out and copied the gestures she'd shown me. And was I glad!" Tony stuttered slightly as he spoke.

Mama smiled at him. "Well in those early days of our small Bratsvo socials people were asked to do a turn and some children had learned short poems. I wanted Tony to do that."

"I hated it but tried, just to please Mom, you know what she's like." He winked at me.

"Paula called you little big-head but your brother was delighted, urged me to try you out at Bratsvo. I wasn't sure, you were only three ....."

Tony interrupted. "A huge success. Never looked back. And it's gone on for years. I think maybe Paula was right." He grinned.

Mama remained serious, shook her head. "Mrs Knabel said it was wrong to let you recite because you couldn't possibly understand what you were saying. I didn't agree, saw it gave you pleasure and, more important, confidence. And that's one thing an immigrant's child needs. Like I tell you children, you have to learn to stand up for yourself and what you believe." This was a favourite theme of hers.

"That's right, mom," Tony was serious now. "But it wasn't that easy for me. They ganged up on us, called us 'hunky' and other names. It was a different, threatening world when we weren't among our own kind." At his technical school he'd had a rough time.

He looked at me. "I guess it's easier for Frieda. When she stands on that platform facing all those people, recites in three languages and they applaud like mad it must give her confidence. She can't help being so good, can she? Always was a show off." He was teasing now but somehow, I felt uncomfortable.

Mama gave him a reproachful glance. "Don't you remember that big concert in East Pittsburgh. May 1915. She wasn't four yet."

My brother and I exchanged amused glances. We'd heard this before but it had been mama's big moment, a memorable and important occasion for her.

"You wore a white dress with a red sash and I had on my best navy skirt and white blouse, for I had to be beside you on the platform as you stood on a chair. The hall was packed and when you finished they clapped and clapped. As we walked down the middle aisle people reached out to touch you. Some must have thought you weren't real." Mama laughed happily and we laughed with her.

But I had to tell her. "I'm not going to recite again, Mom. I'll soon be at high school.

She was upset, hurt and I tried to soften it. "Maybe someday I'll be a real speaker like Ella Reeve Bloor. Then you can be proud of me again." I'd recently heard 'Mother Bloor', now well into her seventies, was fascinated by the row upon row of beads which encircled her wrinkled neck. Yet when she spoke it was with a fire and passion which brought the audience to its fee. Tony came to my rescue.

"She's right, mom. You have to face it. Frieda will soon be making speeches for the Young Workers' League."

In the end mama accepted my decision and perhaps also for the first time realised I was no longer a young child but an adolescent.

Chapter 6

Latimer and Allegheny High Schools

Loud laughter rang out as I walked through the open doors on my first day at Latimer Junior High. A cluster of girls stared at me, giggled, whispered together. Had I caused this mirth? Why?

As they strolled away with an occasional backward glance my eyes met those of a slight pretty girl standing alone. She came towards me. "Don't mind that stuck up bunch. They're always making fun of people."

"You know them?"

"Yeah, from grade school."

"Why did they laugh at me?"

A long pause, "It's your clothes. Black satin don't go with them grey cotton stockings."

I looked at her worn blue dress with red edges. A safety pin held together the seam which had come undone under one arm pit. Two more safety pins held up a part of the hem.

Her face turned red. "Go on, say it, what about my dress. My other one's in the wash and I had the babies to feed this morning, no time to sew this up." Her voice was defensive but she managed a twisted smile.

"I'm sorry, I didn't mean to make you feel bad. But you're not immigrant like me, are you?"

"No, shanty Irish they call us. There's twelve in our family, not counting mom and pop. Three older ones go to work, bring in a little money. Mom hides it because my father drinks." It came out in a rush, as though she was saying to me – now you know, take it or leave it.

"Well, they call me 'hunky'. Let's stay together." She smiled, nodded.

By now the foyer was crowded with fourteen year old boys and girls. A bell rang, silence was called and we were assigned to our classes. Peggy and I were not together but met again at lunch time in the large hall where a pianola banged out popular tunes. From her during that year I learned to foxtrot and we danced every day despite derisive glances.

Mama agreed when I told her I had to dress differently and soon I wore a grey skirt, plain white blouse and navy sweater with pockets. Cotton stockings were all right with oxfords. I'd copied Kitty, the one American girl who always smiled and said hello. There were girls who wore silk dresses and expensive silk stockings, slip on shoes with low heels, not lace ups. Though they seemed to regard this as the height of good taste, I decided Kitty and I were more suitably dressed.

Excited by all Latimer had to offer, I concentrated on my lessons. Mr Cameron, my English teacher, made Shakespeare come alive as his sonorous voice read aloud the speeches of Brutus and Mark Antony, put before us the vivid image of the fickle Roman mob, the white clad senators, the splendid buildings. "Choose which speech you want to learn and next week we'll act the forum scene."

Mama listened as I walked about the house repeating 'Friends, Romans, Countrymen" and importantly explained to her that this was from a play called 'Julius Caesar' written by William Shakespeare.

"He was a real man, you know, a Roman general," she answered. I looked at her in amazement. "Where did you read that, mama?"

She reddened, laughed, "In those Books of Knowledge we bought you children." That evening she pored over my copy of 'Julius Caesar'. A remarkable woman, my mom.

At school Mr Cameron praised my Mark Antony speech. After class he asked me, "Have you ever read anything else of Shakespeare's?" I shook my head. "I'd never heard of him before. But the words are wonderful, aren't they?" As a teacher many years later, I remembered him when at times I too experienced the pleasure he had then shown.

I was into everything, side-centre in the basketball team, hurdles champion in the inter-city schools' races, a reporter for the Pen and Ink Club which produced the school's monthly magazine.

Most teachers were friendly and in the whole of that year I had only one clash, in my civics class. A four page printed bulletin of world news was distributed and discussed once a month. In one issue there was a photograph of Shapurji Saklatvala who had been elected a member of the English Parliament. The teacher drew particular attention to this picture. "What a sinister man, look at his dark glittering eyes, you can see his is a fanatic."

Up went my hand. "He has dark eyes and skin because he is from India. The eyes of some boys in this class glitter, especially when they're angry. That doesn't make them sinister. I also don't see that being a communist makes a person a fanatic. I know a communist whose mother belongs to the Daughters of the American Revolution." There was laughter as this sparked off a good argument.

Years later when I spoke on the same platform with Saklatvala at the Battersea Town Hall in London I told him how, as a schoolgirl in far off Pittsburgh, I had defended him. He laughed heartily, "I didn't know I was so famous."

As summer vacation neared, Peggy told me, "I've got to get a job right away. My mom's carrying again. Sometimes I feel I could kill my pop." A quick gesture as she crossed herself. "I didn't really mean that but he's killing my mom."

She'd been a bold spirit, ignored as I did the slights and insults we'd met during these months. But the odds were against her for she didn't have the encouragement I received from my family.

Peggy was close to tears as I put my arm around her. "Come on, I'll buy you an ice-cream. When she looked at me with that twisted smile I tightened my grip. There was nothing else I could do.

At the end of the school year three kinds of small golden badges were awarded, for a high standard in school work, for sport, for all round participation in school activities. A much coveted special badge combined the three and to my intense surprise and pleasure I received one of these. Next year I'd be in Senior High.

☾

That first morning at Allegheny Senior High was a confusion of new faces, teachers, long corridors. Weary, hungry by lunch time I found the cafeteria, chose my food and picked a table at random. As I put down my tray a voice said, "This side is reserved." The ever present chip on my shoulder grew larger as I looked at the many empty places. "Who made that rule? I'll sit here, I'm tired."

No reply from the girl who had spoken. Hostile glances as she and her friend picked up their trays and moved down the aisle. As I ate my hot dog I wondered how, on this very first day, they had labelled me. Was there something in my appearance which made them recognise me as a child of immigrants, a 'hunky'? I shrugged. Perhaps Kitty, the Quaker girl who though friendly was one of them, could tell me if I ever met her again.

Each day I returned to that table but as though a signal had been given no one joined me. During the second week a short girl with black curly hair and large dark eyes sat down opposite me. "I've watched you from the other side. They froze me out. I'm Bella, Jewish."

"And I'm Frieda, Croatian. So glad you came over. It's nice to have someone to talk to."

I'd noticed another girl who sat on the other side but even so had a table to herself. "How about us asking her?

Looks like she's been frozen out by everybody." Bella protested. "But she's a negro."

"And what are we, a Jew and a hunky. Are we so different? She seems a nice person." Bella wasn't sure but didn't protest as I walked over to her table. Helen, tall, slim, pretty nodded and walked back with me.

"You'd expect Jews and hunkies to be nigger lovers". The voice was loud and heads turned. I hoped Bella would now understand.

But she didn't. These two girls became my close yet separate friends for Bella found it hard to overcome her reservations about black people.

"My folks want to meet you," Helen said to me one day. "Can you come tomorrow after school and stay for supper, will it be all right with your mom?"

"Fine as long as she knows where I am." As we walked to her place Helen asked me, "Why did you come over to me that day?" "You were alone and I knew the reason, we're socialists."

"So that's why. We've a few white Quaker friends but our church is most important to us. My pop's a doctor, says its best for our people to stay clear of politics."

I thought of Ben Carruthers, a black active communist, but said nothing.

"How do you find the teachers?" I asked her.

"Friendly, pretty fair. Maybe they're all Quakers and Socialists," she laughed.

Helen's home had carpets, comfortable armchairs, a well filled bookcase, paintings not photographs like on our walls. After supper Helen played the piano and her brother the violin, strange, wonderful music. For the first time in my life I heard Mozart and Beethoven.

As Helen walked me to the streetcar stop I said, "You've a lovely home and your parents understand about music and art. You're lucky."

"Yes, among our people I am. But my skin is black and that'll always hold me back."

I had no answer and knew that some of our friends too had prejudices against negroes. Not everyone held my mother's views.

So close was the municipal park at the back of Allegheny that we treated it as part of the school. In spring and summer we sat on the grass in the sun, when winter came we skated on the small frozen lake ringed by fairy lights.

Often Bella and I walked across North Park to her home above the family grocery store. On my first visit Bella asked, "Do you know anything about Jewish customs?"

I shook my head. "I've only met Jewish people at Socialist meetings."

"Well I must warn you. My grandma won't like you. She still follows the old ways. But mom and pop told her you were to come."

"What's wrong with me?"

"Nothing, except you're not Jewish. Grandma will gather up your plate and cup as soon as you're finished and you'll have the same ones when you visit again."

"Do you think I should come if she doesn't want me?" "Oh yes, but don't feel insulted or get mad. She's old and it matters to her."

It happened just as I'd been told and all the while I ate her grandmother hovered near me and whispered in Yiddish.

As we walked to Ohio Street Bella asked me, "Why are you so quiet? Something wrong?"

"No, I was just thinking how funny it is. They look down on you at school because you're Jewish and your grandma looks down on me because I'm not."

We smiled at each other then raced across the park.

I was fifteen in this first year at senior high school and soon realised that a kind of social scale existed. Americans who went back many generations were fewer than one might have expected. But it was they who were most polite, smiled at us as they passed for they were so very sure of their superiority. To Germans with parents or even grandparents born in the States we were invisible, as we were to the Irish. The calumny to which the forebears of the latter had been exposed, as barefoot and starving, they arrived in droves during the potato famine in Ireland, had long since been forgotten.

The rest of us, Jews, blacks, first generation immigrants' children, few in number, were excluded almost entirely from the social life of the school, controlled by the 'sororities' and 'fraternities' we were never invited to join.

Of course I minded as I listened to their talk of parties, dances, boyfriends and cars. Still in my skirts and sweaters I now envied the fine silk dresses, silk stockings and smart shoes which seemed obligatory in those circles.

Years later I read 'Middletown' by Robert and Helen Lynd, a study in depth of a small town in mid-America as it was in 1924. With a population of 38,000 it had only one high school.

The book described the pressure on children and parents from lower income groups as they tried to keep up with the affluent who set the trend.

I realised then it had been my good fortune to have lived on the outskirts of a large city as I escaped from pressures, different but just as strong, to my totally dissimilar environment on the Hill.

It has been possible for me to shrug off these 'exclusions' as I took full advantage of the many clubs and societies open to all and in time to become President of the Maths Club and Manager of the Basketball Team.

Soon classes started in earnest. There was more homework as we toiled that first year at basic subjects about which we had no choice. More Shakespeare but also poetry. Yet our little round English teacher seemed bored with us. He did say to me one day, "Your composition on autumn is well written. Read Shelley's Ode to the West Wind."

He sensed my bewilderment, asked, "Never heard of Shelley?" As I shook my head he rummaged in a drawer, handed me a small volume. "You can keep that." But never once did he ask me what I thought about the poem.

Later a rather different English teacher became my favourite. Miss Heck, middle aged, comfortable, with bobbed hair and large brown eyes, wore grey skirts, old sweaters, sleeves pushed up to the elbows. She introduced us to Jane Austin, the Brontes and contemporary American women writers like Willa Cather. Poetry too, Walt Whitman, Robert Frost, Edna St. Vincent Millay but also the English poets.

In the German class I forged ahead and lost the colloquial dialect I spoke at home.

It was my Chemistry teacher, Mr Hole, tall, heavy, a bit run to seed, who gave me a shock. When he asked to see me after school I thought it was about my work which I knew should be better.

Through his thick glasses he looked at me. "Frieda, socialism interests me. Tell me about the free love you practice, how do you go on?"

So that was it. Seventeen at the time I could hardly believe this, felt vulnerable but my voice was even as I answered, "It's a myth, put about by people who wish to discredit us."

"Still, one reads of Greenwich Village ......"

Suddenly I was very angry. "I know nothing of that. This is Pittsburgh, a city of coal and steel. I'm sorry to disappoint you but we socialists and communists are very respectable people."

He drew back as I slammed out of the room. On Monday I dreaded going back to his class but he acted as though nothing had happened and marked me higher than I deserved.

My greatest discovery was the debating society dominated by final year students. I listened, learned the rules and when I was seventeen started to take part in debates.

As we discussed possible motions for debate at one meeting, Gus, tall and arrogant, put forward 'That anyone, by hard work and application, can achieve success and wealth.'

The president turned to me, "You'd like to oppose that, Frieda?"

"Yes, it's an excellent subject."

Somehow rumour had spread there'd be fireworks. The room was packed. Gus opened, spoke of Henry Frick but picked as his prime example the greatest of all early local industrialists, Andrew Carnegie. Had he not started as a poor boy, built up a huge fortune, become a great benefactor, used his enormous wealth for the benefit of the community? There was a Carnegie Museum, Library, Technical College and many other institutions.

Confident, so sure he was right, Gus performed as he finished, "Anyone who works hard can get on. Only the lazy and shiftless are left behind." He sat down with a smug smile.

At home one of my most unloved nicknames was 'shrimp' and as all five feet of me rose the contrast was so great that some of the audience, with a glance at Gus, burst into laughter which I joined. With a smile the President introduced me, "Frieda may be small but you'll hear every word she says."

I'd worked hard on this debate, anticipated my opponent's approach and even his choice of hero. In an even voice I started, "First, I will read you a paragraph from the Report of the

Commission on Industrial Relations set up by an Act of Congress in 1912.

> 'Have the workers secured a fair share of the enormous increase in wealth which has taken place in this country .... largely as a result of their labours. The answer is emphatically NO.'

I paused, turned to my opponent, "I wonder if Gus has ever heard of the 14th Amendment to our Constitution. He should read it. To refresh your memories it says in part,

> 'No State shall ....deprive any person of life, liberty or property, without due process of the law; nor deny to any person within its jurisdiction the equal protection of the law.'

Now listen carefully to what the Commission goes on to say, and I quote,

> 'It is quite clear that the 14th Amendment not only has failed to protect personal rights but has operated wholly for the protection of the property rights of the corporations.'

What an indictment that is. One must ask – how did Carnegie become a rich man? How many tens of thousands have been maimed and killed in his mills? How many widows has he made? How many fatherless children? Not all the libraries and museums by which he tried to purge his conscience can make up for that."

I stopped, looked again at Gus. "Has my worthy opponent never heard of the Homestead strike where a pitched battle was fought between steel workers and Carnegie's hired Pinkerton thugs? The men wanted shorter hours for it was at the end of the twelve-hour shifts that most accidents occurred. But this Carnegie refused to grant. He was not concerned with people's lives but with his profits."

A beefy lad who'd been lounging against the wall could take no more. "You've no right to speak like that about Mr Carnegie. Your kind don't belong in this school. You should be in a factory among your friends."

There was a deep silence. The President rose but I waved him back and turned to my interrupter.

"My father was in a steel mill for many years. And yes, many of my friends are in factories though their proper place would be here for they are clever people."

I looked again at the audience. "Shouldn't there be some way by which brawn without brains is transferred to factories while the intelligent who have no option but to work there are given the chance of an education?"

It was spur of the moment stuff but there was a roar of laughter and applause from some of the audience. There were also cries of 'shame' from others.

The young man's face went crimson as he lunged towards the platform. His friends pulled him back. The President banged his gavel then said to the glaring youth, "I must ask you to leave the room. You chose to insult the speaker and she had every right to reply in kind. The debate will now proceed."

But the rest was an anti-climax as his friends followed the furious young man while, in spite of the President's attempts at order, the room continued to buzz with laughter and talk. He bowed to the inevitable, closed the debate without a vote.

The news spread, people smiled at me in the corridors. Perhaps my own prejudices had stopped me from meeting those who might sympathise with my views. Or perhaps it was just that the angry young man was not popular.

Towards the end of the Autumn Semester I was told to see the Principal. Why had he sent for me? What had I done? Not the debate, that was months ago. Endless corridors, outer office, inner office and I stood before the head of these two thousand strong schools.

"So, you're Frieda." Mr Smith smiled as I answered "Yes Sir."

"Sit down, I've something to ask you."

Surprised, I sat on the edge of a hard chair. This didn't sound like the prelude to punishment.

"Although you're due to finish in June we think you should graduate in February. You've accumulated enough credits with high marks to put you second in that year group."

I was silent, somewhat confused. At least I asked, "And if I stay till June?"

He shrugged. "Who knows? I advise you to choose February. Coming second is very good. You'll graduate with high honour."

"Can I go to Pitt if I do that? My parents want that for me."

"Oh yes, the University has a February enrolment. Can they afford it? It's a pity there's only one scholarship. There should be at least two."

I smiled then. He seemed on my side, knew about me. "I think my parents will be pleased, they'll find a way."

He nodded. "Tell me tomorrow. You've done well here, Frieda." It was high praise and I left his office somewhat dazed but happy. Mama and papa were delighted and as it turned out, it was a fortunate decision.

On graduation day I had to make the closing student speech, give thanks where due, extol the virtues of teachers and school. My draft was passed to Miss Heck with certain amendments, then I had to memorise and be word perfect.

All went smoothly until my peroration.

"We who graduate today must give thought to that majority who have not had the benefits enjoyed by us during these last years. We who have been fortunate to receive so fine an education must look towards a society where there is sufficiency for all, where no child need leave school at fourteen to supplement the family income. High school should be a right not a privilege.

We are the youth, the future of this country. It is for us to strive and reach that goal which Thomas Jefferson wrote into our Declaration of Independence. It is for us to regain some of the early values which time has eroded. Let us remember those famous words:

> 'We hold these truths to be self-evident, that all men are created equal, that they are endowed by their Creator with certain unalienable Rights, that among these are Life, Liberty and the pursuit of Happiness.'

As I sat down to a good round of applause and the beaming faces of my parents I became aware that on the platform something was amiss. The Principal was listening to Charles Kline who, attending in his capacity as Mayor of Pittsburgh, was speaking somewhat forcefully. Mr Smith's controlled expression revealed nothing but I could have sworn, as his eyes met mine there was the ghost of a smile and a half wink.

The Mayor's was the last speech before the distribution of diplomas. Near its end he gestured in my direction. "I must praise the idealism of our young friend. We need to make allowances for the naivety of youth which still has so much to learn. In the real world there is equal opportunity for all, the nettle has but to be grasped."

Shades of the Debating Society! But I sat back and smiled, glad to have made some impact on the 'first citizen of Pittsburgh', something I'd never considered when I wrote that speech, which could hardly have been called 'radical'.

Chapter 7

Sacco and Vanzetti

For years my parents had been associated with the campaign to free Sacco and Vanzetti. Throughout the early twenties I was often taken to meetings where demands were made that these two men be given a new trial. I helped papa put leaflets about them under doors in the streets of Troy Hill. Their case had become nationwide, then worldwide.

In 1927, a schoolgirl of sixteen, I became actively involved in frantic last minute attempts to save them from the electric chair. For the date of execution of Sacco and Vanzetti had finally been announced.

These two Italian workers had been arrested on 5 May 1920 during the hysterical peak of the Palmer raids and charged with robbery and murder. It was a blatant frame-up and rallied not only the radical left but also the Jeffersonian democrats in the United States.

Sacco and Vanzetti were philosophic anarchists and close friends, active together in labour movement struggles. Bartolomeo Vanzetti, a fish peddler, read widely – Marx, Gorky, Darwin, Zola, Kropotkin, Hugo, Tolstoy. Nicola Sacco, a shoemaker, was primarily interested in his family and garden. He raised flowers as well as vegetables.

Accused of killing a man during a payroll robbery at the Braintree shoe factory in Bridgewater, Massachusetts, they were able to provide foolproof alibis. Sacco had been working at his job in the shoe factory at the time the hold-up occurred. More than twenty witnesses testified that Vanzetti had been miles away from Bridgewater on that day.

In the packed courtroom much was made of their political views and during Vanzetti's trial Judge Thayer included such remarks as – 'This man, although he may not actually have committed the crime attributed to him, is nevertheless morally culpable because he is the enemy of our existing institutions'. Subsequently fifteen pages of the court records, including such remarks, disappeared and were never found.

In the anti-red hysteria of the times, the opinions expressed by the judge inevitably led the biased jury to bring in a verdict of 'guilty of murder' against both men. The foreman remarked, 'Damn them, they ought to hang anyway'.

Subsequently one of the Federal agents assigned to the case, Fred J Weygand, issued a sworn affidavit which stated:

'I am thoroughly convinced and always have been and believe ..... it has been the opinion of such Boston agents of the Department of Justice as had any knowledge of the subject that these men (Sacco and Vanzetti) have nothing whatever to do with the Braintree murder and that their conviction is the result of co-operation between the Boston agent of the Department of Justice and the District Attorney.'

Despite appeals from many quarters a new trial was denied by the same Judge Thayer who had originally sentenced them.

Then in 1925 a young Portuguese criminal signed a note saying, 'I hereby confess to being in the South Braintree shoe company crime and Sacco and Vanzetti were not in the crime.'

A distinguished Boston attorney investigated the confession, appealed again for a new trial and again the appeal was dismissed by Judge Thayer.

A hard fought campaign to save these two men continued without success for seven long years. On 10 July 1927 Judge Thayer sentenced them to die in the electric chair.

There was an avalanche of protest throughout the world. So huge were the number of objections and requests for clemency which poured into the United States State Department that the date was twice postponed.

In many European cities, Paris, Madrid, London, Basle, huge demonstrations took place and also in Mexico City, Havana,

Buenos Aires. There were protest strikes in Denmark, Australia and South Africa. Impassioned pleas from Bernard Shaw, John Galsworthy, Albert Einstein and other prominent people were sent to America.

Only the Governor could now save Sacco and Vanzetti and committees throughout the country made a tremendous effort to get a reprieve. But on 3 August, Governor Fuller of Massachusetts denied a plea for clemency for Vanzetti and the date for execution was finally set for 23 August 1927.

As that date approached we were all in a high state of tension still gathering signatures, still sending telegrams. There was time for the Governor to change his mind.

I went every day to the Pittsburgh office, ran errands, addressed envelopes, made many cups of coffee. At home the first question was, "Is there any news? Will he listen?"

"He's got to, "papa stormed. "Millions of people know they're innocent. How can he let them be murdered?"

But mama sat quiet and at last in a low voice said, "No, papa, they will die. They are working men, foreigners and radicals. That is why. Innocent of course, but they will die anyway."

My mother's views were also those of millionaire Robert Lincoln O'Brien, owner of the Boston Herald, who in a privately published document wrote, 'The momentum of the established order required the execution of Sacco and Vanzetti.'

I cannot clearly remember that last day, so great was the confusion, urgency and clamour as telegrams, phone calls, enquiries poured in and a constant stream of people filled the office. As evening came without news a crowd began to gather, all hoping to hear of a last minute reprieve.

Twelve o'clock approached and there was still no word, people turned to one another – 'they must be reprieved' was repeated over and over again. But just past midnight we were told that Sacco and Vanzetti had been killed in the Charleston Penitentiary, near Bunker Hill, where the first major battle of the American Revolution had been fought.

Moans, cries of 'no, no', women fell to their knees and prayed, sobs and angry shouts came from every side.

"Godam bastards" papa repeated over and over again. But mama, who so rarely cried, stood still and made no attempt to wipe away the tears which ran down her cheeks. I leaned against her, wept into her shoulder as her arm came around me.

We were not alone in our grief. Such scenes were repeated in every large city in the United States and in many other countries.

Harvard Professor of American History, S E Morrison wrote: 'When Sacco and Vanzetti were electrocuted on 23 August, 1927, a cry of horror at the injustice of it went round the world and those citizens of Massachusetts who loved justice remembered John Adams and the Boston Massacre case and Judge Sewell's retraction in the case of the Salem witches, and hung their heads in shame.'

That is how we felt, horrified, spent. A sense of bitter anger and despair that the protests of millions could be so ignored and these innocent men put to death in this brutal way. We sat quiet as my brother drove our old Maxwell back to the Hill. At last he said, "It's like in the olden days when men were left hanging on the gallows for all to see. The deaths of Sacco and Vanzetti were meant to be an example, a warning."

It was not till 1977, fifty years after the execution, that the state of Massachusetts publicly declared that Sacco and Vanzetti were not given a fair trial and named 23 August a Memorial Day for them.

Chapter 8

Anniversary of 'Radnicka Straza' (Workingmen's Guard)

"We let him die!"

Papa's passionate protest rang out above the laughter and noise. I made my way to where he sat with his cronies. On the white cloth stood bottles, glasses, bowls of walnuts."

"No, no, no" Paul Hanas shook his head. "He was a sick man when he came over. That prison in Mitrova did for him."

"We did for him," retorted papa. "He worked all hours, took only eight dollars a week. We let him do it."

Peter Skrtic, respected, perhaps the most learned of the group, intervened and spoke directly to my father.

"You have a point Paso. I did try to tell him not to burn up so. But he was young, full of fire. He'd come to do a job for us and by God he did it well. That's how we must remember him."

"There was no-one. We had a little learning. Some of us were socialists even in the old country. But we were only working men." Skrtic spoke gently, as to a child.

Hanas, the great collector of newspaper clippings and statistics, capped him. "That's right. Of the Croatians who came over in those early days only one in two hundred was skilled, only one in a thousand a professional man. In every four of our people there was one who couldn't even read or write."

Papa added his bit. "Glumac was educated, knew how to edit a paper, use words, write articles." His eyes shone. "He was a wonderful speaker too, made everything so clear."

As the talk became general I stopped listening. How bold they had been, this small group of immigrants who had set out to create a socialist paper. I wanted to know more. Tomorrow I'd tackle Uncle Pete who was staying over. He'd been even more involved than my parents.

With the years he'd become a solemn man who rarely laughed or joked. I'd always been a bit afraid of him but on Sunday morning I approached his chair.

"Uncle Pete." Gravely he looked up from his newspaper.

"It's what you were talking about last night. Why was the paper so important to you? What was Glumac like?"

He held up his hand. "One question at a time, Frieda. It all started long before you were born. Things were different then."

"How do you mean, different?"

"Immigrants were flooding into the United States by the millions. That stopped after the war. There's a quota now."

This didn't interest me but I realised I'd have to let him tell it his way.

"We came to work, to earn money. Some, like your father and I had a trade. But most were from the villages. They went straight into the factories."

"But they didn't know anything about machines."

"Learn on the job. That's how it was. The result was terrible accidents as men were injured by unfenced machinery or fell from high platforms without railings. The toll was high. Nobody cared and there was no compensation. You see Frieda there were so many people coming over, if a man got hurt or killed there was another to take his place."

"And the socialists organised them, "I interrupted.

My uncle smiled, seemed to realise I really wanted to know. "I wish it had been so simple. There weren't many Croatian socialists, only about twenty of us in Pittsburgh. Most were tailors who'd lived in cities. Even your father, a bricklayer, did not work in steel mills till much later. So how were we going to get through to these raw young men? After much discussion we decided that a Croatian Socialist newspaper was the answer."

My uncle laughed. "That same year, 1907, Eugene Debs whom some of us had barely heard of, wrote a pamphlet 'The Aims of a Workers Press' and in that he said that a socialist newspaper was vital, a way of teaching workers to think, helping them to get together and fight for their rights. Well, that's what we were going to do."

He seemed pleased that, in their own way, the Croatian socialists had come to the same conclusion as the foremost socialist in the United States.

"But that came later. Our first step was to raise enough money to make a paper possible."

He paused, eyes distant. Finally, I broke the silence. "There were other Croatian papers though. Pop always gets mad when he talks about 'Narodni List' (People's Paper)."

"Your father gets excited about so many things but yes, there were such papers. They used our people, made money out of them, twisted the truth. Even steamship companies issued papers in many languages then, including Croatian."

"And pop tells stories about how you went 'na agitaciju', to sell the paper in the boarding houses."

He smiled broadly. "Your papa was far better at that than I could ever be. You must ask him about those days."

"Well tell me then about Glumac and how it all began."

"We got together with Croatian socialists in Chicago where a printing press was available. The Slovenes were already publishing their paper 'Proletarac' (Worker). But we needed an editor."

"So Glumac came," I exclaimed.

He shook his head. "It wasn't as easy as that. We wrote first to the old country, to the Agricultural Workers Association of Croatia and Slavonia in Zagreb asking for help with an editor. They advised us to abandon the project, no-one could be spared."

"How could they? Maybe they weren't socialists."

"I'm not sure, half and half I think. We were very discouraged, didn't know what to do next. Then came a letter from Glumac to say he'd edit the paper. It gave us heart."

"But you knew nothing about him?"

"Very little except that he was a twenty-three-year-old Serb imprisoned for some time in Mitrovica. As a student he'd been too free in spreading his views. It solved our problem but we had to raise a great deal of money to make it possible. In June, or was it July, 1907 we had a fundraising meeting at the Czech Hall in Vinial Street on the North Side of Pittsburgh."

Uncle Pete paced up and down. He stopped in front of me. This was not the solemn glum man I knew. He was transformed.

"Frieda, it was a wonderful meeting, an exciting historic meeting. There were some fifty of us, not all socialists. Mokrovic was there, Banjanin, Franjo and Pavel Hanas, Anton and Maria Horvat. You know them all. The moving spirit was Tomo Besenic who was in touch with Chicago. But it was Tomo Sokac I'll never forget.

He stood up in front with a hundred one dollar bills in his hand, let them fall and spread all over the table. 'A start. I've begged, borrowed,' he stopped, smiled at us then went on, 'but not stolen to get things going.'

We laughed, some cheered. We'd never seen so much money. Almost everyone added a dollar and agreed to try and give another once a month. Plans were made for dances, picnics, concerts to raise money. So that's how it started, Frieda." Uncle Pete sat down.

"I can appreciate now why you always talk about it when you're together."

"Not me," he protested.

"But papa and the others like last night."

"You can understand that. We were young, involved, eager, felt we were doing something important, and that was true. We did something else too that day in 1907, Frieda, just as important. We formed a Socialist Party. Called ourselves the Croatian Workers' Organisational and Political Association. The Serbs and Slovenes were doing the same. Later we all got together in the South Slav Socialist Union of Allegheny."

Mama's voice came from the back. "Dinner's ready."

"But what about Glumac?"

"That can wait but your mother won't." His arm around my shoulder, Uncle Pete and I went together into the dining room.

Later in the afternoon I sought him again. "You promised."

"There's not much to tell. We gave him a great welcome though to some of us he seemed so very young. Glumac was too thin but none of us realised he already had tuberculosis. I'm sure he didn't either.

We took him to steel mills, coalmines, Croatian boarding houses. It was interesting how freely he spoke with young men near his own age. He studied English and his knowledge of

German was a big help. So many people in Pittsburgh still spoke German in those days."

"Did he go to our picnics, dance and sing like papa?"

My uncle smiled at me. "Oh yes, he was an excellent dancer, the girls flocked 'round him. However, he was a serious young man, kept saying 'I want to get the feel of this country', asked questions about everything.

We didn't see much of him after he left for Chicago. But he must have worked hard for on 25 December 1907, the first issue of the Radnicka Straza (Workingmen's Guard) appeared. That was a wonderful day. And that's about all I can tell you, Frieda."

Alone one evening with my parents I said to my father, "Uncle Pete told me to ask you about the long ago times when you two first went out to sell the paper. He said you could tell it better than him."

Papa laughed. "That was nearly twenty years ago, when the first issue came out. We decided to go to Jaska Street, a great many young Croatians lived there."

"Where's that? I've never heard of it."

"It's that part of East Ohio Street just after we turn up to Troy Hill. Most of the men came from Jaska in the old country. Even the cops called it that. There was one policeman, Ryan, who must have had a kind heart. He made the rounds every Saturday night to pick up the drunks and put them to bed."

I laughed. "No place to laugh about, Frieda," said mama. "It had the worst boarding houses on the North Side, run by really tough 'burting bosses' who tried to keep tight control over their boarders. They made their own wine and beer, sold checks on pay day so the men could buy their liquor for the week."

"And the boss's lady acted the part of wife to the boarders, for money of course," papa chuckled.

My mother gave him a stern 'not in front of the children' look.

Slightly abashed he said, "She's old enough to understand. These young men were uprooted, did the menial labour in the mills. So they spent their free hours drinking, looking for women."

"Did you ever get inside one of the houses?"

"We got thrown out of quite a few. There were fifty to sixty men in one boarding house. They worked shifts, used the same beds, long tables, hard benches at meal times, no comfort. That first time we didn't really know what we were going to. Your mother was near her time, just before Tony was born. She was frightened for us."

Mama smiled, "I couldn't stop you though."

"The paper had to be sold. We went again and again on Sunday mornings. Once when we started talking to the men outside the proprietor came. He began shouting at us, called us 'cincilisti', syndicalists, trouble makers. I shouted back 'why are you so afraid of what we have to say? Why don't you let them decide if they want to listen to us. They're not your slaves but fee men who can make up their own minds'.

The boss started down the steps toward me. Peter moved closer. One man stood up, 'he's right. I want to hear him'. The 'burting boss' turned threateningly but some of the men came to stand beside him. The big bully backed off and went inside. We sold a few papers, answered their questions, even exposed the boarding house's racket of selling inferior liquor."

Papa had clearly enjoyed it. He and mama reminisced and I listened.

As time went on the paper created quite a stir. It published in full the names of factories where accidents had occurred, what injury the victim had, how the lack of compensation led to suffering among wives and children. That page became a very popular feature and more and more copies were sold.

"Papa also insisted that going to saloons to sell the paper was very necessary," mama said wryly.

"But it was Maria. That's where they met their friends. The saloon was a social evening of course but the saloonkeeper did a lot of business for the men, especially with steamship tickets to bring over wives and relations. I remember once when we went to that Jaska Street saloon the bartender ordered us out. I called out as loud as I could 'he doesn't want you to know what a shif-carta (steamship ticket) really costs. It's all here in the paper. You're paying too much.' This so interested them that half the men followed us out. We sold all our papers except one which we read to a group who were illiterate. The angry men trooped back into the saloon but we didn't wait to see what happened. Next time the bartender didn't order us out. We sat and talked to the men."

Steamship companies which used saloon keepers as their agents were outraged by these revelations. Factory employers exposed by the paper attacked the Radnicka Straza as did some of the national press.

However, as the paper became more widely read the hard, slogging work of those who had started and sold it brought its rewards. Socialist Party membership increased, evening classes were held to teach immigrants to read and write. Campaigns were waged against debarred attorneys and defrocked priests who came to America intent on exploiting their own people. The paper's circulation grew.

But the young talented editor of Radnicka Straza drove himself to the limit. Hanas was visiting one evening when I asked him about Glumac.

"Ah, Glumac. His articles were brilliant, forceful and written so simply that everyone could understand. He worked too hard, had to write, edit, proof read and do the lay-out, in fact everything. His health suffered and by 1912 he was exhausted. On Doctor's orders he went to a milder climate. Todor Cvetkov took over but the touch of Glumac was greatly missed. In 1913 he again returned to edit the paper."

Papa jumped up. "I wrote to him. I'll get his reply".

Hanas laughed. "I thought I was the only one who saved letters and clippings."

"Glumac is one of papa's heroes, like Eugene Debs. He talked a lot about him when I was little."

Papa came, waving the letter. 'This was written only a few months before he died. It's dated 26 November 1913.

Dear Comrade,

I was pleased you thought of me. My health is now no better than in February 1912. During the first months in California I improved considerably and gained nearly twenty pounds in weight. But then regressed...

Your advice that I should not work too hard I will not be able to follow. We have not got a single person who could carry out the editing of Straza. Comrade Cvetkov helps me but I have to work every night till ten or eleven o'clock and sometimes all day Sunday. I shall perish! "

My father was visibly moved as he finished reading. "And he did". His voice was harsh.

Hanas nodded. "Prophetic words. He had to give up and go to his friend Peter Piric's farm in Cedar Lake, Indiana. There he spent his last days. When did he die, Paso?"

"In January 1914. Just thirty years old."

Papa and Hanas sat silent. For them the memory of that gallant young man remained ever green.

The old Croatian speaking pioneers were dead. The younger generation became Americanised. But above all the McCarthy era left its mark on many Croatian communists and socialists who together with their children had suffered greatly for their beliefs.

Nevertheless, those early days of the birth of the Croatian Socialist Party and its paper 'Radnicka Straza' deserves a place in the history of the American labour movement.

> Note: - The Radnicka Straza (Workingmen's Guard) was banned during World War I. It reappeared on 1 April 1918 as Znanje (Knowledge), then on 24 July 1922 as Radnik (Worker), Glas Radnika on 24 September 1935 (Voice of the worker), Radnicki Glas on 26 May 1936 (Worker's voice). It was a daily, a weekly, a twice-monthly, depending on the political climate. It was last known as 'Narodni Glasnik' (People's voice) from 7 December 1940 till it ceased publication in 1978.

Chapter 9

Back to Beginnings – Sex, Love and Birth Control

Homework finished, I stretched out on the sofa. The handsome face of Glumac looked down at me from the wall opposite. I now knew why he'd come to America. But why had my parents, so many relatives, left their homes for this unknown land?

Mama looked up, smiled. Most evenings, supper cleared away and the day's tasks ended, she sat reading in the rocking chair.

"Shall I make coffee?"

"And bring that apple cake. I just want to finish this chapter."

She put down her book and when I returned. "Anything happen at school?"

"Not really. I've been thinking a lot about what Uncle Pete told me last week. Glumac came to this country because he was a socialist. Why did you come? Who did you go to? When did you meet papa? I hope you fell in love, not like Mrs Millar." She was our new neighbour.

"Poor Mrs Millar was a 'sent for'. Her brother's friend at work paid her passage from Germany on condition she married him."

"Mr Millar? She'd never seen him, didn't know him?"

"Many women came like that, Frieda. Some marriages were good and others........" she shrugged. "Mr Millar is a violent man. She's frightened of him. He beats her and even though she's near her time he forces........" Mama stopped, looked at me.

"You were going to say forces her at night when they're in bed together," I interjected.

"How do you know about such things?"

"I'm not a child anymore, mom. Peggy at Latimer told me. There are twelve children in her family, another on the way and the house is small. Her mother cries sometimes in the night but the father takes no notice. She hates him."

"I don't like talking about this, you're too young."

"But isn't it better to know as I grow up? At least you told me about periods. Some girls were scared stiff, thought they were bleeding to death."

Reluctantly she smiled.

"Why did Mrs Millar agree? She didn't have to come over here."

"Why did any of us come? Because we were poor. Everyone wanted to go to America where there was work."

"But papa's not like our neighbour. You're not afraid of him, I know that. You met in Oakmont at his Aunt Ujna's didn't you?"

"Yes and we were married from her house. He was twenty-five and I was twenty-three.

"Weren't you married before? I've heard papa say he fell for an attractive young widow."

Her expression changed. "I told your father when he proposed to me. That was only fair. But I never talk about it."

I was silent, but soon she continued, "Papa's a good man except for his awful temper."

Quickly I answered, "He soon gets over it then he's so sorry. You know, mama, listening to him I've learned to swear in three languages, he just goes from Croatian to German then English."

She laughed but also scolded. "Don't practice it on anybody."

Mama stood up. "I'm tired, it's bed for me.

"You haven't answered my question, were you in love with papa or was it just easier to be married?"

"I'll tell you more some other time." She kissed me and left the room.

That 'other time' was a great many years later when the United States authorities returned my mother's passport which they'd confiscated during the McCarthy witch hunt. She was seventy-five when she arrived to stay with us for a year. We'd kept in touch through letters, photographs and the occasional expensive phone call. Now we were able to talk long and often.

Some years before my mother's visit I had left my husband, bought a house with borrowed money, taken in lodgers. I kept my local authority clerical job and somehow managed, happier than I'd been for years. Charlie Brewster, organiser for the Essex Party, came often to the house and a mutual attraction developed.

Recently he'd moved in with me and though we lived together openly my husband still refused a divorce. I'd wondered about mama's reaction but she grew to like Charlie and he her.

During our evenings alone together she talked of the past, reminded me how as a child of eleven I'd gone with her to Yugoslavia third class from New York to Dubrovnik. We'd shared a small stateroom, the food was good and there was even a small library. She compared this with the ship in which she'd first travelled to America.

"I left from Bremen. There were a lot of us, all pushed into the bottom of the boat. It was terrible. People have written books about it."

"Yes, the steerage conditions must have been awful and it seems from what I've read that it was much the same in all those early ships. Millions experienced it."

Mama nodded. "Bad for everybody, much worse for women who travelled alone. There weren't many of us. Our quarters had only a flimsy wall which separated us from the men. We had to use the same toilet. It was best for two women to be always together. I met Anna on board and we stuck together like glue. Her sister had written how it would be. Some men were decent but many made stupid, insulting remarks to us. So, we spent a great deal of time on the little bit of deck allowed us. The stewards who should have protected us were sometimes the worst. It was an enormous relief when we finally reached Ellis Island."

"Did you have any trouble? So many people did."

"No, I easily passed the health check. Then a badge with my destination was pinned on my jacket and I had to pay for a lunch box out of the ten dollars all immigrants had to have before they could enter America. I was ferried to the Battery, taken to a station and put on a train."

"Your step-brother met you? He was the only one in the States, wasn't he?"

Mama laughed. "He wasn't there and that's when my troubles began."

It has been harrowing for this tired twenty-one year old as she waited hour after hour in the enormous Cathedral like Pennsylvania Station in Pittsburgh. A friendly ticket collector, a German speaker, saw she was a 'greenhorn' and after some discussion put her on a train for the small town of Oakmont where her step-brother lived.

At that station she again waited, on an open platform. Her dilemma became worse as she discovered from the station master that the address she had was for a post office box, not a house.

"When a factory whistle blew and men poured through a gate near the station I ran over, asked for a German speaker and found one. 'From German?' he asked. 'No Croatia.' He and his friends took me to a Croatian saloon. The proprietor knew my step-brother so at last I got to his boarding house.

More than twenty men lived there, shared rooms and beds as they changed over in day and night shifts. It was no place for a young woman. But Jovanka, the 'boarding missus' came from my province, Srem, and was very helpful. I was starving.

She made me a huge meal of egg on steak and fried potatoes and soon I felt better. That night I slept with her. Next morning she took me to an agency and I got a live-in job."

"What about your step-brother?"

"He was never very bright. Hadn't taken in my letters and the telegram still lay in the post office box.

On my first Sunday off Jovanka took me to Mrs Millivoj's home where all the Srem people gathered. She was much older but became a real friend, helped me to a better job and through her I met your father, who was her nephew."

"You must have met other young men, a lot more of them over there than women at that time."

"I could have had my pick but no-one appealed to me till I met papa. Him I liked straight away. Not just because he had wavy hair and was very good looking." She smiled at me. "He was so full of life, always led the Kolo and the singing. And me, I felt like a little brown sparrow. I'd never even learned to sing or dance."

"But papa courted you?"

"After a while. I think his aunt may have influenced him. She liked me. A year after he came we were married from her house on 1 May 1905."

"And the wedding night mama?"

She countered with 'how was yours?'

"The first I want to forget but not the second, good with Charlie. Only I wasn't young then and it was different."

Wedding portrait: Sebastian Truhar and Maria Pichler (my father and mother), 1905

She nodded. "We were in love and young. But I said to him 'you're aware I'm a widow and know what to expect but no children yet.' He bowed, said 'on my honour Maria' and we laughed. You see, Frieda, your father was no innocent. He'd worked in Vienna and Budapest and though we never talked about it I'm sure he'd had experience of women. I just took it for granted."

I made coffee, hoping no one would disturb us for I wanted to hear more.

"In those very early days, though we were happy, life became difficult because papa earned so little. I went cleaning, took in washing, still it wasn't enough. The crisis came one evening. Papa pulled off his heavy boots, slumped in our armchair. 'I can't endure it Maria. It's hunky do this, that. I fetch, carry, push wheelbarrows, sweep up, all for eight dollars a week. I'm a craftsman not a boy.' He buried his face in his hands.

Your father was always a highly strung man, I realised he was near breaking point. I had to think for both of us, made him quit his job and we moved to Pittsburgh, where we shared two rooms with my brother Peter. Papa vainly searched for work. He didn't

Group photograph of Maria's and Sebastian's wedding

Photograph of handwritten notes on the back of the wedding photograph sent to me from Paula (my sister)

then know that the American Federation of Labour Bricklayers' Union operated a 'closed shop' and few outsiders were admitted.

Tired and bitter, he announced to me, 'I'm going labouring in Jones and Laughlin steel mill, they always need men.' My answer was sharp, 'No, it's got to be a bricklayer's job.' I'd seen what happened to those in steel mills, constant accidents and deaths.

It was then I decided to take in boarders like the woman who lived underneath us. We moved to a bigger place and Peter found three decent men who shared a large room. The money from them and help from your uncle kept us going.

It was a year of depression, illness and frustration. I had to fight to keep your father out of the steel mills and finally, through a friend already in the Union, he got a bricklayer's job. Years later he did work in steel mills but as a skilled craftsman.

Sisters and brothers followed us to America. We had to find them jobs, look after them. Within a few years most of them had

*Allegheny, Pittsburgh Pennsylvania, 25th November 1905:
Back row from left: Vera (Maria's sister), Mila
(Maria's sister), Apolonia (Sebastian's sister)
Front row from left: Nick (Sebastian's brother),
Pete (Maria's brother), Sebastian, Pascho (Maria's stepbrother)*

married and moved to other parts of the city or even further afield.

I listened intently as mama spoke, got a notebook, asked questions, jotted down names, dates, happenings.

"Why are you doing that?"

I laughed. "Maybe someday I'll write a book about our family. We've done interesting things I want my children to know. And these times, before I was born or remember anything, are important."

"If you do that you must tell the truth not just the good side but how hard it was for our people in those days."

"I will, mama, believe me if it ever happens."

Friday was my one free day, stolen from the busy life at Goldsmiths College where I was now a student. My mother had crossed the Atlantic to be with me, she needed to talk and I was

Father's side of the family outside House on the Hill, 1928: Sebastian (my father) back row fourth from left, me directly in front at age 16 next to my mother (Maria) second row right, Paula (my sister) end first row right, Tony (my brother) front row third from right with tie. Others unknown

certainly interested. So on Friday afternoons we sat alone, cosily together as it had been in my childhood.

"Strange isn't it, that Paula and Tony have the same birthday, 10 January, just a year apart."

"I never expected to get pregnant again so soon, thought I was safe while breast feeding Tony. It was then I decided two children were enough."

"So how did I happen? I was the third."

My mother remained silent. "It's a long story, have you time now?" she said at last.

I nodded, "It's Friday mom, my afternoon off."

"Where to start? If that letter from your father's mother hadn't come you wouldn't be here. That's made you sit up." She smiled.

I was certainly very curious, didn't want to miss a word.

"Papa didn't get the letter till after supper. I thought it might upset him and it did. It was only one page. He looked at me. 'She's not well. I suppose the old bastard lifted his hand to her once too often. She wants you to come, bring the children, before she dies, she writes.' Your father was very miserable. At last he said, 'Will you go? She wants it so much. I'll borrow the money..........'. 'No need,' I told him, explained that my 'house' money was enough for a one way ticket and he could send me more. He was relieved. 'You can go to Ilaca, see your mother.'"

Mama was silent, resumed with some difficulty. "I always knew, Frieda, that in spite of all the hardship I had as a child, your grandmother loved me. She had no choice but to send me to service, I was the eldest girl. But I remember how she cried when I left."

"Yes, when she visited us long ago in the old farmhouse, she wanted to be only with you. But how did papa manage while you were away?"

"The men ate with my friends Kata, who had rooms above us and also took in boarders. She had payment for that but they slept at home. So I left with an easy mind.

Paso's house in Vukovar was sumptuous by comparison with my home. His mother's welcome was warm but the father scarcely acknowledged me or the children. I ignored him, helped with the chores. My mother-in-law was afraid, rushed to do his bidding, but not once during my stay did he attempt physical violence though he was often abusive. She was very happy at my visit as we spoke long about all her children in the States.

As our departure neared I decided to face up to the old man. When he was alone I said to him, 'You expect too much of her. The doctor says she must have rest.'

'Who gave you the right to call the doctor. He's very expensive.' I replied, 'Don't worry, I paid him. As to what gives me the right, I'm Paso's wife, she's the grandmother of our children. Can't you see how frail she is?'

'There's plenty of work in her yet, I have it hard too,' he was very angry. But I wasn't afraid of him. 'You haven't born all those children, six still alive, what do you know about how a woman feels.' Amazed at this frank talk the old man's eyes blazed as he moved toward me. I stood my ground and his hand dropped.

'It's time you realised this. When I'm gone someone must come to help. You can afford it. Leave her in peace for the few years she has left.' He turned, stalked away. Nothing could soften him. He'd scarcely looked at his grandchildren. But their presence had made a difference to the grandmother even though nothing might change.

The leave taking was sad. I promised to write often. High on the wagon seat my father-in-law stolidly waiting to take us to the railway station. The children and I climbed aboard, turned and waved till the grandmother could no longer be seen."

"In Ilaca we received a rapturous welcome. I hugged my mother, Christine, her little girl, Lena and the wild-eyed, mentally retarded boy. But for this child who could never have passed through Ellis Island, they'd all have been in the States. It wouldn't have mattered then that Christina's husband had walked out one day and never come back. My mother had been adamant she must stay for Christina had always needed direction. We knew she was right.

I enjoyed working beside my mother in the fields. We spoke of my brothers and sisters, she wanted to know every detail.

Then she asked, 'you are happy, Maria?' 'Yes, as happy as people can be when they are poor. Life can be hard there, mother, for we are strangers to the American people and they do not always treat us well. But we have met interesting Croatians and learned many new things.'

'You go to mass and confession every Sunday?' I was silent, did not want to upset my mother but neither would I lie to her. 'No, we have left the church. In America it helps the rich not the poor. We manage well without it.' It was hard for my mother to understand as I tried to explain we were socialists now and the priests considered such people evil though to us they were the kindest and best people we had met in America.

'I will pray for you,' was her answer. 'You will come to visit, mother, when Christina's children are older and she can be left alone with them. They you will see for yourself.'

Pichler family portrait, 23rd November 1903, Croatia: Back row from left Maria, Peter (Maria's brother), middle row from left Vera, Mila (Maria's sisters), front row Kristina (Maria's sister), Grandma Pichler (Maria's mother), Begev Blum (Maria's half-brother)

I was time to go back to Paso and Pittsburgh. Now I travelled as an American for during my absence papa had been to night school, learned about the Constitution and obtained his citizenship papers which automatically included me."

Mama sat silent. I watched her, remained quiet. Slowly she spoke again. "I'll never forget how happy papa was when he met us at the station. He hugged us all and was close to tears. At home I told him about the visit. He nodded. 'Your letters made it clear the old man hasn't changed.' 'He never will. I suggested she come to America but her answer was the same as before, 'he is my husband, this is my fate.'

'The old, God's will, rubbish.' 'Yes, I couldn't persuade her yet it was good I went, she so enjoyed the children. I'll write every week and we must take a family photograph which she asked for.'

Life returned to normal. The boarders moved back. Some weeks later I realised I was pregnant. All day my thoughts raced for I had to make up my mind.

I'd been sure two was enough but now I wondered. Maybe it was because papa was so loving to the children and me. He's been a long time alone. 'Never even looked at anyone else, not like some I could mention,' Kata had said. I smiled, felt it couldn't have been otherwise.

Tony, so solemn sometimes, his big brown eyes wide as he listened to the talk of grown-ups. And Paula, never still, under the table as she hugged her father's legs or on his lap with her arms around his neck. Children were hard work but made for happiness too, a bond between husband and wife if the man adored them as your father did.

That was the bright side. For nine long months I'd get bigger and bigger, then the pain of birth. And I wasn't as young now, in less than two years I'd be thirty. So, my thoughts ran. There were other good reasons why I should not have this child. Could I manage the extra work, the toddlers, the boarders? Another baby meant a move to larger rooms, more rent. There'd be the midwife, other expenses.

For days I pondered, my mind on little else as I did the chores. The boarders noticed the change, tried to cheer me up. The kindly Topol said, 'Tell us your troubles and we will help you. I'll compose a song – To the lovely Maria – will that make you happy?'

I smiled at him. 'It's not a real problem and you can't solve it. Thanks for the offer.' It was then I realised it was indeed not so formidable a matter as I was imagining."

Mama laughed, "Also as I was pregnant, I needn't worry about getting pregnant and papa would be happier, for a while at least. He too had been worried. You know, Frieda, your father was an industrious and able man. In those days he did not take for granted but appreciated that my work with the boarders contributed to half our income. On social occasions he became merry but never drunk, like the husbands of some of my friends who had to be coaxed away from more drink and even became violent.

So that's how you came to be born at 6.30 on the morning of 4 August 1911. It has been a hot night. You were a large baby, eleven pounds and the birth was difficult. Papa stayed up and Mrs Ranczak, our Czech midwife, told me he was shaken, flinched when I cried out. At first I didn't like that, then thought well it's good he should know what women have to go through at child birth. The midwife insisted I stay in bed. I was very weak, had lost a lot of blood. Slowly I recovered. By October the boarders were back."

Me as a baby

Mama smiled. "They were interested in you and there was a long discussion about your name. Topol suggested Miroslava, celebration of peace, but I thought ahead to school and we compromised on Frieda, nearest to Germany for peace. That's on your birth certificate and only later at school did you become Frieda. I guess the teachers thought we couldn't spell."

It was surprising to me that my mother spoke so freely about these events in the past. Yet I understand that to her I was now also a woman who had experienced childbirth, could sympathise and understand.

I hugged and kissed her, "Thanks for letting me be born, mama," which she hugely enjoyed.

The quiet of the afternoon ended abruptly as my son Pat, home for a weekend from Oxford, burst in followed quickly by Margaret. Mama treasured their hugs and kisses, was pleased when they praised her cooking. A casserole simmered in the oven and her special apple pie was already baked.

Pat, now twenty after National Service, spoke of his first year at Balliol, the good things and the bad. Margie consulted him about her grammar school, not at all sure she liked Coborn Foundation.

The next Friday afternoon we sat contentedly before the open fire. "You've never told me about how it was after I was born."

"Hard years, Frieda. We had to move twice as boarding houses multiplied and streets became crowded. Paula and Tony went to school, you to Kindergarten. The years seemed to fly by and who knows we might never have moved to the Hill but for Topol. You know about him?"

I nodded. Then mama surprised me with the question. "You are happy with this man, even if he is younger?" "He makes up for much I've missed." "I can see he loves you from the way he looks at you. Papa used to look at me like that, then he stopped." Such intimacy was more than I'd expected from her.

"Why, mama?" "I didn't understand then. From the beginning I should have talked to him freely about everything as you say you and Charlie speak to each other. But it was hard in those days. People didn't mention 'such things.

"Mother, even with Pat I couldn't speak freely about personal matters. When I tried he'd walk out of the room, just wouldn't listen." "But he never loved you. I knew that from the beginning. You were young, a virgin, a communist, just what he wanted. Love didn't come into it. And what you felt wasn't love either, he was your 'movie star'. It soon faded, didn't it?" She'd known I'd be unhappy, had strongly opposed the marriage.

"And you and papa stayed in love with each other?"

Her lined face smiled. "You remember you asked me that when you were around fifteen? I couldn't tell you then what came between us. But I've changed too, I can speak of anything with you now. Tony had noticed things weren't right between papa and me. You didn't?" I shook my head.

"I knew the reason, remembered our happier days and decided that night I'd speak frankly to him, try to make things better. Your questions at that time had brought back so many memories. I left you because I had to be alone.

In bed, propped on two pillows, I waited for him. The front door banged and soon he was in the bedroom. He didn't even look at me, just undressed, got into bed and lay with his hands clasped behind his head.

I spoke first. 'Paso, what's happened to us? Do you remember our early days? Where have the years gone?'

He answered reflectively, 'In hard work, Maria, settling into this house, raising our children. And we became socialists which gave more purpose to our lives. As for our early days,' he turned to look at me, 'many nights I lie here and remember but I thought you had forgotten.'

'I've forgotten nothing.'

'Then why has it been so long, why have you refused me so often?'

Mama seemed to remember every detail of that long ago evening. Now, still indignant after so many years she said, "Frieda, he was blaming me. I spoke out as never before.

'Fear of pregnancy, nothing else. Because of you our birth control method hasn't always been successful. I gave myself several abortions you know nothing about. The midwife says it might kill me if I do it again and she'll not help me.'

Papa looked at me, his eyes wide. He was speechless, appalled. He went quiet and I waited.

'Maria, I'm so sorry. I know I must withdraw but it's so hard and it's true I've not always done it.' I didn't relent. 'It's harder for a woman to give herself an abortion or bear a child every year. And you refuse to try those new rubber things Peter mentioned. I heard him telling you but you laughed at him.'

I'd never been so frank before. That night we talked a long time. Then he put his arm around me and said 'on my honour, Maria' as he had on that first night of our marriage. We laughed and things became better."

She sat silent and I didn't interrupt.

Those abortions, I'd shuddered as she described the hooked steel instrument, like a long crochet needle. What desperation she must have felt and what courage it had taken.

Victorian values, Catholic doctrine, fundamentalist Puritanism worked against those who sought to introduce birth control. An American pioneer in this field, Margaret Sanger, was imprisoned after she opened the first Birth Control Clinic in Brooklyn, New York in 1916. It was closed by the police as a 'public nuisance'.

When even educated women were at such a disadvantage how much more so were the women among whom my mother lived. She'd known very well that in her circles many children made for greater poverty, the evidence was all around her.

But not all women were as strong as my mother, though it had cost her dear as she took drastic action. The withdrawal method or abstinence were the only answers at that time but most men refused either and their wives had little or no say in the matter.

Thank goodness papa had been different, not like Mr Millar or Peggy's father. Even so my mother had found it difficult to talk with him about this. Yet she had spoken, made him understand and to this day was glad she had done so.

"You're a brave woman, mama. I could never have done that to myself."

"Frieda, you've never had to." It was long ago and she could now smile as she said it.

That was to be our last conversation about 'the old days' as my mother was soon to return to the States.

Chapter 10

The New Brick House

During the boom of the twenties my father made plans to strike out on his own. He had learned to read blueprints, felt that his years of experience in the building trade were a good foundation for success. Friends with the necessary skills would work with him.

My mother was against it. More widely read than papa she followed political articles in Radnik which gave warning that a prosperity which ignored large areas of deprivation could not in the end continue. The paper pointed out that this mania for buying stocks on the instalment plan, called margin, didn't represent reality. Free of illusion, the left realised this might lead to an almighty economic crash. Though papa in conversation agreed, he did not see that it in any way concerned his own small proposed venture.

Yet mama faced a dilemma. My father had sweated in steel mills, come home cold and wet from building sites. Had she any right to interfere with his plan, which might give him an easier life?

The crunch came when papa announced at the supper table, "A bricklayer should have a brick house, not this old wooden place. I'm going to start building soon on the flat land behind the well. That will give a good experience for my new scheme."

I laughed. "You can't do that, papa. This is a wonderful old house. We'd lose our lime tree, the barn. And what about the view, that green hill on the other side of the Millvale."

"My boxing ring is in the barn and the pigeon cote. Our Aylers Club meets here," Tony protested.

Mama decided to shrug it off. "Papa's joking. He can't want to move away from this airy, open place. We've put so much work into it."

His loud angry voice interrupted, "Yes I do and I'm going ahead with it."

Her manner changed. "Paso, I'm utterly opposed to your plan. This house can be modernised for a fraction of the cost of a new house. It's not just what you want. I too have worked hard, scrimped and saved. And just as we're breaking even you want to lumber us with a new pile of debts. It's unnecessary and it's wrong."

"Mama's right," I butted in and Tony too spoke up.

My father was beside himself with rage. He snatched the empty platter from the table with both hands and flung it on the floor.

"I don't give a damn what any of you think," he shouted and stormed out of the room.

This violent interruption of temper though rare was not new to us. It might be sparked off by some trivial incident and we'd learned to sit silent as he raved and swore. In a few minutes it was over. He'd look sheepish, assume a false jollity, but never apologise.

Mama's reaction had always been a withdrawal from us all. A stillness came over her. She went about her tasks without speaking except when necessary and never to my father. This could last a week or more, a miserable time. But as we helped mama pick up the shattered pieces of china we knew this was different.

Papa had for some time become more and more authoritarian. When my sister and I argued with him he rarely lost his temper, for we'd learned to handle and humour him. But, proud woman that she was, my mother wanted justice and would not stoop to this.

In earlier days when she'd looked after boarders to keep the family going during papa's times of unemployment there was greater equality and far more discussion between them. Often it was her point of view which had been accepted and acted upon. This had continued through most of my childhood as they'd worked amicably together in house and garden.

But almost imperceptibly the relationship had changed. As his earnings increased and he became a master builder, papa began to consider his opinions always to be the correct ones.

"What will happen now?" I asked mama.

"I don't know, he has become a stubborn man." She was very upset. We were soon to learn that none of us had a say as papa went ahead.

"Why don't you go on strike?" I said to her as I helped in the kitchen where mama cooked large meals on Saturdays and Sundays to feed the men who'd come to help papa dig the foundations.

"You have a lot to learn, Frieda. Your father now acts like he is God but we depend on him and what he earns. Where can I go with you children". This is my home. But don't think I do this willingly. He is wrong, big-headed, spends money like water on something we don't need or want."

The work went on for a long time and it was during these years that my sister married and left home.

On some evenings I sat on our porch where the men gathered after their hard day. Among them was a young carpenter, Steve Mesaros, who later became known as Steve Nelson, Commander of the Abraham Lincoln Battalion in the International Brigade during the Spanish Civil War.

At last we moved into the new house. The rooms were smaller, the bathroom didn't mean much as we still had no 'city' water. It was a poor exchange for our rambling old farmhouse.

My father's temper didn't improve as increasing debts had to be met by even harder work on his part. Mama bore the full brunt of his irrational behaviour. One day she turned on him.

"Papa, if you go on shouting and carrying on, I shall leave you. I am a good cook and can still get a job in one of the rich houses in Sewickly. I've enquired into that. Paula is married, Tony old enough to earn his living and I'll look after Frieda.

You just do what you please now and I have to put up with it. I've had enough. I am your wife not your servant and unless you change I'm going. I give you six month's notice."

For my father it was a great shock, especially that she'd made enquiries and clearly thought it through. Though he shouted and blustered he knew mama meant what she said. As the weeks went by he became more conciliatory, consulted her, listened to her suggestions. Though she still felt strongly about the new house she did not reproach him, it had been built and there was no going back on that. So again they sat down, talked together as 'two people should' and returned to the more balanced, happier relationship of earlier days.

My mother asked him one question. "Why have you been going on like this, yelling and swearing, shouting at me, thinking only you know what is right?"

To which, somewhat shamefacedly, he replied, "That's how I thought a man should behave."

"Only after you become the 'big earner' which made you feel so important. You weren't always like that."

In fact he'd bitterly condemned his own father for harshness towards his mother, whom the old man had frequently struck. Now he has been doing the same, using verbal assault rather than physical violence.

Yet he was a socialist, said my mother, and should have acted differently. But like so many early socialists, communists and trade unionists, it was the 'brotherhood of man' they were working towards and somehow the equality they wanted didn't always stretch to women, especially those in their own homes.

Many women didn't question this role of subservience which had for so long been their lot, but my mother was made of sterner stuff though it took even her a long time.

However, things went reasonably well until the Wall Street crash of 1929 when my parents were faced with problems more difficult than they had ever previously experienced in America.

Chapter 11

University – The Liberal Club

On 12 February 1929, I became a student at the University of Pittsburgh. Mama was near tears on that first morning. "I still can hardly believe you're really going to college."

Hurriedly I kissed her and escaped. This ambition mama had nourished was about to be realised but I didn't want to be overwhelmed by her emotion. She didn't understand that alongside my delight I also had doubts and fears.

As I entered the 'hallowed portal' it seemed more like a building site than a campus. The new ambitious Cathedral of Learning was going up. Bill Albertson, nearing the end of his second year and the only other communist there, took me under his wing. We scarcely knew each other for he lived near the University whereas I had an hour's travel to get there. Bill initiated me into the ways of the campus, spelled out rules about classes, clubs, showed me the library.

"There are a great many societies, over a hundred and thirty but I hope you'll concentrate with me on the Liberal Club. Ever since it was founded the pressure's been on. We've reason to believe they'll act this spring to try and get rid of us once and for all. Are you taking Economics?"

"How did you know?"

"We all do it, part of our political background I suppose. I'll let you know about the next meeting of the Liberal Club." With that he disappeared to his part-time job in the college cafeteria and I saw little of him during these first few weeks.

There were few women in my economics class. Most of the male students were established Americans who saw it as necessary grounding for a business career. Rarely at a loss for words, I mingled easily, spoke up in discussion, enjoyed the relative freedom, so different from high school.

To my surprise within a week the young man in a seat next to mine asked for a date. Bob, short, slight, blonde was one of the 'aryan' types who at high school wouldn't have given me a second glance. The 'necking' sessions in his car were both tender and passionate as I responded to his kisses.

But Bob belonged to that part of American youth outside my experience, one of the affluent hedonistic products of the prosperous twenties who enjoyed comforts, luxuries, indulgence unknown to me. Sexual satisfaction was what he expected within days of our first date. Much as I'd enjoyed our passionate exchanges I wasn't ready for this. He coaxed with loving persuasion, used to having his own way. When I still refused he became angry, distant. The brief encounter was over.

It left me bruised, hurt but also reflective. What might it have been like, that act to which all this passion inevitably led? Had I missed something good, as he said, wonderful? For Bob was clearly an experienced lover. He'd wanted it desperately, promised I too would enjoy it. I'd never know now.

Our dating hadn't lasted long, I had not become too deeply involved and so was able after a time to put it behind me. Soon, as before, I laughed and joked with the other students.

As he noticed Bob's aloofness, Al, a six-foot gangling man with slicked down hair and horn rimmed glasses came to sit beside me.

"I've never met a communist before. I can't believe some of the arguments you put up in class." "Like what, for instance?" "All this talk that only a socialist society can meet the needs of the poor. There aren't many such people, surely. After all, times are prosperous."

Scarcely believing what I heard I looked at him. "Where have you lived all your life? Here in Pittsburgh? Don't you ever leave this plush east end to explore the rest of the city? Why this sudden interest in my views?"

Somewhat haltingly he answered, "I've never really thought about these things before. Of course I've been to theatres and restaurants. But I've not really looked elsewhere, as you say." "That can be remedied. You have a car so come to my part of the world, see places in which people like mine live and work. But on a weekday, so we'll have to cut classes, OK?" He nodded.

I took him to the Hill District, the Jewish ghetto of Pittsburgh with its mean streets, little sweatshops and tenement buildings. Then across the Allegheny River, down East Ohio Street where we went to see the multi-occupied houses in one of which I was born.

We returned to the other bank lined with steel mills where flames rose and men ran as molten steel poured.

I pointed out Heppenstalls. "My father worked there for years repairing still hot furnaces for the next shifts, putting bricks back. That's his job, bricklayer. When he couldn't take any more he found an outside job but that meant less money."

We drove through Millvale where the small factories which gave it that name belched smoke. I pointed to three small cinemas.

"That's where we spent our Saturday, a nickel for the show, a nickel for an ice-cream cone. Sometimes in June I had to bring baskets of roses down here to sell – five cents a bunch.

I pointed upwards to our Hill. "That's where we live but no car can get up this way. We'll have to go back to East Ohio Street, then to my home for coffee and cake, you've earned it. And remember, my parents are immigrants and mama's English is poor."

Al had asked few questions. As he steered his large car carefully up our uneven mud road he said, "It is a different world yet we live in the same city." I smiled at him but said nothing.

Mama in a clean apron was ready for us. The coffee pot was on the stove, strudel on the table. In her fractured English she said, "It's so nice someone from Frieda's college should come to our house. I'm very pleased to meet you."

"Bathroom's upstairs, Al. You can have a wash after all that smoke."

When he came down the Hill kids had surrounded his car. I went out. "You can look but don't touch. It's a rich man's auto."

Al smiled wryly at my words, followed me into the parlour as my mother brought coffee and cake. She soon excused herself. "I got to make supper, papa will soon be home from work."

Exhausted, I was glad when Al rose. He bade my mother good-bye and as I went with him to his car said, "I'm beginning to understand why you feel as you do. Now you must come to dinner at my home and perhaps you'll understand me better." I agreed and with another smile he left.

In class Al asked, "How about dinner at my home on Thursday evening at eight?"

"Look, each day on the street car it takes me an hour to get her and an hour to get home. Then I have a long walk up to our Hill. I'm afraid it's not on to come twice to this part of the world."

"I should have thought of that. We'll make it dinner at six and afterwards the theatre. I think an hour and a bit will be quite enough for you with my mama." "Doesn't she want me to come?" "She doesn't understand. It's hard to explain to her." "I suppose I'm an 'undesirable influence'." He reddened. "Something like that. But I want you to come." I almost asked 'why' but bit it back. Unless she was downright rude I'd be very polite to his mama. We agreed to meet at the cafeteria after classes.

He was there when I arrived, drove to an enormous house set well back among trees and shrubs. We walked through a spacious hall into a large elegant room whose long windows revealed flower beds and a lawn which seemed to stretch on forever.

His mother greeted me. She was nearly as tall as her son but gaunt, somehow lacking in grace, I though, even though she wore a soft flowing wine coloured gown. Around her neck hung a ruby pendant, rings sparkled on her fingers. Black hair was piled high in Edwardian fashion.

Al worked hard to keep the conversation going. When dinner was announced we entered the long sombre dining room panelled in wood. On one side was an elaborately carved sideboard, in the centre stood a large oval table on which at the far end placed for three had been laid. Our conversation now was a polite exchange about the early spring, the need for rain, the possible premature blossoming of roses.

"I want to exhibit but the rain must come before the bud opens or the rose will be flawed. Have you roses in your garden?"

"Yes, two long rows, some of them wild. Mama says they are two tightly bunched but I like to see the colours intermingle." "Your mama is right. Each rose bush should stand alone. In a bed, yes but separate." Al smiled and I wondered if he remembered my story about selling roses. His mama's lips pursed as I smiled back.

It was the first time I had food put before me by a servant. I looked with interest at this unobtrusive person who came and went so quietly. How mused my mother would be.

As dinner ended Al looked at his watch. "Time we were going if we're to make the theatre." I said good-bye to his mother. A maid showed me into an elaborate, ornate bathroom. From the hall, as we walked out, I glimpsed a very large room to the other side, complete with jutting balconies.

I stopped, raised an enquiring face to Al. "It's the ballroom," he explained. "My, it's quite a spread you've got here." I said to him as we got into the car.

He looked keenly at me, then shrugged, opened his two hands palms upward, but said nothing. It might almost have been an apology.

I regularly attended Liberal Club meetings. Now Bill Albertson, President of the Society, wanted me to become secretary. This slight intense man with straight black hair, dark eyes behind horn-rimmed glasses looked down at me as I protested.

"I've only just got here. There must be others." 'It's difficult. The Club's well established, we've over fifty members but few are willing to take office now the authorities are bearing down on us. I wasn't keen on being president, sophomore year's important and my work in the cafeteria takes a lot of energy."

I remained silent. "I didn't think you'd hesitate. There's not much to do, only a matter of keeping minutes and records." "It's not that. I didn't want to get involved so soon. I'm enjoying the freedom here after high school. You don't understand, do you? Going to university was something you never questioned."

"That's true and although we're hard up I always knew I'd go. My mother's a graduate, studied in Russia before the war." "Well for my people and me it seems a miracle I'm here at all. Could I be expelled?" "I don't think they'll go that far. They just want rid of the club and lately we've had a lot of harassment from the authorities."

"Why just now?" "Money. This grandiose sky-scraper scheme needs a lot of donations from the big industrialists." "And the Liberal Club threatens that?"

"That's how they see it. But not just our society. Quite a few of the faculty, like Fred Woltman, are under pressure. He's an assistant instructor in Philosophy. You and I are the only two communists here among thousands. But not the only ones with strong views about how the world should be. Arthur McDowell, vice-president of the Club, believes Christians should be out among the poor, helping them, not sitting in churches. He's going to be a preacher. Fred Woltman is a civil rights campaigner.

There are many among the students and teachers who might be called liberals or Jeffersonian democrats if you prefer." "I've heard that term used before. Does it mean an organisation of followers of Thomas Jefferson?" "No, just people who believe in his ideas. After all, he wrote the Declaration of Independence. Somewhere in a letter to a friend he said 'I have sworn upon the altar of God eternal hostility against every form of tyranny over the mind of man.'"

"You memorised that?" Bill grinned sheepishly. "I like quotations and that one appealed to me. And that 'tyranny over the mind of man' is what they're trying to impose here on students and faculty. What they don't like is that our Club believes in 'free speech according to the Constitution' and we take it as a right."

"And Fred Woltman, what did he do?" "You remember the 1927 miners' strike, Frieda?" "I'll say I do. I was out every Saturday either on relief or in the company towns." "Well, Fred wrote an article for the American Mercury which condemned the use of the State police system and certain actions of the police. He also criticised the coal police employed by the companies. Dean Steig told him his article had made Governor Fisher 'as mad as a hornet' and that keeping the Governor's favour was a matter of 'bread and butter' since there was a possibility he might cut off their whole appropriation.

You won't believe this but he actually ordered Fred not to write or talk about anything which might make the Governor and what he called the 'wealthy classes' angry because it was they who were financing the great Cathedral of Learning."

"But they can't issue orders like that," I was indignant. "Fred's still fighting his case with them." "What'll happen to Woltman?" Bill shrugged. "He's a great guy. Got real courage. You know what old Gow said to him?"

"Who is Gow?" "J Steele Gow, Executive Secretary of the University. He said to Fred that the people of 'the community' are conservative and don't agree with his ideas. Woltman asked him 'You mean the trustees?' When Gow said 'yes' Fred suggested they were in the main the coal barons and steel kings representing their own interests and not the peoples. Gow was furious.

People like Woltman and Professor Bill Nunn, who did part of that article, strongly believe that to abandon investigation, research, writing and speaking or other work on controversial subjects is wrong. Nunn's off to a New York university and the grape-vine says other professors have been warned."

"So it's very serious then." "Yes, and the students have to fight in their own way, through the Liberal Club, which is the one thing we've got." Ruefully I said, "You've certainly spelled it out, haven't you. I'll have to revise my ideas. To me university meant a wonderful place where I could learn and absorb so many things I don't know. But the conflict goes on, even here."

That night I lay awake a long time. I did not fully accept Bill's assurance that there was little possibility of trouble, even less of expulsion. I realised that active participation in the Liberal Club put me at risk. Yet it was clear from what Bill had said that these steel and coal trusts who waged war on miners and steel workers also had their grip on the university.

My childhood memories of the big steel strike in 1919 in and around Pittsburgh were still vivid. Our friends Matt and Frank had been beaten up and arrested, lucky not to be among the twenty-two murdered nationwide by the steel trust guards. I couldn't hold back. At the next meeting of the Liberal Club I was elected secretary, unopposed.

Almost every day Bill and I met. Before long it was assumed I was 'his girl'. I shrugged it off but he seemed to think it was a good idea. When he kissed me I didn't respond. "Someone else?" "There was, it's over."

He didn't ask questions. As we worked together I grew to like and respect him though clearly he wanted more than that.

"You must meet my mother," he said one day. "You'll find her interesting. She was an illegal revolutionary in Tsarist Russia." I didn't have the heart to tell him I didn't want to meet his mama or any mama so we arranged I'd go to an evening when he wasn't working.

There were two large upstairs rooms and a small kitchen. How pleasant it was, white walls, bright curtains, gay rugs on plain floors. In each room, piled high with cushions, a divan served both as bed and settee. In years to come such places became familiar to me, almost standard furnishing among hard-up radicals.

Bill's mother, slender with greying bobbed hair and a pence-nez perched on her nose, wore a straight skirt, white blouse with a black velvet band around her neck. She held out a languid hand when he introduced me, still holding the book she had been reading.

"So nice of you to come, Bill had talked much about you." The accent was strong but the English good, unlike my mother's. To her son she said, "In the oven beef stroganoff and sour cream is in the ice box." Then a vague smile as she drifted back to the divan and opened her book.

Bill pulled out a plain wooden table which doubled as a desk. Expertly he laid knives and forks, cut rye bread, filled a jug with sour cream. With a flourish he produced a bottle of boot-leg wine and carefully poured three glasses.

"You are a naughty boy," said his mother as she joined us at the table but smiled fondly at him as she ladled out the rice and main dish. My remark that it was delicious was acknowledged by a slight nod, but conversation was difficult.

"Tell Frieda about your early days." But his mama had other ideas. She waved this away with "It was all so long ago" and went on to talk about pellagra "such a dreadful thing".

"Yes, a diet restricted to hominy and grits must inevitably produce a deficiency disease. It is sad for the children in the south". I answered pompously.

Her eyebrows went up, the languid pose disappeared. Bill hid a smile. Had she hoped I would be ignorant on this subject so her son might understand I was just a silly girl? Her aloof manner had chilled me though I remained polite. The grey eyes now shrewdly assessed me as Bill desperately tried to keep the conversation going. But she gave him little assistance and soon returned to the divan and her book. I helped Bill clear the table and wash the dishes. Deftly he put everything in its place.

"You will make coffee?" from his mother. "No, Frieda has a long way to go." Gladly I said good-bye to his mama. Bill was silent as we walked to the street-car stop. "I'm sorry, she's not always like that, she was in one of her moods," he spoke angrily.

I laughed. "Don't you understand? She wants you to herself with no intrusion from a brash young thing like me." "Well she can't have that." He pulled me to him and kissed me fiercely. For the first time I felt genuinely sorry I couldn't respond.

By April of that year, 1929, our Club reached crisis point. Professor Harry Elmer Barnes of Smith College, sociologist and author, had accepted an invitation to speak at the Liberal Club about the Tom Moomey case.

There was a nation-wide campaign to secure the freedom of this man who had already served thirteen years in San Quentin prison, California for a crime he did not commit – The San Francisco Preparedness Day Bombing in 1916. His real offence was that he was a labour leader, as was Warren K Billings, another of the accused.

The trial judge, the prosecuting attorney and most of the jury were now saying he should be pardoned. Many witnesses admitted they had given false testimony. Freemont Older, editor of the San Francisco Bulletin at that time joined the protest as did noted political science professors including Thomas S Barclay, G H Stuart who signed a petition to the Governor asking for

Pittsburgh Press: *cutting bottom photo from second left Bill Albertson, me, Arthur McDowell*

'unconditional pardon'. Even the Pi Sigma Alpha Chapter of Stanford University added its voice.

In spite of all this, a farcical scene was now enacted at Pittsburgh University.

On Thursday, 19 April the Registrar of the University granted a permit to the Liberal Club to use a room in Alumni Hall on the following Monday at 3.30pm.

On Friday the 20th a printed notice stated the purpose of the meeting – a discussion of the Tom Mooney case.

The permit was withdrawn.

On Monday, 22 April Liberal Club members, professors and students went to the Alumni Hall room. William Dauffenbauch, one time prison guard, blocked the door.

Speaker and audience adjourned to the steps of Thaw Hall. Dauffenbauch ordered the meeting off the campus.

Members of the Liberal Club together with some twenty-five of the Pitt faculty then moved to a parking lot.

Dr Harry Elmer Barnes addressed his audience from the running board of an automobile. He outlined fully the facts of the disgraceful frame-up of the two men, gave details of lies and now retractions by witnesses in the Tom Mooney case.

A Pittsburgh Press column ended its story of the meeting with the words – 'These are the facts which officials of the University of Pittsburgh are trying to suppress from free men in a free country in an allegedly free institution of learning.'

A slightly humorous twist appeared in the Press editorial:

'Dr Harry Elmer Barnes is reported to have smiled broadly when he and the Liberal Club of the University of Pittsburgh were barred from the university building and campus....It has been revealed that three of the text books written by Dr Barnes and his associates have been, and are being, used in the class rooms of the university .... Wonder if Pitt can produce any more good jokes.'

The Pittsburgh Sun-Telegraph wrote – 'It is getting dangerous to think in these United States much less to talk out loud'

Even the New York Telegram commented – 'Down in Pittsburgh the University is in an uproar because some of the students wanted to hear a man talk about the Mooney case ..... it is obvious that someone needs to.'

But the Pittsburgh Press was by far the best with a great deal of comment and exposure of pressures and threats against faculty members.

A cartoon depicted the confessions of 'false witnesses' in a courtroom. In one corner of the cartoon, behind a 'University of Pittsburgh' plaque a mortar board and gown administrator shouts to the student body 'You can't learn about that here'.

Pittsburgh Press *cutting*

The editorial said: 'A much heralded function of a university is to teach students to think for themselves.... This would soon be a sorry land if the vast army of young men and women graduated from our universities every year ill equipped, with no thoughts excepting those planted by powers behind the scenes, pulling strings on university instruction.'

In the Liberal Club there was excitement, exhilaration. The stupidity of the authorities had made this an incident which was being discussed throughout the country.

We decided another meeting of the Club must be held and on Friday 26 April, in defiance of the authorities we trooped into our regular room in Alumni Hall. Bill was in the chair and went on as he would have in any previous meeting. What happened next is best described by these excerpts from the Pittsburgh Press report.

> 'That a meeting was to be held had been advertised. A throng of other students choked the corridor. The whole university knew the meeting was on.
>
> William Dauffenbauch who had dispersed the Dr Barnes meeting naively asked Albertson if a meeting was being held. On being firmly told that the Liberal Club was in session he asked the meeting to disband.
>
> 'No' came in defiant chorus.
>
> Dauffenbauch retired. The discussion .... Continued ....
>
> Dauffenbauch returned. With him was Dr A H Armbruster, dean of men, flushed and nervous. He commanded the Liberal Club members to disperse. "We will discuss your suggestion," said Albertson with dignity. "There is no time for discussion," said the dean. "Get out of here! You first!"
>
> Albertson, unperturbed, asked the Club what was its pleasure.
>
> Elliot Finkel moved to adjourn. "We need the university more than it needs us."
>
> The secretary, Frieda Truhar, shouted a vigorous "No". Fiery, defiant, she scorned surrender.
>
> Out came the Dean's notebook. "Who are these people, Bill?"
>
> Finkel again moved to adjourn. Motion carried.
>
> "I wish to state," said President Albertson, still with dignity, that the Liberal Club has held an official meeting."
>
> Applause from the student observers.
>
> "Will they be expelled from the university?" a reporter asked the dean.
>
> "Oh, be sensible, be reasonable," he replied.

But on May second the expulsion of William Albertson and Author McDowell, a first year divinity student, was announced as was the dismissal of Frederick E Woltman from the faculty.

The expulsion and dismissal had been confirmed by the University Board of Trustees on May first but had not been discussed with the faculty of the university, as prescribed in the rules governing the institution.

As for me, I was summoned to the office of a woman I'd never seen before. Large, formidable, she made her pronouncement. "In view of your extreme youth (I was not yet eighteen) and your short time at the university you are on this occasion to be given a warning. If you persist in your activities it will be expulsion. Do you understand?"

I nodded, and said nothing. Resentment I certainly felt but also a great wave of relief that I was not to be expelled.

Pittsburgh Press *cutting: from left William Anderson, me, Arthur McDowell, Attorney Ellenbogen*

That same day my economics teacher who had shown an interest in me and my views asked me to stay behind. He went straight into the attack. "For God's sake Frieda have some sense. Your whole future here is at stake. Remember the sacrifices your friends are making."

I looked at him thoughtfully. "I'll think about it." I knew I couldn't heed these warnings. With others in the Liberal Club I collected signatures on a petition against the expulsion of Bill and Arthur. Nearly a thousand students signed. Fifty members of Philosophy classes taught by Fred Woltman signed a petition against his dismissal.

To no avail. A subsequent appeal against expulsion by Bill and Arthur was refused. Woltman was not reinstated.

The American Civil Liberties Union now got involved. On May tenth, through its counsel Harry Ellenbogen, it drew up a refusal for a Mandamus action against the university following a refusal to reinstate the two expelled students. The papers were to be filled in an effort to force the reinstatement by court action.

At the same time, through the chairman of its education committee, The Civil Liberties Union placed the matter of Woltman's dismissal before the American Association of University Professors. At least five members of the faculty of Pittsburgh University also registered protests with this Association and asked for an investigation of conditions at Pitt.

The due process of law and investigation ground on but there was no reinstatement. The summer holiday began. We dispersed, determined to continue the fight next semester in the autumn. For me that time never came as the Wall Street crash ended my university education.

Not till 1985, in a letter from Pittsburgh, did I learn that the Liberal Club affair at the University of Pittsburgh was in many respects the beginning of the decline of the Chancellor, John Bowman. As the result of a similar but more extreme action – firing Professor Ralph Turner of the History Department – the University was blacklisted for about two decades by the Association of American University Professors. Bowman was ultimately investigated by his own trustees.

Chapter 12

Gastonia Comes to Pittsburgh – A 'Keystone Cop's Arrest'

Summer holidays brought the Liberal Club campaign at the University to a halt. The Civil Liberties Union continued their efforts towards reinstatement.

In my local Young Communist League branch, I was made aware of a very different kind of struggle, not for free speech but for the right to live without fear of hunger.

From the strike bound textile workers in Gastonia, North Carolina, Albert Tetherow had come to Pittsburgh to raise funds, relief and support. A weaver in the Loral Mills, he was one of the 'poor whites' of the Southern states, reputedly descendants of English immigrants who had come to America many generations ago.

Something about his hands was odd. A tiny finger sprouted from each little finger. As I looked up his eyes met mine. "I'm sorry, I didn't mean to stare."

He smiled, "It's all right, I'm used to having folks take notice of that. They say it comes from marrying too much with our kith and kin." Albert's voice was soft. His lean, almost wizened face, the undernourished body in its shabby clothes spoke eloquently of the harsh world in which he lived. It was there that children, with their swollen bellies, died of pellagra.

He'd come to our meeting to tell about the strike, ask for our help. There was no rhetoric, his story was simple and grim.

"We didn't want a strike. But we just couldn't make do. If we dare ask for more we'd be out. So when we heard about this new union we sent a letter and the men came. Our people was angry, the children always hungry. So the union men helped us get a committee. We wanted all Gastona mills to shut down and most did. We got us a union hall, an old place by the railroad. It was a kind of camp where we met and stored the relief.

One night just after fresh relief supplies come, vigilantes with rifles broke into our camp. They spilled the flour over the railroad tracks, poured kerosene on boxes and tins and put fire to them. They wrecked the union hall, broke windows, pulled off doors."

"What did you do?" a voice interrupted.

"What could we do, we had no rifles. If one of us moved they fired in the air above us. Pleased with themselves they was, laughed and joked as they left." He was bitter, the humiliation of that night still with him.

We waited, silent.

"But sure as hell we knowed they'd be back next relief night. So we set us up a guard of thirteen each with a rifle. We was on duty night and day. Like we thought they come again. But this time the bastards wore deputy badges and the chief of police was with them.

When our sentry challenged them, they jeered, shot him in the arm. Then the shooting started on both sides. The police chief was wounded. Later he died."

His next words fell among us like a bomb shell. "They've arrested seventy of our men for murder."

"Seventy. Sweet Jesus," someone said. "Were you there when this happened, Albert?" "Yeah, that's why I'm here now. The Committee thought I'd best be out of the way for a while."

We were outraged, all started talking at once. Dave called us to order then as always felt the need to instruct and inform.

"The strike in Gastonia is being led by the National Textile Workers Union, a new progressive organisation which we support. And if you read our paper you'll know how difficult it has always been to get any trade unions set up in the South. Organisers from the North have been tarred and feathered, dumped in the woods, some even lynched. This is going to be one tough battle in Gastonia."

"We know that. How can we help," Elsie called out impatiently. "A Gastonia Relief Committee is being formed in Pittsburgh. The best thing we can do is work with them, give them our time." Albert nodded, "Any meetings you want me to speak at I'm willing."

I asked Albert about Ella May Wiggins. Even to us in the north she had become known, inspired both men and women in Gastonia with her songs and speeches.

Albert's face lit up. "She's got grit, goes round to other mills trying to get them in our union. Makes up her own songs and has all of us singing them."

"Sing us one, Albert," we begged. He smiled shyly. "I ain't much of a singer. This one's called The Mill Mother's Lament."

> We leave our homes in the morning
> We kiss our children goodbye
> While we slave for the bosses
> Our children scream and cry
>
> And when we draw our money
> Our grocery bills to pay
> Not a cent to pay for clothing
> Not a cent to lay away
>
> How it grieves the heart of a mother
> You every one must know
> But we can't buy for our children
> Our wages are too low
>
> It is for our little children
> That seem to us so dear
> But for us nor them oh workers
> The bosses do not care
>
> But listen to me workers
> A Union they do fear
> Let's stand together workers
> And have a union here

From her birthplace in the Appalachian mountains Ella May Wiggin had been trailed by her family to mining and lumber camps wherever work was to be found. Married to a logger by the time she was sixteen, she bore nine children four of whom had died. After her husband was crippled in an accident they moved to the cotton mills. For ten years she'd worked as a spinner, the sole provider for her family.

Sometime after this meeting a sad faced Albert told us Ella May was murdered by the vigilantes on her way to the Union Hall in Gastonia. No one was tried for this killing. Seven strike leaders received sentences of up to twenty years for the earlier shooting of the police chief. I took Albert to a Bratsvo meeting, spoke in Croatian then introduced him. His appearance, his simple speech moved the audience and they gave a large donation to the strike fund.

But knocking on doors for 'relief' contributions during this beautiful summer of 1929 did not produce results. Prosperity was reaching its height. There was an awful complacency, a terrible illusion among many people who were daily and faithfully repeating Dr Coue's formula for 'infallible' success, 'day by day in every way I'm getting better and better'.

In these months before the Wall Street crash the very mention of poverty among the poorly paid was denounced as unpatriotic and un-American. Prosperity was permanent, wonderful and few wanted to hear about those whom it had not touched.

When the YCL next met Albert was again among us. Dave and Mike, our organisers, were both away. The attendance was poor, just a few seventeen and eighteen year olds.

I opened the meeting. "We're not getting anywhere with the relief collections. We ought to do something big and public. There's nothing in the papers about Gastonia.

"So, you got any ideas?" Harry was always negative. 'Don't go over the heads of the Relief Committee. They know what they're doing." "Look, we help at the Relief Committee. But I think we should have our regular open air meeting next Saturday night. We could put up big posters about Gastonia. It's warm weather and lots of people pass that spot on Ohio Street near North Park."

"You know we can't do that. They stopped giving permits." It was Harry again. "So we ask for a permit and if we don't get one we have the meeting anyway. Would you speak Albert?" "Sure. Like Frieda says, things are a bit slow. I sometimes don't feel I'm doing my job here," he was rueful.

We made our plans. I asked for volunteers to speak. "I'll chair the meeting. There's Albert and we need two more." Danny raised his hand. Harry didn't agree but neither did he want to be left out.

"Ok I guess I know more about what's going on in Gastonia than anyone here except Albert." "And you speak so well," I encouraged. He'd always been a bighead but sometimes that had its advantages.

There was a volunteer to bring the platform and another to give out leaflets. Everyone would help make the posters.

We applied for a permit and as expected were refused. Eight of us turned up on the Saturday but none could have envisaged the strange twist our meeting was to take.

The police were not prepared. They didn't know we were coming for the Party had informed them, though not us, that with a lawyer present a test case of this new ordinance against granting permits for street meetings would take place at a future date.

As I climbed onto the platform there wasn't a patrolman in sight. "The reason for this meeting is the Gastonia Textile strike. Wages are so low that the children haven't enough to eat. Men and women need higher wages so their families won't go hungry."

As I raised my voice passers by glanced over, saw a young woman and stopped. Soon a small crowd gathered so I introduced Harry.

He started by contrasting 'this spurious bubble of prosperity' with the hardships in the mines and mills. As he went on I got impatient, tugged at his trousers. "Get onto the Strike." A solitary policeman pushed his way into the crowd.

"Where's your permit?" he asked slowly.

"You didn't give us one," I answered. "But we've always held meetings here before and consider the new ordinance an infringement of our right of free speech." This phrase had been prepared well beforehand. "No permit, no meeting. Close down. You," he shouted at Harry "come along with me."

Earlier we'd decided that whatever happened it must be peaceful. So when Harry was challenged by 'the law' he did not resist arrest. The crowd grew as the cop led him around the corner to the little jail in Federal Street, two blocks away.

A soon as they were out of sight I scrambled up again and introduced Albert. "Here is a man from Gastonia itself, a striker who will tell the truth about what is happening." The crowd became quiet.

Albert was already on the platform and immediately began, "I am a weaver. I work a long day and at the end of the week I get eleven dollars." There was a kind of mass release of breath at this simple statement. That was a boy's wage in the north. People moved closer to hear the soft southern voice.

He told them of big-bellied children, of women working in humid mills for nine dollars a week. He spoke of men and women laid off and beaten up when they wanted to start a union. "It's our right by law to have a union but the bosses won't talk to us. They just send their vigilantes."

The raid on the union hall, the destruction of the food was vividly described. "That hurt us most because our kids is eating better on relief than they ever ate when we was in work."

Fifteen minutes had passed and now the policeman came running, bellowing at the top of his voice. "Hey, I told you to stop down. Now don't go on with this or there'll be real trouble." A huge arm yanked frail Albert off the platform and marched him away.

I couldn't understand it. Why had the policeman come alone? The crowd was growing, excitement rising. As I climbed back to introduce Danny I said to him "Don't go on about the political situation but about Gastonia."

And he was good, bringing in the miners, which was closer to home, but linking them with the struggle in Gastonia. He surprised himself and me as he spoke forcefully for fifteen minutes.

The patrolman returned, again alone. "Now what?" I said to Elsie who was giving out leaflets. "He can't just arrest Danny and walk off with him. He must realise we intend to carry on."

"Maybe he thinks he can handle it himself, doesn't want to call anyone in. That little jail has only two cops on duty." "Or else he's plain dumb," I answered. Whatever the reason, off he went again with Danny.

Now I was on my own. I told the large crowd, "It is the new ordinance which is illegal. In the First Amendment to our Constitution it states,'... that Congress shall make no law abridging the freedom of speech or of the press or the right of people to peaceably assemble'. There's more but that I remember from my school days. And if Congress can make no such law how is it that our own municipality feels it has that right. They refused us a permit, that's why we're being arrested.

Our meeting is about Gastonia. Whatever happens, remember what the striker from there told you." With my eyes on the corner around which the policeman would come I carried on as best I could.

When again without support he reappeared the crowd could scarcely contain itself. The loud laughter infuriated this tall burly man who roughly pulled me from the platform. The two blocks to Federal Street prison became a procession as the crowd realised there was no one left to speak and followed us to the jailhouse.

"She don't even reach your shoulder but mind she don't escape," one wit jeered.

It was my first arrest. Propelled along by the red faced cop I felt a real heroine. The others greeted me with a cheer.

We'd expected we might be jailed but not in such a 'Keystone Cops' fashion. Even Harry was elated. "A mighty blow for free speech," he shouted. "I thought it was about Gastonia. Albert you were marvellous," I called back. The woman attendant ordered, "Shut up you bitch. I'd rather have a hooker in here than a red."

But nothing could stop us as we sang 'The Red Flag' and 'Solidarity Forever'.

My amused father stood bail for me and the others too were released. Together on the pavement we marvelled yet again at the extraordinary turn the evening had taken.

Next day one paper had the headline 'Pitt Co-ed held in Communist raid' with my picture on the front page. I felt doubly a heroine. But more important was the very good coverage of the

Strike which also appeared on the front pages. In spite of the Ordinance people had heard about Gastonia and now they could also read about it. When we appeared in court on Monday we were fined.

A few weeks later the Party went with its 'test case' meeting. It was to be at the same place and again on a Saturday evening. Long before it was due to start patrolmen surrounded the area. They were joined by a squad of mounted police who galloped to the spot then rode backwards and forwards, their horses rearing in front of those who had gathered to see what was happening.

As more than fifty of us appeared to set up the platform and support the meeting, twenty-eight were immediately and violently arrested. Amid scuffles, the crowd scattered.

I felt glad we'd held the earlier meeting despite the Party's censure. Our decision was justified for we'd been able to publicise the terrible conditions of the Gastonia textile workers.

But sadly the strike was nearing its end and not in victory. Albert was recalled and we were all sorry to see him go.

Chapter 13

The Wall Street Crash – Marriage

From the dining room came the creak of the old rocking chair. "Mom?" There was no answer. I walked across the room, sat down beside her. "What's wrong mama?"

"Everything's wrong. No work, so many debts. How will we ever pay them?" "Didn't papa get the job at Heppenstall's?" "They're firing, not hiring. He's out again looking." Then angrily. "We should never have built this house. He didn't listen."

"No, he was the only one who wanted it. But that's all past now, we can't undo it." "It's you Frieda. No more college. Soon we won't even have the carfare." Her voice was bitter. "It's all right mom. I went to the office today, told them I wouldn't be back. It's not your fault."

And indeed, suddenly for thousands, then millions of people there was no work. 'No help wanted' signs appeared at factory gates. Men tramped from place to place, shocked, incredulous that something which had happened in far off Wall Street could so easily affect their everyday lives.

Just a few months ago many had been riding high. In 1928 Hoover had voted in as President on a wave of prosperity with his slogan 'a chicken in every pot, a car in every garage'.

Papa came in, weary, dejected. "Nothing Maria. I talked to some men just come from Detroit. At Fords they turned water hoses on those who wouldn't leave the gates." He turned to me, "I'm sorry, Frieda." "It's not just us pa."

In vain I searched for work. Papa came home one evening, told me "There's a girl wanted in an engineering workshop on the south side. Bozo knows the foreman so if you go right away you might get it." Again he said, "I'm sorry."

A small old fashioned place, it employed some thirty women. The two-storey building was in a narrow alley and the shop, reached by outside stairs, ran the length of the top floor. I opened the heavy door, entered a long room lit by electricity. Windows were few and high.

The foreman approached, "Ever been in a shop like this?" "No, but I can learn." "Sure, Bozo said you were bright," he smiled. "When do I start?" "Monday morning. 7.30 sharp. Half day Saturday." He paused, "Fifteen dollars a week."

Fifteen dollars! I earned more at spare time work when I was at high school. I nodded, thanked him. A girl smiled at me as fleetingly she glanced up from her machine. I smiled back, felt better. It'll be all right. You'll get the hang of it I told myself. But deep down I felt fear and dismay. What a different prospect from the bright hopes I'd had only a few months ago.

When I reached home mama was again in the rocking chair. Always before when things were difficult she'd coped, found ways. Now the catastrophe which had overtaken us and millions like us was not to be overcome by sheer hard work and determination. This had overwhelmed her. Because she could not act on life she felt defeated. Although I was young, self-centred, not very perceptive, I understood something of this. I felt sorry for my mother and for myself too.

"I got the job. It'll be ok, easy really." Her face lightened, she looked at me searchingly. "It won't be too hard for you? You'll be able?" "I start Monday morning, got to be there at 7.30. It takes nearly an hour with changing street-cars. It'll be alright, don't worry. Anything to eat? I'm starving."

Mama rose, put the coffee pot on the stove and began to fry eggs and bacon. She didn't speak, just shook her head.

On Monday morning I was early and stood waiting inside the door. A few women were already at their machines. The foreman nodded, indicated a row of hooks where I could hang my coat. As they hurried in, the girls looked at me, one winked.

The foreman pulled a lever and with a loud clamour the place came alive. Women bent over their work and Bill, as I came to know him, had almost to shout above the noise as he led me to a drill press, showed me what to do.

I had to take a small place of metal from a box, put it in a jig, then dip my fingers in a lubricant which I applied to the drill. My foot came down on the clutch pedal which connected the power to the drill. As I pulled down a lever the drill bit into the metal, curls of steel dropped as two small holes appeared. Then out of the jig and I discovered I was making holes in hinges.

Slowly at first, then more quickly, I repeated these five movements again and again and again. In all my life I had never experienced anything like the dirt, smell, discipline and tedium such work demanded.

The noise stopped at twelve o'clock as Bill pulled the main lever. I could scarcely move. All of me ached.

I stood for a time, stretched arms and shoulders. The girl next to me had disappeared immediately. She smiled when she returned. "There's toilets and a place to wash at the back. You can eat here. You'll get used to it. I been in worse. Bill's ok. Long as you work he'll leave you alone."

As I ate my sandwiches she said, "You got nothing to drink. Here have some root beer. Home made."

Grateful, I lifted the bottle and drank. Katy was married. She chatted cheerfully but for me the hour passed as though it had been a moment. Much too soon the wheels whirred and I started back on the drill. Minutes, hours crept by and long before five thirty came I felt I could not go on. Yet somehow I stayed tied to this machine. When the screech and din at last stopped I was still, didn't move.

The other girls were gone in a flash. Slowly I walked to the coat rail. "It'll be better tomorrow." Bill was being kind.

After the streetcar the long walk in fresh air revived me, made it easier to face my mother. I didn't feel so noble or brave as that morning when I'd told myself I'd be the only one bringing in real money. Yet I felt some satisfaction at having survived the day.

Yes, I was tired, it was all right, I could do it, could I have a bottle of root beer with my sandwiches, would she be sure to get me up early.

I ate my supper, went to wash. This night I was too weary to rid myself entirely of the white flecks of lubricant which had flown off the drill and covered my skin and hair. The stuff had the texture and feel of soap flakes. It permeated the shop, hovered in the dust. I was in bed and asleep by eight o'clock.

The next day was easier, soon I acquired a certain rhythm and after a time it became almost automatic but I needed to keep my wits about me, not drill holes into my fingers instead of the metal, as I nearly did on one occasion. The work was just sufficiently demanding to make it impossible to lose myself in my own thoughts.

One Saturday morning when I'd been in the shop for well over two months, Bill pulled the lever at eleven o'clock. The machines ground to a halt as we looked up in surprise. There was still an hour to go.

"Anything wrong, Bill," a girl shouted. He waited, looked down the aisles. Gradually the talk petered out, all eyes on him. "It's bad news. This is your last day. The place is closing down."

There was a stunned silence. Next to me Katy started to cry, she had a little boy, her husband was out of a job. What she earned kept them going.

"Why, why? I suppose you'll be alright." "No, it's over for me too. The furniture factory don't need our hinges and brackets. They've gone bust."

To this there was no answer. An older woman angrily cried out, "What are we supposed to do, starve? The god dam bastards shutting factories everywhere. We can't even keep stinking jobs like this."

As a young communist I felt somehow inadequate. Shouldn't I stand up and tell them capitalism was the cause of this misfortune, this unemployment? But I didn't. The sheer boredom and monotony of the work had built up in me a frustration and anger difficult at times to control. Though taken aback at this sudden announcement, the immense feeling of relief which swept over me as I realised I was now free of this place made any such political gesture seem irrelevant. I'd not have left the job voluntarily but I could not feel sorry it had ended.

For the first time on that long street car ride home, I thought of my friends, the girls from the Hill. They had not gone to high school and college after grade school but straight into Heinz Pickle Factory. Whole days were spent putting pickles into jars or labels onto cans, every minute of every hour of their working time, for weeks, months, years.

Maybe, I thought, for my parents' sake I'd have to go back to work like that if I could get it, but not for long, not for ever. Somehow I'd find a way to finish my education.

☽

Pat Devine had arrived in Pittsburgh as Communist Party organiser for Western Pennsylvania when I was nearly sixteen. We girls in the Young Communist League looked him over, agreed with Elsie's observation, "Not bad, good looking, but isn't he old?" With that we dismissed him.

In late 1929, with university and factory behind me, I joined others of the League in work among the unemployed and was in constant contact with Pat.

During those first weeks and months after the Wall Street Crash people blamed themselves for being without work, asked where they'd gone wrong, as though what had happened was their fault. There was no unemployment pay, and relief from city or county was minimal. By the beginning of 1930 thousands of workers and poor farmers faced starvation. Financiers in far off New York jumped from tall buildings, 'small people' who had joined the speculators and invested all they possessed committed suicide.

A bread line formed off East Ohio Street on the North Side where a compassionate parson had opened a soup kitchen. The men were given a bowl of soup, a piece of bread. For some this was clearly a last resort. Still well dressed, they looked ashamed, embarrassed.

We'd seen near starvation in coalfields, knew of hungry children in southern textile areas and felt strongly that this feeling of self blame must give way to anger and action. Our leaflets, given out with the parson's permission, were headed – 'Don't Starve, Fight'. More and more bread lines appeared.

But leaflets were not enough. Somehow these men and women, isolated and bewildered, had to come together to talk, exchange experiences and give thought to what they could do, in fact, organise. Thinking back I believe the beginnings of the Unemployed Councils which gradually came into being may have started with evictions when people could no longer pay rent.

Although there weren't many of us, we had a group prepared to go anywhere, any time, and we in the YCL identified with the pre-war Wobblies. So, one day I found myself in the Hill District where Ben Carruthers was trying to stop an eviction in his neighbourhood. When we arrived the furniture was already on the sidewalk, spilling into the narrow street. Three young children pressed against a small, tearful woman who clutched a 'turkey rug' to her breast.

Ben, tall, lean, greying said to the people who had gathered, "What happened to Mrs Lewis might soon happen to anyone here. So let's get the furniture back into the house, then go to City Hall and ask for relief. Else, where these kids gonna sleep tonight?"

No one stirred. Ben lifted a chair. A few women hesitantly moved forward. Our group came from the back, picked up what we could and followed Ben into the house. More people joined and soon a steady stream of objects were carried in. Pat had arrived and now helped with a heavy wardrobe.

Suddenly people whispered to each other, retreated quickly to their doorsteps. Down the street came the landlord, a tall burly man. Ben went into the house with the woman and children. Pat waited in the entrance, smiled and said a few words. Together they entered the house. Nothing happened for what seemed a long time. Then the owner appeared and without a glance at anyone walked away. Ben and Pat emerged, people again came forward.

Ben announced, "Mrs Lewis can stay for now as her husband's away looking for work. She could do with some help." Neighbours hurried into the house.

Our YCL group was elated with the outcome but Pat's was a more sober assessment. "It's temporary. He's a small landlord and showed sympathy. But there'll be a next time."

I was impressed with Pat's quick and decisive reaction to events, admired his courage. He took on the police, the city officials, even the mayor when the occasion arose. I invested him with all the glamour many girls of my age saw in film stars and there grew in me a kind of hero worship for him.

One morning Pat asked me out for coffee. We suspected a microphone in the office, our mail was tampered with. So I expected another request to take messages to various small towns where we had members.

As we sat opposite each other in the café he said, "Why don't we get married?" I laughed. "Stop kidding. What is it you want this time?" "Just what I said, to marry you."

Speechless, I was dazzled by this handsome assured man with his strong personality.

"Why not?" He went on. "We see each other every day, believe in the same things, work well together. I'm sure we'll make a go of it." His blue eyes sparkled as he smiled at me.

Still in a daze I went home, proudly announced to mama, "I'm going to marry Pat. He asked me today and he wants it to be soon because he's so busy."

Mama sat very still. Her large brown eyes held mine until I began to feel uncomfortable. "You didn't think to talk it over with us first? Pat must have advised you to do that." Her voice was gentle.

Bewildered, I answered, "No he just said to tell you." Then defiantly, "He's wonderful. You've heard him speak. He always knows just what's to be done, brave too, tells the cops where to get off."

"So he's a fine revolutionary. But you know nothing of the private man, what he'd be like as a husband. He's too old for you, Frieda, thirty-one to your eighteen."

Mama paused, went on slowly. "Pat strikes me as very old-fashioned; he'll always have to be boss. There won't be equality, I warn you. Remember when papa thought he was God. I see something of that in Pat."

"But you don't understand. Everybody liked him and he picked me."

"Yes of course he has great charm. But has he ever before today shown you that you're special, hugged you, treated you with warmth? At least papa and I were in love when we married.

To me it seems Pat sees in you an attractive young girl, a good communist and of course a virgin."

She looked at me. "You still are?" "Yes I am. Pat asked me that too." Mama's face became grim. "If you'd answered no he wouldn't want to marry you. At his age he's had other women but he's the kind that has to be first with a wife."

I remained silent, remembered how insistent Pat had been about this. And suddenly I had a feeling of unease. When he kissed me in the quiet dark corridor under the office it hadn't been at all like with Bob whose kisses had been long and demanding as his hands strayed over me. I'd responded too and knew that but for the fear of pregnancy I might no longer be a virgin. But surely marriage would bring even more than I had earlier expected and wanted. Recalling Pat's handsome face and charming smile I banished doubt.

"Mama I'm sure marriage with Pat will be wonderful." With a wry smile she replied, "It's rarely that with anyone. We'll talk again tomorrow."

But to my surprise she said no more. Year's later mama told me she had lain awake for hours. Convinced this marriage would not be a happy one for me, she realised however that I was infatuated with this persuasive older man and felt certain she could not dissuade me. Mama wanted no coercion, no estrangement. At the same time she reflected that in the midst of this unemployment and hardship there was little future for me at home. At least marriage might offer some resemblance of financial security.

"I felt so sad, sorry for you. It was clear to me he was not in love with you but you'd satisfy his needs. Frieda, at that time you didn't even begin to understand that you were 'in love' with the 'hero' not the man. Such people in their personal lives are often very self-centred, everything must revolve around them. I've seen it so often in the movement, even among our Croatians. But this was not something I could tell you. Understanding would come only with experience, I believe had he really loved you it might have worked in spite of that, for women are very adaptable but they do need affection."

We were married by a Justice of the Peace in a civil ceremony on 13 February 1930, he in a blue serge suit and I in a beige waistless 'twenties' dress and cloche hat I had borrowed from my brother's girlfriend.

Mama hugged and kissed me, papa too with tears in his eyes. We went back to our house on the Hill for a meal with relatives and close friends, the kind of celebration which the times allowed. Papa produced a bottle of wine laid down when I was born. Alas, prophetically it was sour and we had to be content with our everyday variety.

At last Pat and I were in the two small furnished rooms which were now home. He laughed as he dropped onto a sofa, kicked off his shoes.

"It's been a long day and I've had too much of your father's excellent wine. Be a good girl and make us some coffee."

This was not what I expected. He was supposed to sweep me into his arms now we were alone, kiss me passionately in the way Bob had. Silently I went into the small kitchen, prepared coffee, set the tray on the small table and sat down beside him. He turned to look at me. "It went quite well, didn't it. Especially as your mother doesn't really approve."

"She thinks you're too old for me." A little smile as he said, "We'll see about that."

In the large double bed I waited. There were no sweet words, no tender embrace or searching long kiss, no feel of his hands on my body, caressing, exploring, arousing. Indeed, my virginity could no longer be in doubt as Pat laboured long to achieve his climax. Then with a sigh he rolled away, leaned back, closed his eyes.

It is hard now to describe adequately how that far off romantic eighteen year old felt. Emotionally shattered, my body one large ache, tears streamed down my cheeks as I turned to Pat.

"Did it have to be like that?" But already, breathing deeply, he slept. As I pulled away from him one thought pounded through my head, with Bob, whatever I might think of him, it would have been very different.

The next morning Pat seemed utterly unaware of what I felt as he picked up the paper and sat down to breakfast. Confused, miserable I was too much in awe of him to mention the previous night. I'd been fluent enough with young men of my own age but he was so much older, an 'important man' in our Party.

Though I had expected equality, an exchange of views, a personal life of love, laughter and fun, I was soon to learn that his charm and jollity was reserved for public occasions. He made it clear, without many words, that I was to make his meals, provide clean shirts and be 'available' in bed if he so desired. That I might want something different never occurred to him.

Why didn't I just walk away? That question haunted me for years. But at the time, together with most married women of my

Pat Devine and me

generation, I accepted and gradually got used to Pat. In spite of my 'domestic' duties I devoted even more time to the YCL, in present day terms 'sublimated my sexuality' in hard work for the movement.

☙

When the Trade Unity League, a Party created left-based organisation, announced that 6th March 1930 was to be a day of protest by unemployed throughout the country, the United States Government and Mayor Kline of Pittsburgh denounced it as a 'Moscow plot'. The city police stated they'd arrest those who were organising it. As he read this in the Sun-Telegraph Pat said, "Now they'll try to pick up all the Party and TUUL leadership."

"What are you going to do?" "We're ready for them. It's all worked out. The others and I will disappear, not come near home or office, sleep in a different place every night. If the police ask where I am you don't know, which will be true." With this he was gone.

It was the first I heard of such preparation. This incident so soon after our marriage was to set the pattern for years to come. Pat never discussed anything of importance with me, nor did he ever ask for my opinion.

The YCL had been allocated the job of distributing leaflets throughout the city and beyond. These gave details of time and place for the demonstration. Most were received in silence, slipped into pockets. Daily the press found something to say which informed many about what was happening.

The day before on 5 March, a group of us went by street car to the huge Westinghouse plant in East Pittsburgh. We each had one gate to cover with leaflets which asked those still employed to support the workless. As people streamed forward after the whistle, ready hands stretched out.

A loud voice shouted, "Hey you, just stop that and get the hell out of here." I pretended not to hear. The irate copy came up and pushed me.

"Keep your dirty hands off me. This is a public sidewalk and I've a right to stand on it."

"You got no rights in this town." He grabbed my arm, steered me to the small local jail house, muttered angrily under his breath. As he showed me through the door he called out, "Another of those God damn agitators with their God damn stuff."

Thrust into a small room and locked in, they hadn't even bothered to search me or look in my purse. I rubbed my aching arm as I paced up and down, worried that we might be held over and miss the next day's demonstration. Within minutes I heard "More bastards" and the voices of my friends but before I could cry out the sounds faded.

The cell, if one could call it that, was below street level, the only light came from a grating in the sidewalk. I listened to the many footsteps which passed overhead. On a slip of paper from my purse I wrote a note, our names, the phone number of the office. In this I wrapped two dimes. Through the small air-opening in the grating I called and called. At last an impudent young face appeared.

"You can't get customers while you're in there." "Listen, I got pulled in outside Westinghouse giving hand-bills for tomorrow."

His face changed and my hopes rose. I stretched up the wrapped money. "Could you phone this number, tell them we're in this jail. I've written down the names and there's enough there for a phone call." "Ok sorry for what I said." The young face smiled and our hands just met as I strained up and he reached down.

He'd do it or he wouldn't. But it was a lucky chance and some hours later a suspicious patrolman led me out of the cell. "How the hell did this man know you was here?"

The lawyer winked at me. The only possible charge was violation of a city ordinance and we were soon bailed. Our relief was great and with much thanks to our friend, we found a café for a quick coffee. By the time I got home I was exhausted, just enough energy for a meal, a bath. Then bed with the alarm set.

Far too early I was walking down Federal Street, across the bridge then slowly to the Driveway, a broad expanse in front of Pennsylvania Station, the assembly point. On one side towered a wall with a railway bridge above it. It was seven-thirty and though police were in evidence there were not many people hurt. Almost immediately I bumped into Max, our Party District treasurer, a tall, round, middle-aged bachelor.

"You're early." I laughed, "What about you?"

We made our way into the station, too soon to be standing about. I'd known Max since I was a child but had rarely seen him cheerful. It was quite in character that he now exuded gloom and pessimism. "Not many will come. The Repressive Power of the State is a Mighty Instrument in the Hands of the Ruling Class. The Capitalist Press has carried out its Role of Intimidating the People." Max always talked Party jargon in capital letters.

"Max, as usual you're full of woe. I bet there'll be at least ten thousand." Dolefully he shook his head.

Small groups gathered on corners, by nine o'clock more people arrived. When it was nearly time for the meeting to start the surrounding streets were almost blocked. Still crowds poured in until, as the press confirmed, some fifty thousand people were thronging the heart of the city. I'd never seen anything like this before. My spirits soared and even Max was beaming.

Promptly at eleven o'clock the leaders of the demonstration, Pat in the forefront, appeared on the high wall beneath the railway bridge. Police were jeered as they tried to close in from the other side. On hands and shoulders Pat was passed to the centre of the packed Driveway.

Still held high he called for unity for the workless to gain relief and unemployment insurance. As police pushed through the crowd he announced a march to the City-County building where these demands would be put before the civic authorities.

"Don't be provoked. We want an orderly demonstration. Our best way to fight is to organise."

With a mighty surge we swept forward down Grant Street, the very magnitude of the crowd creating its own spirit of elation. Traffic was at a standstill. Mounted police appeared, galloped straight into the crowd then leaned forward as they swung riot sticks, beat marchers and observers alike. For a wild frightening moment a horse reared above my head. Nearly under its hoofs, a young man pulled me away just in time. Beside me a woman screamed as the horse thrust against her.

But it wasn't all one sided. Policeman's night sticks were grabbed, some of the Cossacks pulled off their horses. Near me a man shouted, "Kill the police, kill them." I called out, "Pay no attention. He's one of the bastards planted to cause trouble."

"Defend yourselves but look out for those who want to cause a riot. They're police spies," one of our people shouted. True enough, the 'kill' man slunk away.

The mounties retreated then rode singly through the crowd, beat heads where they could. This running battle between police and marchers continued all the way down Grant Street in the block between Liberty and Seventh Avenue. Often marchers had to withdraw as blood streamed down their faces. Foot police now joined in and the odds seemed against us. Clubbed to the ground, people lay inert until friends pulled them away. I saw one man hit repeatedly by the same cop who, with each blow, shouted 'Goddamn red'.

Despite swollen faces and cut lips we regrouped, again and again. A glancing blow on my shoulder made me wince but this was as nothing compared to bloody heads around me. We were determined not to be driven from the middle of the streets.

Strangely there was a lull as ambulances clanged into the fray but many who were hurt melted away for they feared arrest after hospital treatment.

Motorcycle police now appeared, made many arrests. A strongly built young man struggled with two policemen and a third had to come to their aid before they finally bundled him into a side-car.

The drivers of motor cycles, not to be outdone by the mounted police, revved up their machines as they snaked through the marchers, spreading fear and confusion.

It was a fierce, unbridled attack by 'the law' on its own townspeople.

Many had by now left for the sidewalks, but a sufficiently large number remained in the middle of the streets. It was still a march. The pain in my shoulder increased. I began to feel dizzy, faltered. An arm went around me. It was old Max. "Hold on Frieda, we're nearly there."

The City-County building had become a fortress. Doors at Grant and Diamond Streets were locked. Police walked up and down the cleared sidewalks at the Grant Street entrance, displaying tear gas bombs. Above their heads city employees leaned out of the windows.

The Ross Street entrance of City Hall was kept open, guarded by criss-crossed hoses attached to nearby water-plugs. There was no way we were going to get anywhere near the 'city fathers' with our demands for unemployment relief.

Slowly people dispersed but the feeling was not one of defeat. Isolated unemployed realised they were not alone.

Nationwide it was the same. On that day well over a million people demonstrated throughout the large cities of the United States.

The Pittsburgh Sun-Telegraph reported (6 March 1930):

> In New York, Police Commissioner Grover Whalen drives his police at a crowd of 40,000.
>
> In Detroit, mounted police gallop full tilt into a crowd of 50,000.
>
> In Washington, tear gas disperses fighting groups in front of the White House.

In the next few days Pat was very busy. Mayor Kline issued a statement which Pat answered amid newspaper headlines, 'Kline-Devine Views at Odds'. We issued leaflets to counter civic authority and press attacks on us. But most heartening of all, Unemployed Councils began to emerge as people realised the need to work together.

This was the beginning of the struggle for Government aid. It was to continue till Franklin Roosevelt became President in 1932, accepted responsibility for relief of those without work and through his 'New Deal' began to provide jobs.

In the early summer of 1930 Pat was assigned to New York for national work among the unemployed. So after a farewell party with comrades, goodbyes to my parents, especially my sad though resigned mother, I arrived in New York City shortly before my nineteenth birthday.

Chapter 14

New York – Lawrence Textile Strike

Even during these depression years New York remained the 'mecca' of American Youth, the glamour city where somehow dreams of wealth, even fame, might still be realised.

Though these were not my ambitions I was eager to see Broadway, Fifth Avenue and Greenwich Village, home of prominent, charismatic Party people who had spoken at our Labour Lyceum rallies. Their very appearance and sophistication had left an impression of something different.

Just such a man was Willie Weinstone, tall handsome, immaculately dressed who often came to speak in Pittsburgh. Black eyes flashing, his deep eloquent voice brought round after round of applause. I clapped till my hands hurt, stood at the edge of the inevitable group which surrounded him after he left the platform, watched as he walked away with Celia, a woman I knew from the Hill area.

"Does he always go to her place for supper?" I asked my sister who had been married for sometime. She looked at me curiously, must have decided that as I was nearly fifteen it was time I knew. "No, they go to a hotel to be in bed together." She smiled, "Celia seems to bloom afterwards."

I smiled as I thought of this on that long ride to New York. Perhaps I'd meet Wille Weinstone. He might even notice me, make me 'bloom' as Pat never had.

From the beginning I disliked New York, it was so big and crowded. In Pittsburgh I'd been among many people whom

I knew well. It was there I'd grown up and after marriage the nearby presence of my parents had been a comfort. Here I felt isolated, very much a provincial girl.

We found a furnished room but I saw little of Pat who was spending long hours at meetings. Soon he disappeared for long periods, sometimes weeks, to other parts of the country. I had no skills, unemployment in New York was as great as in Pittsburgh. Very much alone I found a public library and Child's cafeteria where meals were cheap.

Pat suggested I take a crash course in shorthand and typing. A competent stenographer could always find a job in the Party.

For a brief moment I felt a surge of rebellion. Had not the German comrades in Pittsburgh called me 'die rote Rosa' after Rosa Luxemburg? I saw myself leading battalions into struggle not typing the proclamations. However, I realised this wouldn't happen in New York. After two months I mastered Gregg shorthand, improved the typing I learned at High School and got a job in the National Party office. I made new friends and took part in the local YCL.

Pat and I had little personal life. This was not unusual among 'full-timers' for we took the Russian Party as our model, and the tasks and demands of our Party always came first.

But not quite always. One day Pat was already in our room when I returned from work. "Something the matter?" I asked, for this didn't often happen. "I had a cable this morning from Scotland. My mother's dying, they want me home." "Can you get away?"

"Head office won't grant leave, will say I can't be spared. But I'm going anyway." "You can't do that. Speak to them again." I was shocked that he'd even considered this. They could be persuaded, I was sure. "No good talking. My passage's booked, I'm off tomorrow." "And what am I supposed to do? This room costs a lot."

I was sorry about his mother but indignant at his utter lack of thought about how I'd manage in his absence.

"You're working, you'll be alright." The next morning he was gone.

A week went by, then a month. The letter I'd sent remained unanswered. When I could no longer meet the rent from my salary I moved in with my sister who was now also in New York. "Probably he'll never come back, that would be good riddance," she said.

As time went on without word from him I decided to go home to Pittsburgh, an attractive prospect. But just then Pat returned. His mother hadn't died but he very nearly had. On a visit to a friend in England he'd become ill with Pneumonia, and had to stay put. Two of his sisters travelled from Motherwell to nurse him. His condition had been serious and, even after the crisis was past, recovery had been slow.

"But why couldn't your family have let me know? I wrote but got no reply. You left me stranded and I had to go to my sister's."

Pat was startled and for the first time since I'd known him his face flushed, he became ill at ease, embarrassed. "I received no letters. Can't understand it," he mumbled and before I could go on hurried away to clear things with the Party.

Years later I was to learn that the friend in England had been Nancy, to whom he'd been engaged but who'd refused to marry him unless he returned to the Catholic faith and gave up his communism.

Had his illness at her home been the reason for his family's silence? Or had they hoped Pat might never return to the States? That may have been their reasoning. Yet though I'd hardly missed him, enjoyed being with my sister and her friends, I resented his lack of concern about me during the whole of his absence.

Pat now simply assumed we'd find rooms again and I'd move back with him. "After what's happened I'm not sure I want to do that," I told him. After a pause he said, "Well I'll stay with your sister and we'll see how things go."

But she was a match for him. "Surely you can't expect her to welcome you with open arms after the way she's been treated. In any case, there's barely room here for Frieda." Pat was furious, almost prepared to force his way in.

When he came again and again to sort out his problems at Party headquarters where I worked, I kept out of his way. He'd committed the unforgivable, gone off after permission had been refused. His long silence had indicated he might not return. Someone else was doing his job. Nevertheless he was an able man, a good organiser, an excellent speaker. They came up with a solution which was also a kind of punishment.

The Party controlled National Textile Workers Union, based in New Bedford, Massachusetts, was in a mess. Two previous secretaries had been arrested and Bill Murdoch, the most recent, deported. Even before the Wall Street crash the textile workers were excluded from the prosperity of the twenties. Now, in the depression days of the early 1930's, when so many were out of work, the Party's instructions to Pat that he rebuild the Union was a tough assignment.

But he'd feared stronger disciplinary treatment and seemed delighted, full of enthusiasm. Throughout his life Pat had always felt he could do a Party job better than anyone else. He was undaunted by this task he'd been set.

Pat sought me out in the office, told me his news, assured me I'd love New Bedford. I said I'd think about it. Pittsburgh beckoned but my sister made me realise a return to my parents might mean an added burden for them.

"You've got a job here, that means something these days. You won't get one back home so it's best you remain in New York. But I'm afraid you'll have to find a place to live. The baby's due in a few weeks."

I'd known I couldn't stay with her, was dismayed at the thought of living on my own in a small room in this city where I still felt an outsider.

Pat asked me to an evening meal, tried hard to persuade me. "We've not been together much since we married. It'll be fine, a small town, not a large city. We'll see more of each other, talk together, work together, as we did before our marriage in Pittsburgh."

I remained silent. The handsome smiling face radiated confidence as he switched on the old charm, spoke with assurance. Did he mean it? Had his absence changed him? Might it be better this time? I certainly wanted to get out of New York. After all, as he said, we were married.

My sister bitterly reproached me. "He's not changed. Pat's more than thirteen years older, will always treat you as subservient. We're different, equals, nearly the same age. But Pat will dominate you as he did before. You've already told me how you feel after only a few months with him and now you're going back for more of the same."

I listened, had to agree it might be so. But people could change, that was part of our philosophy. With mixed feelings I decided to go, in retrospect perhaps for my own selfish reasons. It was something new. Though it might be a hackneyed old saying, I did indeed feel that, 'the view from the next hill might be greener.'

New Bedford, on the Atlantic coast, had once been a whaling centre. But cotton manufacture had later become the chief industry for the large harbour, which was admirably situated to receive the shiploads of raw materials. Now there were many mills, not only cotton but woollen and silk.

Yet it was not as I had imagined, grim and forbidding as were the many small steel towns around Pittsburgh. In that autumn of our arrival I found tree lined streets, red leaves of maple, the gold horse chestnut. Even the poorer areas had for me an openness and charm. And there was the sea, so easily accessible.

We were warmly welcomed by the Portuguese family with whom we stayed. Because he'd tried to get the union going in his mill the father had been blacklisted, fired. However sympathetic, those using the economic crises as a way to force 'speed-up' into the mills. If they succeeded there'd be many lay-offs while those who remained would be given more machines to tend.

For some days after our arrival Pat sat in the Union Hall with the unemployed millworkers, getting a picture of the local set-up. I sat and listened.

After a good deal of talk as the men explained the close cooperation between police and bosses, Pat said, "It's clear everyone in this town's got to know the Union is back and it's come to stay."

"But we told you we been trying. That's how we all got fired." "So, what we got to lose? What's holding us back from a little action? We just sit here and talk." This from young Rodrigo.

"Leaflets headed 'No speed-up' could be given out at every mill," Pat said. "They won't take 'em. Stoolies everywhere."

"Yeah, but they'll know what's in them. We can hold them up."

"Open air meetings?" suggested Pat. "They won't stop but they'll hear us if we keep saying 'no speed-up' often enough".

"Cops'll pinch you straight away. It's happened to us."

Pat didn't push it. "Tomorrow I'm going to City Hall, find out about local ordinances. There are a lot of things we can do which are not against the law, even if the cops don't agree."

The boldness of this move led to more animated discussion as Rodrigo agreed to go with Pat.

Of enormous importance was the support of Big Jim Reed, a lanky six foot pioneer from Providence, Rhode Island, whose forebears went back to before the American revolution. Though a professional man he declared himself on the side of the millworks and became President of the Union. Through him Pat met progressive, liberal people who were concerned about the treatment of the spinners and weavers. A sympathetic lawyer offered his services if ever needed, others were prepared to stand bail.

But it was uphill work, recruitment to the union was slow as police denounced us 'outsiders' and 'trouble makers.

Inevitably these Portuguese men saw me merely as the wife of this 'important' man who was my husband, there to smooth the path for him. Reluctantly I accepted my role for there was no alternative. What Pat had promised didn't happen. Nothing was ever talked over with me. As my sister had predicted he again saw me as provider of meals, clean washing and sex. Despite this, I resolved to take part in whatever happened, donkey work though it might be.

The Portuguese family with whom we stayed was large and our room was needed. They had been very kind. I thanked them, insisted they take money for our keep, and went house hunting. Lack of funds limited choice. The low rent asked for a large room and kitchen behind a barber's shop seemed to me very reasonable. The back door opened onto a small fenced yard, and added attraction after the cramped quarters in New York.

Leaving the door open, I was cleaning the room when to my astonishment I heard a cacophony of yells, whistles and cat calls coming from a few small boys leaning on the fence. Now who put them up to that, I wondered as I chased them off. Back in the Union Hall I told the men they asked me where the place was and as I described it burst into loud laughter but became flushed and embarrassed when I asked for an explanation. I appealed to Pat but he too was evasive. In the end he said, "It was a cat house."

"What on earth is a cat house?" He gave me a long look. "The room was used by local prostitutes." I considered this. "So what" I thought. It was light, airy and I'd spent a long time getting it clean. The rent was cheap and it was near the hall. We'd stay. Pat shrugged. It wasn't something he'd bother about.

When I again saw the men in the Union hall I said to them, "You know I think I'll be quite capable of dealing with any guy who knocks at the door." There was dead silence. Rodrigo laughed for I'd told him of the large broom I'd bought, remembering mama's rout of the priest. But the older men remained puzzled as I had meant them to be.

In Fall River, a nearby town of many mills, it was impossible to hold a public meeting. The police closed us down before we even got started. So with the help of middle class friends we bought a low-priced derelict house surrounded by a small garden and yard. Laden with picks and hammers, a group of us, all young, started an enthusiastic demolition job. When the cops questioned us we said it was our private property, not their concern.

Finally the debris was cleared away and we held our first open air meeting. The platform stood in the centre of the now empty lot with the Union banner at the back and 'No Speed Up" placards around it. Windows were raised, heads popped out, the curious gathered on the lot as Pat and Rodriego explained why we had done this. The police were taken unawares but didn't interfere.

There was always a good attendance on 'Liberty Lot'. At a meeting I chaired the speaker was Dick who had come from New York to 'help with the youth'. Years later I unexpectedly met him in London. By then he'd made his million in the rag trade but as we reminisced, he referred to those times as 'the best days of my life'.

Pat was often away in other textile towns. My search for work had been fruitless and when little was happening I went to the library. Not worrying too much that the books should be 'proletarian literature' I read indiscriminately, Oliver Onions, O Henry, Booth Tarkington, Edith Wharton, Willa Cather. My three books bought with third place prize money won in a city-wide high school oratorical contest, were always with me. From The Complete Shakespeare, The Oxford Book of English verse and Walt Whitman's Leaves of Grass I memorised poems and prose passages. Time passed slowly during that cold New England winter.

At the turn of the year rumours abounded. The mill owners were going to make their move.

※

When the crunch came in February 1931, it was not in New Bedford but in Lawrence, an up-state town near the New Hampshire border. Lawrence had been the scene of the bitterly fought textile strike led by the I.W.W. in 1912, etched in folk memory, which had turned wage cuts into wage increases for 30,000 mill workers. Now it was happening there again.

The Union office was in a little room above a corner shop. For more than two months Dick, Emmanuel, a local Portuguese, and Edith Berkman, union organiser from New York, had stood outside the mills, tried to give out leaflets, held up the Union paper with its one message, 'No Speed Up'. Dick and Emmanuel were arrested but quickly released as our lawyer intervened. They continued to stand outside the mills, their message, that the Union was alive in Lawrence.

In the end it paid off. Dick was on the spot when it began and from him I later learned the details. One morning some thirty women came to the office.

"Mr Unioni, the son of a bitch bosses no good, we want strike. A tall well built dark woman looked expectantly as Dick. "Who look after children if we must be in mill six o'clock," another indignantly exclaimed.

Though neither Edith nor Dick knew what this was about they asked the women to return that afternoon, bring more people with them. Frantically Edith searched for someone who could tell them what was happening. It seemed that 'Efficiency Engineers' had been introduced into one of the mills. The American Woollen Company was trying to introduce a new scheme whereby two women were to operate nine looms instead of one woman operating two looms. And even worse, they wanted to change shift times.

That afternoon some two hundred mill workers, mainly women, stood outside the office building as Edith and Dick in turn leaned out of the small window and spoke with them. Finally, it became clear that they needed handbills in Italian as well as English to give out at the gate the next morning. There were many nationalities among them but most were Italian and the cry went up, 'We want Giovannetti'. The young Italian poet, one of the strike leaders in 1912, had never been forgotten.

Dick's eyes shone as he told me about it. "The office and stairs were jammed with people who wanted to help. We wrote the leaflet, found an Italian translator. Pat arrived from Boston. All night we turned the handle of our old mimeograph. Next morning the strike was on. Frieda, that was a wonderful, memorable, chaotic day."

Only middle-aged women from one mill department came out at the beginning but when some were arrested the men became angry. The strike spread rapidly to all departments in the three mills of the American Woollen Company. Some 10,000 workers joined that handful of women.

By the time I arrived from New Bedford a large hall had become Strike Headquarters. People milled about, busy with posters or just resting after hours on the picket line. Another group was setting off and I joined them. These mass pickets where so many came together were very important. The law said pickets must not stand outside the gates. Cries of 'No speed-up, No lay-offs' rang out amidst songs in Italian, Portuguese, Polish and of course some sang 'Solidarity Forever – For the Union Makes Us Strong'. Police were much in evidence but we were not stopped.

After some hours I returned to the hall. The Strike committee had been meeting in a smaller room and now for the first time

I saw Pat, Edith and Dick in action as they laughed and joked with helpers and strikers.

Pat came over. "I didn't know you were here. Let's have some lunch. I've got just half an hour before the big meeting." In the cafeteria I asked him, "Why didn't you get in touch? Did you expect me to stay in New Bedford?" "Honestly Frieda, I was so busy I forgot all about you."

When people from Boston, New York and other towns were being called in to help he'd forgotten me, forgotten that I too in the past had been active, a good speaker. How sorry I felt for myself, my pride more wounded by this than by the personal side. Yet he seemed to see nothing wrong in what he'd just said.

However, this was neither time nor place for an angry scene. I asked how things were going. "Peaceful so far but it's early days. Jim Reid tells me the State Militia's been put on alert. The local priests are working hard on the women, mostly Catholics. But I don't think they'll get them back. The main trouble is that for years there's been no real organisation, only a few stalwarts. We're starting from scratch. Well, we'll see better how it's shaping this afternoon at the big strike meeting."

He looked at his watch, rose. "I'll have to get back but no need for you to rush." Then as an afterthought, "New York's sending Alf to head the Relief Team. You could work with him on that."

I sat back, raging. Of course relief was important but as always I wanted to be part of the action. It never occurred to Pat, yet he'd praised me highly back home. Why was it so different now we were married? I'd leave him, go back to Pittsburgh. But not in the middle of a strike.

I slowly made my way to the hall, arriving as Edith Berkman was speaking. She was an impressive, handsome woman with black wavy hair and large brown eyes. The women cheered as she ended with 'No Speed up, No Shift changes.'

At that moment the local Catholic priest entered from a side door and walked up the steps onto the platform. Pat jumped up, stood beside him before he could say a word. "Welcome Father Milanese. But I'm sorry, you cannot speak. That is for our elected strike." There was loud applause as the furious priest walked off the platform and out of the hall.

But he did not give up. His threats during mass had not moved the women and now he came to the picket line. The cry went up, "Get Pat quick. Father Milanese's here."

Pat appeared beside the priest, talked to him politely and pleasantly as they walked along. In a loud voice he said, "Aren't you proud of the brave women from your church who come on the picket line to protect their children?" Again the priest was out-manoeuvred. He strode away, shouted, "You'll all burn in hell."

During the next days and weeks the mill owners made a determined attempt to break the strike. The hitherto peaceful picket lines were subjected to harassment and bullying. Arrests were made. Young soldiers of the State Militia stood in side streets near the mills, nervously fingered their rifles.

But spirits remained high and the mills remained closed. As the employers finally discharged the 'Efficiency Experts' and withdrew speedup and shift changes, the mill workers were jubilant. For them the strike ended in victory.

But Edith and Pat were arrested immediately. Pat had several charges brought against him, damaging American Woollen Company property, conspiring to undermine the State Militia. It was on the last charge, being in the country illegally and having a false American passport that the prosecution concentrated.

During the strike a Scots-American Police Inspector recognised Pat's accent, accurately placed him in Lanarkshire from where he himself had emigrated. Enquiries revealed that Pat was born in Motherwell, had never applied for entrance into the United States or received an American passport.

Like many before him Pat had slipped across the Canadian border. Because this was not a Massachusetts State matter the venue of the trial was changed to the New York District Federal Court.

I was put up by comrades in New York and visited Pat in the somewhat ramshackle small jail. There was a long row of cells like those behind the Sheriff's office in Cowboy films, with the barred front open to view. Every day I brought him food and newspapers. He was annoyed that lawyers did not come more often but clearly to them it was an open and shut case. There was no possible defence. Nevertheless, I followed his instructions, went to see them and those at Party headquarters.

Pat was found guilty on all counts. He had already been in jail for some time when on 28 May 1931 judgement was given. The sentence was harsh, fifteen years in the Federal Prison at Atlanta, Georgia. There was a proviso, that after serving a year and a day he should be deported to Scotland.

In handcuffs Pat looked back, smiled at a group of us who has been present throughout the trial. Soon he'd be on his way to Atlanta. For me there was nowhere to go but home. Exhausted after the months of tension I took the overnight train to Pittsburgh.

Chapter 15

West Virginia Strike

The street car rocked on towards Troy Hill. "End of the line" called the driver. Weighed down by my suitcase I walked through the Hollow, a short-cut to my home and scene of many childhood adventures. Through the open kitchen door I saw my mother. She turned, came to me arms wide. "Papa, it's Frieda," she called out.

He hurried from the garden, hugged me. "So you're back. I phoned this morning but they didn't know anything."

Over coffee we talked, mama's eyes on my face. "You look so tired Frieda." "It's been hard, jail visits, the trial, lawyers. Good to be home again."

My parents too had changed during the year I'd been away. Mama looked more than her forty-nine years, new lines on her face, an expression of anxiety which rarely left her. Always a lean man, papa's face was almost gaunt. My eyes filled but mama put this down to lack of sleep, comforted and patted me as though I were still her little child.

"You go rest. It's a long trip from New York. I'll wake you when supper's ready." I lay on the bed in the little room which had been mine. Clearly getting a job must be my first priority.

That evening was a celebration with papa's wine and a sumptuous meal of roast duck, vegetables, green salad followed by a generous helping of preserved peaches. "Mama, how can you do this in such hard times?"

Papa winked at her as she answered, "We manage." I understood when on the following evening an identical supper was served. My father almost choked with laughter. "Tell her, Maria."

My mother smiled broadly. "I just hope you like duck and peaches, there's a lot more in the cellar. You know we always had chickens and ducks but it got so we couldn't pay the feed bills, not even the grit they need. I looked in the cook books, at last found the answer. Roast, then preserve them in fat. We had to buy the lard but it isn't wasted for I use it again."

Papa interrupted, "Your mother preserved all the fruit and vegetables from the garden. All we need to buy is salt, vinegar, sugar, lard and flour."

"You're a clever woman, mama. It's a long time since I've eaten so well." "We don't always eat like this, have to make it last. It's ready money that's hard to come by." She paused, "At least we have a roof over our heads, so many people have been thrown out of their houses."

I went upstairs, got my purse. "Here's thirty dollars. I saved that in New York when Paula wouldn't take rent from me." I laughed, "Pat didn't know I had it. He always thought he should manage all the money." "Are you sure?" She was troubled, hesitant. I nodded. "I've a few dollars left and I'm going to look for a job soon."

Her face brightened. "I can make it go a long way. Papa gets work sometimes, mostly with bootleggers, building a wall or a garage. People drink when they can so the speak easies still make money."

When we were alone she spoke more freely. "We have such heavy debts Frieda. I don't see how we can ever pay them." "This house?" She nodded. "But I never talk about it. Papa knows he was wrong. You can see it in his face."

Poor papa, I thought, must be feeling very guilty.

After a few days' rest I went to the Party office. Somewhat hesitant, I stood in the doorway. "Frieda", Tony Minerich shouted. He gave me a bear-hug and waltzed me around the room.

The pained expression on the face of the sandy haired man who emerged from the cubbyhole which Pat had once occupied brought us to a halt.

"Carl, meet Frieda. She's one of ours. Pat should never have taken her away." So I met Carl Reeve who shook hands and tried to look affable. I didn't know then that he was the son of Mother Bloor, descendant of old American stock and a heroine to the radical left throughout the United States.

"Pat's in Atlanta Penitentiary then?" asked Carl. "He'll be deported soon. Got fifteen years but only a day and a year to serve and he's done some of that."

Tony, short, sturdy, was one of the blond blue-eyed Croatians who looked more like Scandinavians. But the Slav temperament was there and now he butted in.

"You home with old Truhar and your mom? How are they?" "They're surviving." "And what you gonna do now?" "A job if I can find one." He looked at me. "I gotta better idea. Come have a coffee."

We went to the little place I remembered and sat at a marble-topped table. "Wanna doughnut?" he asked as he ordered. "No. Just had breakfast." He dunked, still looking at me. "Come on, you got something on your mind, Tony. Out with it."

"How about you going in the field as an organiser?" "An organiser?" I was incredulous. Pat had never seen me in that light and my time with him in New York and Massachusetts had somehow diminished the old fervour and drive I'd had in my early Pittsburgh days.

"You'd be great. I've heard you speak." Tony's enthusiasm was heartening. "Let's have another coffee. I'll get it this time. Then you can put me in the picture."

"Well, it started after the 1927 miner's strike. You help in that?" "Yeah, I went out with the Quakers and relief people every Saturday. Frightening it was sometimes when those deputies came nosing in."

"Threatening bastards. They was everywhere." He sat silent then went on, "That God Damn John L Lewis broke every promise – no relief, no organisers from the Union. And the Agreement, only for the Illinois District, nothing for us or West Virginia."

"It was real tough, wasn't it? You, Pat Toohey, Frank Boric, Vic Kamenovich, Tom Myerscough were in the thick of it. I was only sixteen but I remember that."

He smiled at me. "We all got fired and they wouldn't take us on anywhere. The Union was smashed and the son of a bitches in the Company did just what they pleased."

Wages went down from seven dollars and fifty cents a day to two dollars. In some coalfields also excluded from the Agreement, Canada, Colorado where the I.W.W. was strong, Oklahoma, the miners started up local dual organisations.

"In Western Pennsylvania we worked to salvage what was left and build our own Union. Them over there in Moscow had the same idea. Said new unions was needed."

I interrupted. "You mean that Red International of Labour Unions? They talked about that in Lawrence." He nodded, laughed, "They had a conference in March 1928. Sometimes their ideas are not so crazy. But we'd started long before they even thought of it."

I was shocked for I regarded anything from that source as sacrosanct. Tony saw my expression and smiled. "Sometimes people on the spot know best. What else could we do but start organising again. Lots of miners was unemployed, the kids didn't have enough to eat. We had to get the locals started up again."

And dangerous as it had been, in the face of company police, stool pigeons, deputy sheriffs, the militants had set up new organisations.

"By September 1928 we had enough locals to start the National Mineworkers Union, right here in Pittsburgh. We got 15,000 members but it aint enough. We hoped to be bigger and stronger before anything started." "So why a strike now?" "The miners want it. It's been only two bucks a day for an eight- or ten-hour shift. Them bastard coal owners want to cut even that.

The strike just broke out in May and spread like wild fire. Committees sprung up all over the coal field. There's a kind of 'strike fever' even in places where we got no lodge and don't know a single man."

"But Tony, it's 1931, not two years since the Wall Street crash. More people than ever are out of work. Do they stand a chance?" His face was troubled as he answered slowly, "I don't know. But I guess they feel they just ain't gonna be pushed to under two dollars a day."

Tony's eyes were on me. "What about it? Our main problem is we ain't got enough experienced people who know something about miners, company towns, speaking and organising. We're still weak and every single person counts."

"First of all, it ain't like that textile town you just come from, lots of women on strike in one place. You'd work with the women – there's always one woman who stands out, draw her in, she'll know local conditions. But sit in on the men's committee meetings. Miners can be influenced even though most got old-fashioned ideas about women."

"You think I could do that?" "Sure you can do it. What's happened to you? You shoulda stayed here where you belong." I smiled ruefully, maybe he was right. "Ok, I'll try. Women's picket lines?" "That'd be good. And relief, get the women organised. Some places work ok but not where we're sending you. You'll have to speak at meetings, try to set up a local where there's only a committee. The men'll listen to that."

"When do I go and where?" "Right away, to West Virginia. It's always been a tough coal field. Bill Dunne's there already."

At home mama straight away said, "You're sure it'll be alright? You won't be in danger?" I shrugged. "A strike's a strike. Tony Minerich thinks I'll be all right as an organiser." Papa was proud of me. "Who you working with?" "Bill Dunne."

That short stocky man with the bull neck and heavy Irish face was a legendary figure in our circles. My father's eyes shone. I knew what was coming, kept quiet for he so enjoyed telling this story yet again.

"It was in 1917 he led a strike against the bosses of the Anaconda Copper Company. He was chief electrician, didn't have to side with the miners. But out he came. He always carried two guns." "Did he use them?" "Yeah, he sure did. He was editor of the strike paper, the Bulletin. When the Company gunmen come to smash the print machines he fired right down in front of their feet. "Come closer and you'll get it," he shouted. And they didn't come closer."

My father had his heroes and Bill Dunne was one of them.

For a long time that night I couldn't sleep as I argued with myself. The women'll be older. How will they regard me? And to the men I'll be just a young girl. How they look at me depends on how I act, not how old I am, so I'll have to forget myself and what impression I make. Just go in and do the best job I can.

I thought of my earlier life before I married Pat – the free speech fights, the arrests, my high school battles. Then I'd been bold and confident. I could be like that again. And there was always Bill Dunne to consult.

Our base was Wheeling, the capital of West Virginia. Bill Dunne shook hands and introduced me around. I was relieved that many of the team were also young.

"Maria here will work with you. Her dad's a strike leader." We sat together, ate baloney, bread and tomatoes because eating in a café cost too much. Maria was eighteen and her family were Czech. I told her my parents were from Yugoslavia.

"A lot of Slavs where we're going," she said. "Can you speak the language – it'll come in handy." "Yes, Croatian. And you?" "A little, not so good though. My mom wanted us to talk American so she could learn it too."

We took to each other which was just as well for we were to work closely together in the coming months.

A bit apprehensive, we travelled to our first company town. But the women were pleased to see us. In the Miner's Hall we told them what we knew about other places. We worked on relief, organised transport to the nearest large town. The women laughed as we passed out tins. Several small children clung to their mother's skirts and this was all to the good during the collections.

After several weeks' work a sound committee was established. As Tony had said, someone always emerges to take the lead. And when we got to that stage, Maria and I moved on.

In one of the mining towns most of the people were Croatians. I sat in on the Committee meeting and found it was conducted in that language with a quick translation to the few Italians. As Tony had asked, I suggested they set up a lodge and enrol all the miners. Perhaps because I spoke Croatian, they were very friendly and agreed it was a good idea. They knew the name Tony

Minerich when I mentioned it. The women were there too and we discussed relief with them and the men. That was a good experience and it gave me a lot more confidence.

Maria and I suggested to Bill Dunne that we take a group of women from different places to Wheeling to see the Governor of West Virginia and ask him to help with relief. One day in the early hours a relief truck pulled up to the Miners' Hall where we were waiting. We clambered aboard, picked up more and more women on the way until the truck was packed. They were all in their best clothes and very excited. We started singing 'Solidarity Forever' and the younger ones joined in while the older women smiled and nodded.

When we got to the city the truck attracted attention as we kept asking where we could find the Governor. One man hopped on the running board to show us the way. Curious people crowded around us as we stood at the bottom steps of the capitol building. The Governor finally came out, looked down on us but said nothing. I pushed Maria forward for she was to be our spokeswoman. She whispered, "I'm nervous, you do it."

"We'll both do it. I'm nervous too." We marched up, the women behind us, and I began loudly so those below could hear.

"The people of this state are your responsibility. These miners' wives and their children are going hungry. We want state relief." "You're one of those outside agitators, you don't sound to me like a miner's daughter."

I pointed to Maria. "She's a miner's daughter. All these women are miners' wives. I'm a bricklayer's daughter but is that so different?" "Our kids is hungry. Need food, "one of the women shouted. Others joined in – "relief, want relief."

The Governor looked at them, the worn shoes and clothing, the thin faces. "Maybe, maybe something can be done." But no relief ever came from that source.

We sat on the steps, munched sandwiches. Then we got out the collecting tins and went into the main streets of Wheeling. We had no intention of wasting our time in this large city and in fact did very well.

Word came from Bill Dunne that Maria and I were to return to a company town where scabs were being brought in. Anna, a large young Polish woman greeted us warmly. She'd easily taken on the task of relief work and also organised the women to picket.

To us she announced, "Tomorrow picket line. We women go behind men. Show them scabs."

The mine was on a narrow dirt road between two hills. As our line wound its way towards the opening Anna turned to me. "Where's the police? They up to something?"

Sure enough these Chicago gangsters, criminals sworn in as deputies, were nowhere to be seen.

"I tell Matt." She rushed forward, I with her, but as we rounded the corner there they were standing on top of the hill opposite the mine entrance. Outlined against the blue sky, in black uniforms and shiny black boots, revolver ends gleaming from holsters, they towered menacingly above us. They did not move.

Then as the front of the picket line passed the mine opening and turned for the walk back a volley of boulders rolled down the hill, striking some people in the crowded entrance. Another valley and another.

Matt shouted, "Keep women and children away. Go back Anna, Frieda. Stop them. We get bastards."

As he led the men up the hillside a large stone just missed him. We pushed for the rear. One man near me stumbled, fell. When he rose blood poured from a gash in his arm. Trembling, frightened and angry Anna and I shouted abuse at both scabs and deputies. When I looked back the skyline was empty, the deputies gone.

We crowded into the Miners' Hall. The atmosphere was tense with a lot of arguing and interrupting. "What you think, Frieda?" Anna asked.

"I think Matt must telephone papers, tell what happened. Then tomorrow a women's picket line. When they brought soldiers to Lawrence textile strike we had a big picket line with women in front. Soldiers did nothing. We could try – if the women are willing."

"Sure they be willing." Her eyes flashed. She stood up, climbed on a chair and at last got attention. "Tomorrow women go first – only women. Men stay at back. I think scabs not go in, deputies not hurt us." She looked around her. "You all come?" "Sure, sure, ok we come," the women responded.

"You Matt, phone papers. Tell what happened, how they roll stones. Tell about scabs. But not about women picket line. We show them, we surprise bastards." Matt looked troubled. Some of the men shook their heads. "We have to try," Anna said fiercely. "We go early, before they expect." A wonderful, forceful woman, she got her way.

Led by the women it was the largest picket line ever seen at the mine. Because of Matt's phone call, newspaper reporters arrived. The deputies stood silent, glowering, but made no move. As the scab trucks turned back the women cheered. "We do it," they cried. Some were in tears.

That night a harmonica played in the Hall as we celebrated. There was dancing and singing. Maybe it was Matt's phone call and the reporters who had done the trick but it was our victory.

In early August, in face of a great deal of harassment at another mine, Bill Dunne asked me and Maria to go there and try the women's picket line again to stop the scabs.

But this time the police were waiting and gave no quarter. Driving into our ranks with motor cycles, state troopers scattered the pickets. We shepherded the children into a field and left them with the older women.

Back we went, reformed our picket and walked towards the mine. Maria and I started singing – The Union makes us strong .... Younger women joined in, the non-English speakers clapped their hands.

Quiet now the police watched from the side. An Italian woman behind me spat on the ground each time she passed a deputy.

Then the troopers moved towards me and Maria. The women near us held tight, pulled us back, kicked at the police. "Son of a bitch bastards, leave alone" women shouted. There was an outcry in several languages. In the struggle my dress was ripped right down the front.

One of the deputies pulled out a revolver and fired into the air. Get back, get back, you Godamn whores," he shouted. As the hold of the women slackened the police pushed them away, dragged Maria and me, scratched and bruised, into motor cycle side cars. We were driven straight to a large formidable prison building.

It was two days before they allowed us to phone the union office but nobody arrived to see us. In the gloomy cell with its high, barred window, my twentieth birthday came and went. Still no word from anyone. As we were marched out one morning, I asked the large woman warder if I could have something to read. Her smile was not friendly. "Yeah, I'll bring you something."

Later she unlocked my cell and thrust a huge bible at me. "Maybe this'll teach sinners like you repent." For me it was manna from heaven. Raised as freethinkers, we'd never had a bible in the house and now I read every page, deeply interested in the stories, moved by some of the language. But I did not repent.

After a week had passed Maria's mother appeared. In rapid Czech she explained to her that there were many arrests, among them her father. "Speak English", the guard had shouted. "You should have seen how my Mom glared at him. But she gave me Bill Dunne's message – we'll get you out as soon as we can, don't worry."

In these past weeks thousands had been arrested in an organised sweep. Our lawyers found it hard to cope. So it took time. I cannot remember exact words but believe there were charges of conspiracy and assault against us.

At that stage of the strike the miners were facing not only state troopers but local coal and iron police who fingered the militants, Department of Labor agents who combed the areas looking for strikers who weren't citizens. The courts issued one injunction after another to stop picketing. Strikers were beaten up, shot at. Two were killed. Over a hundred thousand men, women and children throughout the coalfields were evicted from company houses.

Worst of all strike breakers began to flood into the mining areas. As the strike weakened, miners trickled back. By the time Maria and I got out on bail the strike was nearly over.

The charges against us might be serious, perhaps lead to a jail sentence. I put this behind me as I said goodbye to Maria and the others. Bill Dunne said, "You two did a good job."

"But they lost," I answered. He nodded, "Like last time and the time before. But they'll fight again, they're a tough breed, miners." "How about their women?" Somehow, I resented Bill's matter of fact dismissal of this defeat after the bitter months of struggle. I'd worked, laughed and cried with these women, some of them were my friends. And now they were returning to even worse conditions.

No longer in awe of him after these hard months I went on. "You make them and their men sound like pawns in the great class battle. They're mothers, fathers, suffering human beings." I was near to tears and he understood.

"Their suffering isn't of our making. Aren't we here because of it, because of what the coal owners are doing to them? Don't you think I too am sad, unhappy that the strike's been lost? But I've seen it so many times before. I'm glad you feel as you do. It is our anger at such injustice that makes us what we are. Don't lose it."

Chapter 16

Farewell to the States

With Bill Dunne I left West Virginia by car for Pittsburgh. My parents were delighted to see me. "I didn't know we'd be bailed today. The lawyer arrived and out we came. Boy, were we glad." They laughed and my father started to ask questions. Mama firmly stopped him. "Food first, talk later. "You're right. Frieda, get some fresh air. I'll pick you a bunch of grapes." From the porch swing I watched my father move among the vines. How fortunate I was in my parents.

During supper my mother's eyes were on me as I again devoured duck, fresh vegetables and salad. "Eat, Frieda, eat. There's lots more in the cellar," she urged. Over coffee mama asked, "What was it like, that strike and the jail?" "You've never been to a coalfield, Mom?" She shook her head. "Well West Virginia was the worst I've ever seen." "How come?" papa asked.

I shrugged. "I dunno. No union organisation after 1927. Bill Dunne told me they were the lowest paid in any mining area even though they'd dug more coal. You could see the poverty in their faces, the skinny kids. All the talk about coal, it's their life, how every day the women worried if the men'd come home, there were so many accidents.

"Sounds worse than the steel mills," papa interjected. "Yeah. They almost enjoyed being on strike. When the relief came the women, who cooked in the miners' hall kitchen, said the kids were eating better than when their men were down the mines." "You ate with them too?" I nodded. "But never like this, mama." She smiled.

"In one company town I stayed with a wonderful Polish woman, Anna. One evening she said to her husband 'show Frieda your back'. He laughed, protested, but pulled off his shirt. His back was like a map with dozens of blue lines and dots. His face too, like that of most miners had blue marks. Anna told me he got that after an explosion and cave in, one of the lucky ones who hadn't been killed. "Poor man," mama murmured. "No mom, Matt was great, one of the younger men who didn't yet have the coal dust in his lungs. Some of the older ones wheezed like a concertina. Matt was a real leader in that town."

"It must be a very hard life." "Yes, but they're wonderful people, especially the women." "And who was in jail with you?" "A young girl, Maria, whose father was in the strike. We were good friends."

I told them then about the manner of the arrest but said little about the jail, the menace I had felt in that vast forbidding building, the oppressive darkness in the narrow cell with its dirty walls which stretched up and up towards a small barred window under a high ceiling. So different from the little neighbourhood jails I'd been in before.

"What did you do all day?" "We weren't real prisoners so we didn't work except to look after the cell and ourselves. I recited poems and verses, sang papa's songs and the ones I remembered from Socialist Sunday school." Because of mama's deep religious prejudices, I didn't mention the bible.

"Is it true the strike's nearly over?" my father asked. "Yes, and lost again. Those God damn coal owners don't care at all about people, real bastards they are." Mama was startled at my vehemence. "You did your best," she said soothingly. But papa, unknowingly echoing Bill Dunne, answered, "Maria, it's right she should be angry."

After a few days at home I went job hunting. As I left for town mama said, "Go Millvale way. Look across the river near the old bridge and at those steep hills in East Ohio Street." "Why? What's happened there?" "Just go see for yourself."

I ran down the short path, walked over the bridge. On an empty lot a squalid town of some twenty make-shift shacks and hovels, covered with tar paper or tin, had sprung up. Large packing cases were held down by scrap iron. I shrank from the smell of garbage and urine. An old woman washed clothes in a large tin can while on the open fire a pot simmered.

As I stood gaping, a younger woman with a baby on one arm emerged from behind the tattered blanket which covered the opening of an up-ended grand piano bar. Her hostile glance made me back away. At the entrance some bitter wit had crossed out 'Car Park' and substituted 'Grand Hotel'. It was the first Hooverville I had seen, and so close to our Hill.

I recrossed the bridge, walked slowly down East Ohio Street. Here, where sloping green mounds gradually became bare rocks, tin stove pipes stuck out of the hillside caves which, with my brother, I'd once explored. Now they were dwellings for the evicted. In modern industrial America the jobless were being driven to a stone-age existence. I remembered the 'Cave Dweller' books of my Socialist Sunday school days. But then there had been no cities, no buildings for those early people.

Angry, frustrated but also feeling helpless, I walked slowly to the next street car stop. It took time before I found work as a counter girl in a sandwich bar. The boss had looked me over. "You got experience?" "No but I graduated high school and can learn quick." "Ok. Give you a try. Two shifts we got. Change over each week. Ten dollars. Tips you can keep." Ten hours a day for ten dollars a week. But I agreed for after weeks of searching I knew how very scarce jobs were.

During late morning and into early afternoon the pressure was greatest. From all sides came a constant clamour, 'ham on rye', 'cheese and tomato on toast', 'coffee and apple pie', hurry up honey, I gotta move'.

Orders had to be bawled through the serving hatch, coffee carried on the run, bills worked out in a hurry. Counter tips were rare. Behind the scenes four young men made mounds of toast, brushed melted butter on bread, slapped in ham and pickle, chicken mayonnaise or some other concoction, deftly removing the cockroaches. The place was alive with these as they swarmed near the heat of the stove pipe. Few of us accepted the free meal of sandwiches.

Near the end of my fourth week the boss called me aside as I was about to leave. "Frieda, you don't smile. The customers want jolly waitresses. You gotta keep that smile on your face." I'd smiled as the shift began but as my back ached more and more the smile disappeared. I was very tired, angrily burst back at him. "Look, you got my legs and feet, my arms and hands, my voice for ten bucks a week. Right? The smile's not included." Even as I said it I knew I'd lost the job.

"You quit right now," he bellowed. "I got another day to go. I'm willing to work it. I want my ten dollars." He held out eight. "That's all you're getting. Vamoose, out of my sight." "Ten dollars or I'll make a sign and stand outside your place. You wanna know what'll be on it?"

He stared at me as though he couldn't believe what he heard, didn't make a move. "Ok I'll write 'Sandwiches and plenty of cockroaches. I know. I worked here.'" As he handed me a ten dollar bill he shouted, "No more God damn high school girls for me."

I got another waitress job as I stressed my experience. It was a small sit-down, two-bit joint with only two of us serving. The boss fussed. "We got regulars, you gotta be nice to them. Times is hard and we wanna keep them." He pointed out three men. I laughed at their stupid jokes. I did try. But the middle guy was hard to evade as he leered, groped and made what he thought were wise cracks, 'how's little honey baby today', 'I like 'em curved with good tits, just like you. When I glared at him he grinned.

One day as I was about to put his food in front of him he reached 'round and pinched my bottom. I banged down the plate. The gravy splashed him and the tablecloth. Then I turned, slapped his face as hard as I could. Loud laughter from men at nearby tables brought the owner running. "You're fired, get out," he shouted at me then apologised to the lecher.

I waited. "I've been here nearly a week. I want my full money." The customers were watching. A voice called out, "She done right." The fat boss looked at the other men, then without another word went to the till and returned with my ten dollars.

Third time lucky and so I was at a bigger café. Though the pay was the same, tips were usually a dime rather than a nickel. The job lasted till the proprietor had to retrench, he and his wife would manage alone. "Sorry girls," he said to us, "You can see we're not getting the customers. I've put an extra two bucks in your pay packets and that's all I can do." They were decent people.

Pat's letters from prison had been few. There was a hint of early release. Sure enough in the new year I received word through the Party that on Christmas day, 1931, he'd quickly and quietly been deported. But no letter came even though he was now a free man in Scotland.

In our home a feeling of excitement had built up. One morning after the post arrived papa shouted, "Maria, we've been accepted." He looked again at the letter. "It says, 'near the old city of Nizhni Tagil a new steel town, Tagilstroi, is being built. Bricklayers are needed on the construction site. Make your arrangements and come as early as possible. Be sure to bring your tools. Write to ......'"

He stopped, looked up, eyes sparkling. My father certainly wished to help build socialism in Russia. At the same time the sale of the house, even at a loss, would help with debts and leave a bit over for a start in their new lives. From the beginning mama had argued against going. "It's best to hold on to what we've got and in some way weather the storm. This can't go on forever. And papa, you're 52 and I'm 50, a bit late for this new life." But pap's determination and the possibility of an end to the burden of debts had finally worn her down. He was jubilant but she seemed sad, dismayed by this strange new move.

What my parents were about to do was not so unusual. During the late twenties and early thirties people from many countries were recruited to work or teach their skills in the Soviet Union. Inevitably socialists and communists were among them. It was during this time that a letter came from Pat. Mama stood beside me as I opened it. "So, he's written at last. Two months since he's been deported."

"Would you believe it, he wants me to join him in Scotland. I'm not going." My mother's answer surprised me. "It will be best for you to go." "But you never liked him," I protested. "You didn't want me to marry him and you were right. Remember you said 'he may be a good communist but what kind of a man is he?'. I often thought of your words for I've not been happy with him. It was not as I expected."

She remained silent for a long time then nodded. "I felt it was like that. Frieda, if we were not going to Russia I'd want you to stay, divorce him. I even talked with Margolis, our lawyer and he said that would be easy." "You didn't tell me. And I wouldn't divorce him while he was in prison." Mama made a face. "So, for once I acted without speaking to you about it. I could see what kind of man he was and Frieda, he wasn't for you." "But now he is," I was indignant.

"We are going to Russia and that changes everything. We won't be here if you need us, if you want to come home. So few jobs, what will you do, how will you live? Sure we have relations but for everyone life is hard these days. Maybe over there it will be different. You've not had much time together in these two years of marriage."

She shrugged, watched me as I remained silent. In all this excitement I'd given little thought as to how the departure of my parents would leave me. Suddenly I felt a sense of desolation as I realised that the security which they'd always provided was gone. 'Home' as I'd known it would no longer be there for me. Mama smoothed back my hair, kissed me. "It might be for the best, Frieda. Think about it."

The next day I went to the Party office. It was very quiet and a vague thought that I might ask for a Party job was never put into words. As Carl Reeve read Pat's letter, I asked him about my position as I was still on bail. "I'll go into it. Come back in a week or so."

It was a time of hubbub at home, relatives coming and going, furniture being sold off, odd articles given to neighbours. Mama was busy and I felt out of it.

One evening she asked me, "What have you decided?" Then before I could answer she went on, "Go Frieda, go. You can see how it is here. He has asked you to come and he is your husband.

Perhaps you expected too much. Most women do but they have to come to terms with what life offers them." "This is not how you talked before. It was 'stand on your own feet, don't be dependent on any man'." "Can't you see it's different now? So many people without homes, without hope, without work. Who knows what the future will be."

I listened, shook my head. How could I answer that? Yet I didn't want to go back to Pat. With a little clear thinking on my part I might have realised a job in the New York Party office was probably open to me. Nearly twenty one now, it was the second time I could have made an end to this unfortunate marriage. Why didn't I? Not till I was writing these memoirs did I fully face this question.

At the office I was told by Carl that the lawyers thought I should take the chance. "So many strike cases are still outstanding. Yours may never be followed up."

Early in April 1932 I jumped bail and sailed from New York for Greenock. In her last letter from the States mama wrote, "You went just in time. A patrol wagon, its bell clanging, rolled up the hill and policemen rushed into the house. 'Where's Frieda, where's she hiding?'. 'She's on the high seas', I told them but they insisted on searching the house. You'd have laughed, they were so mad."

Two weeks after this happened mama also left. The next time I heard from her she was in Russia.

THE OLD WORLD

Chapter 17
Arrival – Life Among the Miners

Eight days on the SS California had been a holiday as I put all doubts behind me, enjoyed the sea and sunshine. Tom, near my age, coached me at deck games, asked me to partner him in the Charleston competition and we won.

As music from the salon became louder on this last Gala Night, I hid in the darkest corner I could find on deck. Tom called my name several times but with arms folded across my chest and knees pulled up I tried to make myself invisible.

Only now when tomorrow was so near did I face the uncertainties of the future. For a long time I sat quiet, listening to the sea, then stood up, straightened my shoulders and joined the dancers.

As the ship docked I leaned on the rail. He saw me, lifted his arm, I raised my hand. Disembarkation, customs, the quay and Pat. We looked at each other. My spirits rose somewhat as I sensed he also was nervous, not as confident as I had expected.

"Was it a good voyage?" "Reasonable, at least I didn't get sea sick." He smiled, picked up my suitcase. His hand on my elbow guided me towards the nearby station. Our journey to Motherwell passed quickly as he talked of his mother, four sisters and three brothers, all waiting at his home to greet me. As my eyes widened he went on quickly to explain we'd leave very soon for East Fife where he worked with the unemployed.

From the station we walked down the main thoroughfare, Brandon Street, turned into Glencairn Street. "Now you'll see our magnificent mansion." Again, that slight unease in his voice.

Under an archway, through a long passage and we were there. A long unbroken tenement two storeys high lined a courtyard. At its centre were a number of wash houses. Outside iron staircases led to small upper flats where on landing and a shared lavatory served two families. From a top floor Pat's sisters waved.

We entered the packed room as curious faces turned my way. Pat hurried the introductions. At last we sat down to a meal, 'high tea' they called it, a cold buffet of ham, salad and cakes on a three tiered stand.

Pat's mother was small, frail. Short frizzed hair encircled a worn face which retained traces of an earlier beauty. A dark blue dress, white frill at the throat, reached to her ankles. The strength and determination which had kept the family together, pushed the younger girls towards university, was evident in her confident bearing. The father was large, jolly, easy going. After a long stint in the steel mill he was happy to leave everything to his wife so long as he got his 'wee dram'.

The mother's eyes were constantly on me, weighing, assessing, judging. I'd expected interest but not this relentless scrutiny. Conversation was forced, helped on by Pat. At one point his mother said, "I believe you're a Pole, Frieda." Pat frowned, was about to speak when I answered, "No, I'm not Polish. My parents were from Yugoslavia and I was born in the States." "Well, it's much the same, isn't it?"

Puzzled, not understanding the prejudice behind this question, I remained silent. Yet the others must have realised this was a snub, for the Polish miners who in those years had come to work in Scotland were at the bottom of the working class social scale, looked down upon by such as my mother-in-law.

Clearly Pat's family was poor. Eight children had been raised in these three rooms, the largest not as big as my bedroom in our old farmhouse. Here the family lived, ate their meals and to my amazement, some of them slept in two alcoves behind a curtain, the 'hole in the wall'. To one side was a tiny, doorless scullery where the cooking was done.

But Pat's mother knew the way to distance herself from those categorised as 'slum people', for when she went out she always wore a hat, the sign of working class respectability. The 'keelies' flung shawls over their heads.

Though I knew nothing of these strange gradations at that time, I felt her lack of friendliness despite the outward show of politeness. His mother had not forgiven me for marrying her 'lovely son Pat' as she called him. But then none of her daughters-in-law pleased her as she clung to her 'lads'.

It was with relief I heard Pat say, "We'll have to be away tomorrow. There's a meeting in Kirkcaldy I've to be at." "You said you'd manage a few days," his mother protested. "I forgot to tell you. I had a message to say I was needed back." It wasn't true and she knew it. Maybe Pat understood her hostility, decided it was best for us to leave. If so, I'd never know for I was to learn that his family, especially his mother, were not to be discussed or criticised.

Early next morning as we left for Fife I was pleased to learn it was a good distance away. I turned my face to the coach window. Yesterday's dreadful 'welcome' from his mother. But it had been worse when we were alone in the one bedroom.

As Pat undressed he said, "You'll like where we're going, it's near the sea." He was trying. Could it be possible he'd now show me affection, even tenderness? I needed that for I felt lonely and somewhat lost. Slowly I searched for a nightgown, then turned to him, "Why did you ask me to come over?"

He half sat up, head on elbow, looked at me. After what seemed an age, he gave that familiar high laugh which meant he wasn't going to take me seriously. "Hell, you're my wife, aren't you. We're married, that's why."

"And that's all?" "Well, why did you come?" he countered. "For the same reason, I suppose. I just hoped things might be different this time." "Things have always been all right. It's you who's been fanciful. But you're older now." Fanciful. I hated that word with which he'd often dismissed all I felt. I undressed, put out the light, got into bed. His long months of celibacy had not brought consideration for me. For him it was an almost instant, urgent release of sexual tension. There was no change of heart, it was for this relief he wanted a wife.

Pat sighed contentedly, smiled, turned on his side away from me. He did not stir as I rose, put on my robe. From the small window I looked long at the starless night, dark as this dreary future I saw stretching before me.

The bus sped on. My thoughts were on Pittsburgh, three thousand miles away. Pat's voice broke in, "Another half-hour and we'll be there."

I closed my eyes, didn't answer. My life must now be here, in a foreign land and it was my own fault, I'd chosen this path. Slowly I discarded my self-pity, my mood changed. They'd not really be strangers, these new folk. An old Sunday school song came to mind, 'comrades awaiting me' – how did it go, there was more, 'where'er on earth I roam, with them I'll feel at home'. It was up to me now. These people belonged to the same movement of which I was a part. I could adapt. I'd survive. How resilient the young are!

The coach dropped us. Soon we were in the miner's cottage where Pat had a room. Our landlady, Nellie Hynds, plump with large brown eyes and dark bobbed hair, greeted us warmly. "You must be famished." Buttered bread, ham and eggs were placed on the table. She smiled at me then busied herself with the teapot while her two young sons, dressed in rough jerseys, knee length shorts and lace-up boots, stared at me. I felt embarrassed for her sing-song Fife speech was hard to understand. The room soon filled and it was clear Pat's charm had worked yet again as laughter rang out. Nellie was in the Party though her employed miner husband was not. I found this interesting.

We were in the village of Denbeath, part of Buckhaven in the Wemyss Estate. The laird owned the land, the minerals, the pits. But this was no stark 'company town' such as I had known in the States. Despite the nationwide depression it was a flourishing community in which the left-wing United Mineworkers of Scotland played an important part. Jock McArthur, the leading union official in this area, was a communist.

I soon mastered the dialect, joined an active group which met at Alice McGrory's house. Here Alice, Nellie, John Boyle, Hugh Smith and other unemployed miners produced pit papers, 'The Spark', 'The Torch', 'The Searchlight', 'The Mash'. Typed, stencilled and stapled, these were sold at pit heads.

Women's Guilds, football clubs, with a successful UMS Juvenile Team, were all part of the social life. Saturday night dances attracted so large a following that at times they spilled over to Monday and Friday. I enjoyed these evenings when in the intervals men rose and without embarrassment sang solo. The 'Rose of Tralee' was very popular. Though I saw more of Pat we still went our different ways for he was most often in Kirkcaldy or the surrounding towns.

During the early summer a large meeting called to denounce the Means Test was held at Port Brae. Led by a local man, Jimmy Ord and Pat, the unemployed marched down the High Street to present a petition. But as their spokesmen sought to enter the Town House the police charged, lashing out with batons. Jimmy was arrested. Pat rallied the men back to Port Brae and led another march, this time to the police station to get Jimmy released. Instead, he and eleven others joined him in jail. The town was in turmoil till the trial. The majority were fined but Pat, the outsider, got sixty days while Jimmy got forty. They entered Edinburgh's Saughton Prison on 22 June 1932.

"From one jail to another. Seven months ago he was still in Atlanta Penitentiary," I said to Nellie. "Will you go to his folk?" she asked. "I scarcely know them, I'll stay here." "You'll need to go to the Broo then." "Why? I asked her, not understanding. "The Unemployment Bureau will have to help you. Tell them your husband's in prison and you've no means of support." "But he led the unemployed march." "Doesn't matter what he did. They've got to keep you till he's free. It's the law." I burst out laughing. "Never in a million years could that happen in the States." So, without fuss or bother I got ten shillings each week during Pat's imprisonment.

Visitors were forbidden but Jock McArthur was going on some legal matter and took me with him as his secretary. Pat, unshaven, presented a strange sight. He wore grey, pinstriped knee-length trousers, a collarless shirt, thick socks up to the knees, clumsy boots and on his head a little forage cap.

When Jock became indignant at this garb, Pat laughed. "It's as bad here as any jail I've known in the States but it doesn't matter. I've got them going and that passes the time." He seemed cheerful enough, laughed at my ten shillings, then went on to explain his new ploy. I smiled as I listened, not at all surprised. For Pat had this quality of being able to arouse in the unemployed, the demoralised, a feeling of self-respect, a sense of their own dignity. In prison conditions which were meant to degrade and demean he was showing by his actions that you must not be afraid to demand your rights.

Before his deportation, while at the Boston centre, he'd come up with the demand that each prisoner be provided with his own kind of food. The Chinese, Italians, Indians, Greeks and others soon caught on and the campaign continued, perhaps even after Pat had been shipped off.

Here in Saughton he had asked for an extra slice of bread and been refused. Now he was taking it step by step through prison procedures as high as he could go. Paraded before the Visiting Committee, Pat embarrassed the officials as he stepped out of the line and explained his request. "I'd like an extra slice of bread because I'm hungry." The other prisoners were delighted and slipped slices of bread under his pillow. On the day of his release Pat was informed that the Home Secretary had denied his request.

During Pat's time in prison I started open-air speaking at the Party's regular meetings in Port Brae. I was usually put up first for my American accent caused both interest and amusement as the crowd gathered. Willie Gallacher, later Communist Member of Parliament for West Fife, was often the main speaker. After hearing me the first time he gently explained Scottish conditions and thereafter helped me with my notes.

In late summer Pat was freed. It was a time of preparation for the hunger marches against the Means Test which were to converge on London. From all parts of Britain the unemployed came and reached the outskirts on 26 October 1932. A million signatures against the Means Test were to be presented to Parliament.

Huge demonstrations took place in Hyde Park and Trafalgar Square. London unemployed and employed came to welcome the marchers. There were baton charges, clashes with mounted police, railings torn up as weapons against them. Many were arrested including Wal Hannington, secretary of the National Unemployed Workers Movement, and the Chairman, Sid Elias. Hannington was jailed for three months, Sid Elias for two years.

Pat was now asked to work temporarily at NUWM headquarters. By late November we were in London. These eight months in East Fife in the warmth and friendship of a small community might well have been my best introduction to this country, but I was very glad to be at the hub, in this great city.

Even before we found lodgings I got a job working with Bill Spence, National Secretary of the Young Communist League, whose office was on the top floor of Party Headquarters at 16 King Street near Covent Garden. But my lasting memory of that day is meeting Beattie Marks, custodian of the general office and the first to interview all newcomers. To her I presented the tiny square of silk which stated I'd been a member of the Communist Party in the United States.

Brusque, unsmiling, she read it then said "Sit down" and left the room. I moved nearer the fire, looked up as pictures of Karl Marx, Lenin, Stalin and a man I later learned was Harry Pollitt, Secretary of the British Party. Beattie returned, the grim face transformed as she smiled at me. "I thought you were all right but I had to check. Harry and Bill will be down soon."

My eyebrows rose and she sensed my question. "Harry's the man you need to see. Bill is YCL Secretary. I'll make you a cup of tea." I'd already learned in Fife that 'a cup of tea' was a form of welcome but felt a bit wary of this formidable little woman who seemed very much in charge here.

Harry, stocky, jovial, entered the room. We shook hands as he bluntly said, "So you're Pat's wife, a lot younger than I expected." Bill who had followed him interrupted, "You're no in work are ye? I've a job for you if you can type."

That afternoon I found a room and kitchen on the Holloway Road and the next morning I was at work. I enjoyed the atmosphere at King Street, the easy companionship of the other women who had jobs there. Beattie and I were to become lifelong friends.

After only four months in London Pat came home one evening very excited, bursting with news. "Hannington's back.

I'm being sent to work with Bill Rust at the Comintern." "You mean you're going to Moscow?" This was quite unexpected. "Almost immediately. You stay, clear up and take the trunks by boat. We may be there a few years. It's all been arranged."

Over my head again but this time I didn't mind, everyone wanted to go to Russia. I'd miss King Street and my new friend in the East End, Annie Silver with whom I worked in the Pioneer Groups. But Russia meant seeing my parents again and that I very much welcomed. Surely the Urals couldn't be that far from Moscow.

Pat gave me money and a list – warm clothing, tea, chocolate, coffee. He'd been well briefed. In April 1933, a year after I'd left the States, I sailed from Hayes Wharf near London Bridge across the North Sea, through the Kiel Canal and the Baltic Sea to Leningrad. As we neared port, I stood on deck straining for my first glimpse of the Soviet Union.

Chapter 18

Moscow – The Luxe Hotel – Depression

My emotions as I disembarked in Leningrad might be compared with those of pilgrims to Rome or Mecca. Many communists have described a similar reaction as they crossed frontiers into the only country where 'workers ruled'. How could we then have known that such uncritical acceptance of a belief, to which we gave unswerving devotion, was to acquiesce in the distortion of the world communist and socialist movements for many years to come.

The briefest glimpse of the city as I drove to the station, drab streets, unpainted buildings, gold domed churches glistening in the late afternoon sun, a sparkling river spanned by a beautiful bridge. Then by overnight train I travelled to Moscow.

Pat was there to meet me. "It's great, you'll like it." "I hope so". Why was he always so sure?

All Comintern foreigners and some Russians lived in the Luxe Hotel which was on the Tverskaya, later called Gorky Street. In the foyer by the stairs was a lift which rarely worked. From a cubby hole a porter watched. No-one could enter without a 'propusk', a pass.

We abandoned our bed-bug infested room on the third floor for an L-shaped room on the first, facing the street. I was to discover this was a matter of status as well as comfort. Down the corridor a communal kitchen with gas stoves and lockers for pots and pans was in constant use.

Our street sloped down into Red Square, beautiful with its huge walls, towers, the long row of fir trees against stone. I marvelled at the Basil Cathedral with its strange Byzantine domes, whorls and minarets. Outside the Mausoleum, where sentinels with fixed bayonets stood guard, long queues of people waited for a glimpse of Lenin. I never took part in this ritual which seemed to me backward and superstitious, reminded me too much of the Catholic church in Millvale where the faithful lined up to kiss a stone effigy of Christ. From the top of the Kremlin fluttered a red flag, illuminated at night. Nearby was the famous Bolshoi Theatre.

Very soon I worked in the Comintern typists' pool and each day walked from the Luxe to the Communist International Headquarters housed in a large building near an entrance to the Kremlin.

"A new girl," shouted one lively woman in German. "Who are you? Where are you from? Did you bring coffee or chocolate?" Millie, known to every Briton or American who had ever stayed at the Luxe, introduced me. It was good to have these new people so friendly. Again, my knowledge of German was useful for the place was flooded with refugees.

In the mornings as I walked to work the sights which had astonished me became all too familiar, undernourished men and women, drunk lying in the gutter. Queues waited patiently in front of food stores. Dreary shop windows, bare of goods, showed red-draped busts of Lenin and Stalin.

At the same time tall new buildings were growing up beside small wooden houses, Red Army men sang as they marched through the street as did groups of office worker volunteers giving their free time to help build the Metro.

We moved mainly among the English and Americans, were mostly with Bill and Tamara Rust and Reg Bishop, the Daily Worker correspondent. Willie Weinstone was there from the States and him I now saw as an old man, not the 'hero of' my teens. Often, I caught a glimpse of the venerated Japanese Santayana.

The evening meal was served in the Luxe Restaurant but we could collect our dinners in containers and eat in our room. On the first occasion, as I closely examined Pat's dish and mine,

I exclaimed angrily, "Hey, how come you have chicken and I have a meatball?" Pat laughed as I carefully divided both meals equally. I was to learn there were three categories of dinners for which we got meal tickets. His was class I, as he was a political worker but as a mere typist I was class III. It shocked me, it wasn't fair, but protest got me nowhere. The food was filling but monotonous. We grumbled, not knowing of the famine in the parts of the Ukraine where people had died of starvation. As a political worker Pat also got a 'pyok' or special food parcel. Butter, eggs, perhaps a chicken or a frozen sudak fish. I'd invite to a feast my typist friends who were not so privileged.

Our ration of sour black bread I exchanged for milk brought by peasant women who waited outside the hotel entrance. In early summer, across Pushkin Square behind the local church there was a little market where sometimes I could buy fresh fruit, vegetables and small wild strawberries. One morning I wandered into the church, attracted by the splendid singing. Small groups, mostly kerchiefed women, stood inside the vast interior. When the singing stopped I quietly retreated.

A bath was a luxury but showers were available every morning, alternate half-hours for men and women. The men too often overstayed their time, laughed as we shouted our protest. One morning we stripped and walked in, pregnant women in front. Red faced men scuttled out.

There were many evening parties with plenty of wine and vodka though the food was most often canned fish sandwiches. These gatherings were held for 'guests of honour', for those whose stay at the Luxe it was a breathing space between bouts of difficult, often illegal, work.

So we lived in Moscow but were not of it, knowing only the Russians and other foreign nationals in the Comintern, travelling from hotel to jobs or shops. Shut off from the life of the city most of us knew little of the outside world, ignorant of much that was happening in this enormous country.

After I'd missed several periods, I had to accept I was pregnant. Dismay and apprehension were uppermost. There were few babies in the Luxe. Here, though loved, a child was still a burden, a liability. Many of those in the Luxe would return to fascist, semi-fascist and colonial countries to carry on under illegal conditions. True we Americans, British and French were not in this position but nevertheless considered ourselves a part of this international band of revolutionaries.

An abortion was possible, they were legal in Russia. But I'd already had one in my first year of marriage when I was eighteen. A talk with Pat, perhaps together we might arrive at a solution His reaction was like a blow in the face. "That's the second time. How the hell could you let it happen?" I stared at him in amazement. Surely this man wasn't as stupid as he sounded. My anger was so great I could scarcely speak. In a trembling voice I emphasised every word. "Pat-you-are-a-son-of-a-bitch."

I stopped, fought for control, continued, "You've a drawer full of French letters. Why don't you use them? The responsibility is yours not mine. You're not much of a husband, God knows, but I never thought you could be such a coward."

I turned to the door, snatched up my coat, ignored his cry of "wait a minute." It was late May but there was still a chill in the air as I walked, half-blinded by tears, towards Red Square. The river for which I'd headed lay in darkness. Reluctantly, I turned back into the lamplit street, walked past the Luxe. In Pushkin Square, huddled in my coat, I sat for a long time on a bench where during the day grannies and nannies gossiped as toddlers played on the grass verge.

Anger spent, I returned to our room. Pat didn't apologise but talked quietly about difficulties and possibilities. I barely listened. "I want a ticket to Nizhni Tagil. It's time I saw my mother and father." He stopped in mid-sentence, nodded, relief in his voice as he continued, "If you decide on an abortion you can have it there where your mother will look after you." But he didn't try to insist.

Three days travel and I was again with my parents. More than a year had passed since we'd gone our separate ways. Hugs, kisses, tears, it was good to be together again. I'd brought provisions from the special store for foreigners in Moscow. Food was scarce. But completely absorbed by my problem, I paid little attention to the primitive conditions in which my parents lived.

When we were alone I told my mother. Her eyes on me, she remained silent for a long time. At last I asked, "What shall I do, mama?" She shook her head. "That's not for me to say". Then after a pause, "What's happened to you? Where is the courage and boldness you once had/"

This seemed harsh to me. I was near tears, looked away, but mama did not immediately soften. Later I heard from her how disturbed she'd been. She'd expected more from me and now I was just a typist, the wife of an 'important man'.

She relented, her voice gentle, "Children can be great happiness but they need love and care. Don't have the child unless you are prepared to look after it." I knew then that she must have heard of the Comintern School for children for foreign communists who could not take them back to their own countries. But this was not so in my case though it had happened with some Americans. We did not speak of it again but Mama understood from her own experiences that the decision must be mine. When it was time to leave I told her I'd have the child. She smiled, "You know Frieda you weren't planned either, but I've always been glad I had you."

Back in Moscow I continued at work. The girls in the typists' pool gave me constant advice though none of them had yet had a child. It was taken for granted I'd return to work after the baby's birth and as my maternity leave neared the Hotel manager introduced me to Zhenja, a sturdy woman in her late twenties, prepared to act as a kind of nanny.

I looked at her carefully, a village woman with fair hair coiled in plaits about her head, small blue eyes, a snub nose and a generous mouth in which metal teeth gleamed. We got on well and she understood my fractured Russian.

On 3 December 1933, when Labour pains began, Zhenja was with me. Swiftly I was taken by car to the hospital. A young nurse helped me undress, put on a gown, then led me into an enormous room tiled in white, a hot place of glaring lights and moaning women.

"Oh my God." I stepped back. She put her arm around my shoulder, held tight, expertly heaved me on to a trolley, smiled and left. There were no screens. Around me under the low harsh lamps lay women on trolleys similar to mine.

No nurse was visible and I seemed a long time alone. A sharp pain gripped me and I shouted loudly. The young nurse appeared, took one glance and called 'bistro', (quickly, quickly). In seconds I was surrounded by people speaking urgently. A cloth was put over my face and I lost consciousness.

When my eyes opened I was on a bed in a small ward. I stretched my hands over my body, felt the flatness of my stomach. It was then I realised my breasts were tightly bound. As I tried to sit up a nurse hurried over.

"Rebjonok", I said in Russian, "Where's my baby. I want to see it." She looked troubled, hurried away, returned with an older woman. Again I asked, "Where's my baby?" The tired face of the head nurse bent over me, as she stroked my hair. I understood some of her words to the younger woman. "Poor thing, here she is alone in a strange land. How am I to tell her the baby is dead?"

At that last word I grasped her arm. "Umer, rebjonok umer?" She nodded, continuing to stroke my hair. "I want to see it," I cried. "Videt, videt."

She looked doubtful, shook her head but a short while later returned with the perfect body of a tiny boy, lean, red-haired and quite still. I looked long then turned my face into the pillow.

Back in the Luxe, I was told to rest. Days seemed endless. I sat alone, miserable. I now know I had post-natal depression but then I'd never heard of it. Nor it seemed had others. I moped, remained tearful and Pat became impatient, as did some of the women.

"It's hard of course but we're living in a world where our comrades in Germany and Italy are giving their lives in the anti-fascist struggle. This is no time for indulging in personal grief. Shake it off, put it behind you." Elsie, an American woman, was always free with advice.

But I realised that before this had happened to me, I might have said something like this to someone in a similar position to mine. What was wrong with me then, that tears flowed if I saw a baby in the street and at night I cried quietly into my pillow so Pat would not hear. I began to shun people and spent long periods in our room.

As Christmas approached there were parties nearly every night. Pat persuaded me to go to an evening in Bill Rust's room. It was a mixed affair with Americans, Germans and Austrians as well as English. I sat apart, watched the dancing and drinking.

A tall grey haired Austrian with a thin, worn face sat down beside me, smiled. "You looked so lonely." And suddenly to this stranger I poured out the whole story and my own feelings of inadequacy and guilt. I repeated to him what some of the women had said and how I could not respond.

This man listened, the only one who didn't say 'snap out of it'. His voice was gentle as he tried to reassure me. "It happens to many women after childbirth even when they have not lost the child. There is no need to feel guilty. Too many of our people harden themselves, stifle their emotions. This does not make them better Bolsheviks although they might think so. We must have compassion, feel for others and their sufferings or why are we communists."

He smiled at me then. "Sind wir doch nicht auch Menschen, (Are we not also human beings)? You must not worry. It is right you should grieve. Heresy to some perhaps. To me this commonsense humanity was a great comfort. I felt a sense of relief and release.

"Tell me more about yourself." So I spoke long and eagerly about my socialist childhood, my communist youth, told him of free speech fights, strikes, jails and demonstrations. "I can see you are not just Pat's wife but an able and committed young woman. Perhaps a change would help, there is other work you can do." With this enigmatic statement our conversation ended.

Some weeks later I was asked to see a Comintern official. Briefly I was told there was need for trustworthy people with respectable passports who could travel to fascist and semi-fascist countries. Contact must be kept with communists working underground. Was I prepared to do such work, very dangerous especially in Nazi Germany. Who at my age would not have jumped at such an offer to serve the 'cause'. I accepted immediately.

It was during this time in February 1934 that Georgi Dimitrov, hero of the Reichstag Trial, arrived in Moscow by plane. Only a week earlier in the German Nazi court he had defiantly taunted Goering as he asked him, "Are you by any chance afraid of my questions, Herr Minister President?"

Now he was here among us in the Luxe, a tall man with dark shining eyes in a strong face and a mane of greying hair above an imposing forehead. We were thrilled, sought to catch a glimpse of him as he came and went.

Jimmie Shields, then Editor of the Daily Worker, was in Moscow for a conference. He asked me to accompany him to the Bolshoi as he had a spare ticket. These were kept for important foreign visiting communists and on this night we sat grandly in the Tsar's box. The door opened and as I looked back Dimitrov, his mother, Popov and Tanev, the two Bulgarians who had been on trial with him, entered. My excitement was great as Jimmie introduced himself and me. All that evening I looked more at Dimitrov than at this performance of 'Othello'.

During the interval when refreshments were served in the room behind the Tsars bock, we were able to congratulate Dimitrov as he smiled and nodded. It was the most memorable moment in my young life and I was the envy of my friends in the Luxe.

At last word came from the Comintern. Kurt explained that though not on the political side, a courier was very important. Without such liaison comrades who worked illegally could not carry on. "You will take them money and often documents. They will send back information. One thing you must never forget. You will be on your own. We cannot acknowledge or in any way help if, for whatever reason, you are picked up by the police. So take care." Kurt spoke gravely and we shook hands.

Masha, a fair, middle-aged woman came into the room, led me to the section which was unusually referred to as 'upstairs'. There all detailed arrangements were made. "You are going to Paris." "But why? That's not a fascist country." She laughed. "Paris is the first step to many places."

My exit visa was on a separate piece of paper, not stamped in my passport. The railway ticket was by way of Poland and

Germany. Money for the journey, expenses in Paris, name of the hotel to which I was to go. Most important, the place of contact, the question I had to ask, the reply I was to receive. All this was explained and I memorised the words.

Lastly, I received a suitcase. "Use this for your clothing. In Paris they will arrange to collect it." Masha turned to a man standing nearby. "This is Volodya." We smiled, shook hands. "I will take you to the Luxe now and call for you tomorrow morning. Be ready by 9.30, the train leaves soon after ten."

Briskly I shook hands with Masha. "Au revoir. And be careful." I nodded. Brimming over with excitement I locked my door and packed the case. Pat was away so there was no need for leave taking. Volodya was prompt. I gave him a happy smile as I set out on a whole new way of life.

Chapter 19

Comintern Courier – Paris – Berlin – Vienna – Shanghai

Paris

The Express sped across the Russian countryside to Negoreloye, The Soviet Frontier post. A quick passport and customs clearance then over the border to the same process in Poland.

All went well and the train hurtled on to Warsaw. A woman entered the first-class carriage, stood by the open window in the corridor. A Polish Officer held, then kissed her outstretched hand. As the train began to move he clicked his heels, bowed. She entered my compartment, smiled, murmured a few words. I shrugged apologetically, smiled and continued reading.

Surreptitiously I studied this elegant person. That's how I must dress. Still in my American clothes, slightly shabby now, I felt like the provincial Pittsburgh girl I was who by sheer chance had left her own environment for the cosmopolitan cities of New York, then London and was now travelling to Paris. There and then I decided on a fashionable silk dress, a smart coat and hat with matching leather shoes and gloves. I'd buy them with my enormous (to me) daily allowance. As this woman did, I'd carry a glossy magazine and a small box of expensive Swiss chocolates. Amusing now, but I soon discovered that clothes mattered in my job. Being well dressed not only gave confidence but also impressed customs and passport people as I crossed so many borders.

Paris at last. A porter, a taxi, I managed it all, pleased with myself as I looked out of the window at this fabulous city. But it seemed a long ride as we sped far from the city centre. The cab stopped before a large house in a quiet tree-lined street. Only a small sign board showed it was a hotel.

I registered as from London then walked up a broad staircase to a balcony with many doors one of which led to my room. Loud voices from below brought me to my door. They were speaking in Russian. These people must be White Russians, implacable enemies of the Soviet Union. Why had I been sent here? Was it a trap?

Door locked, angry and anxious, I decided not to unpack but quickly make contact. I rang, asked for a taxi. It arrived promptly. "Will madam be back for dinner?" I shook my head, walked to the door. No one stopped me.

At the Place de la Opera I left the cab, took the Metro to the address I'd been given, a small shoe shop empty except for a smart middle-aged woman who looked at me inquiringly. In English I said, "I have come for my uncle's shoes." "What colour are they?" It was the right answer, also in English. She waved me into a back room. "I will inform them." A rapid phone call in French then she turned to me.

"Tonight at seven you will sit outside the Café de la Paix on the corner of the Place de la Opera. On the table you will place this Tauchnitz book by Mrs Gaskell. A short thin man with glasses and moustache will sit beside you and say, 'Mrs Gaskell is a very good writer.'"

I felt bewildered. This was Paris, not fascist Berlin. The woman saw my look but continued, "You must answer 'I've read all her books," Have you? " She asked with a half-smile. "I've never heard of her or Tauchnitz." My tone must have conveyed my irritation.

Coldly she replied, "I have my instructions and I am giving you yours. It must go just as I have said." Several times she asked me to repeat the words, memorise them. "It is important always to be correct. You will remember?" I nodded as she gave me the book. "Yes, though I don't understand why it's necessary." She shrugged and I left.

It went as arranged. When he was satisfied Andre paid the waiter and we walked to a less crowded café. There I poured out my misgivings about the White Russians and the hotel. He was angry. "I shall have to report this. It is not good that our people are sent to such places. I forward lists of hotels but still this sometimes happens.

"Not sabotage?" Andre smiled. "No, a relative or former friend recommends it. But it must stop. Go back immediately, ask the taxi driver to wait. Pay whatever they ask then go to this address on the Boulevard St Michel. I'll be there." He hailed a cab.

The hotelier was displeased when I told him I'd met a friend, was moving in with her. Andre was waiting. He carried my case around a few corners and stopped just short of a small hotel. "A girl, Lois, will come to you at nine in the morning. You will accompany her when she takes the case." "How will I know she's the right girl?" I was getting used to this way of going on. "She'll say your name and ask 'Have you read Mrs Gaskell?'" Was he making fun of me? But his smile was kindly and anyway I was too tired to care.

In my locked room I washed and tumbled into bed. Sleep didn't come as I pondered the day's events. Paris was free, wide open, why was it necessary to say words exactly, go from café to café?

Sometime later when I put this to Andre he treated it seriously. "You are very innocent. Our secret service too is interested. We French also have colonies with illegal Parties. Many Europeans from fascist countries have a base here in Paris." "The Germans?" He smiled. "You ask too many questions."

I correctly took this to mean there were German communists in Paris. I was to discover that half the Political Bureau of the German Party was there at this time. Andre continued, "It is important for you to realise that when you are in Berlin or Vienna the people you meet will be risking their lives. They have to be sure about you and such details are very necessary." It was a lesson learned and followed.

My hotel on the Left Bank was well chosen. Young people, students, some foreign, had rooms here. No meals were provided. There was a constant coming and going.

The young woman arrived promptly next morning. "You are Frieda." As I closed the door I asked, "And what else?". Straight-faced she answered, "Have you read Mrs Gaskell" and we both burst out laughing. Evidently the joke had travelled but I didn't mind.

I was to meet Lois many times in the coming months. She took the case, walked with me to the nearby Boulevard St Michel, pointed out a place where I'd get breakfast. "Be in your room at twelve. We'll have lunch together and I'll show you around." Lois hailed a taxi and was gone.

The next day I again met Andre. "You may be here for some time. Things don't always go smoothly. Do you mind being alone? "No, I'm used to it." "Good, it is Spring, Paris is beautiful, enjoy it." I was now left to my own devices except for a weekly meal with Lois or Andre.

For some days I did not venture far. Nearby was the Seine and the Quay close to St Michel had bookstall after bookstall. I'd struck gold for my main concern, where to find books in English, was solved. As I browsed I discovered that Tauchnitz was a continental publisher of English books. My question was answered and in quiet squares and small gardens I spent many hours with Mrs Gaskell.

Soon I discovered the Metro was easy to use, the fare always the same. I made my way to the Pere Lachaise Cemetery and found the Wall of the Communards. Here they'd made their last stand and against this wall one hundred and forty-seven had been shot. During my childhood I'd heard of these Paris revolutionaries of 1871 and even remembered a bit of verse I'd recited –

> Wall of the Communards crying to me
> Thirty thousand massacred in the streets of Paris
> And the blood flowed in the gutters
> And the blood flowed in the Seine.

My mind a jumble of images I walked slowly back to the entrance, past the famous interred here, La Fountaine, Moliere, Hugo, Balzac, Proust and so many others.

Often, I went to the Place de la Opera, sat outside a café, watched the passers by. Sometimes the call of my native land was strong as I abandoned the little French restaurants I'd found and ate hot dogs and apple pie in the nearby American lunch bar.

Then the unexpected happened. A voice called, "Frieda, my God, it is you."

It was Al, the tall rich young man of my brief university days. Slicked down hair, horn-rimmed glasses, expensive suit but still the gangling, eager lad who'd sought me out because of my views.

He was on the American 'Grand Tour'. Was I also alone? Could we team up? He had three more days in Paris. "Sorry Al. I'm married and live in London now." "Gee, wish I'd known. I've just come from there. How about tonight, though. I'll book a table at Maxims."

"My husband might not like that and we're leaving in the morning. But let's have coffee." He was lonely, talked on about where he'd been and what he'd done. After an hour I rose. "I'll have to go now. It's been nice meeting you again."

Al started to protest but I waved and walked away. For the next three days I stayed reading in my room, went out only for hurried meals. "A treat today, we'll go on the river boat," said Andre at our next weekly meeting. "I'd like that. I went alone once." "You do get around. Have you been to Versailles?" "It's obligatory for Americans, isn't it, even when they don't speak French. Our guide's English was reasonable."

Over a leisurely lunch he said, "One of your British people, a Scots woman, was here a few days ago. She was very uneasy, out of her depth. It was decided she should return immediately, empty handed, for the journey was through Berlin. As I had to stay with her till train time, I brought her here to the river."

"Are you telling me that not everyone can do this work? That Paris is a kind of training ground?" He nodded. "Only for full-time couriers. Not if it's a one-off trip. They often use Lenin school students for that." "It's not how it was put to me in Moscow." "No, yet they were right about you. The final decision is ours." My feelings were mixed, irritation that I'd not known this but a glow of satisfaction that I'd passed the test.

Then as even Paris began to Pall I was told I'd be leaving the next day. Lois brought two cases. "Fill them somehow, take all your books, coffee beans, chocolate. Buy more clothes, take back gifts." I laughed. "All right, all right, I'll manage, don't worry."

Andre gave me instructions. "Train to Amsterdam then by plane to Moscow." "Fly?" I gasped. "I'm scared." He grinned. "You'll enjoy it. Anyway, you've no option. It's urgent and what you're taking can't go through Germany."

It was as he said. More quickly than I expected I was airborne. Volodya met me at the airport and we drove straight to the Comintern building. My first assignment was over.

Berlin

During the next months I carried messages and money to the communist underground in Europe. Puzzled when my destination was Czechoslovakia, not a fascist country, I remembered Andre's reference to illegal communist bases and this was true of Prague where there was a Sector Leadership of the German Party at that time. I never learned why I went to Amsterdam, Zurich, Basle.

It was exciting to visit so many new places, successfully carry through my mission. Even the times when things went wrong yet were overcome left me with a feeling of exhilaration. But there were also tedious dull days when I sat for hours in railway stations or alone at evening meals. Sometimes the contact was brief, the face scarcely remembered.

My first visit to Berlin was in the spring of 1934. As the cab drove through the city I was not prepared for the Nazi flags, large pictures of Hitler, swastika arm bands on many brown shirts. Walls were smeared with antisemitic graffiti, obscene cartoons on posters directed against communists and Jews. I was frightened, apprehensive.

After lunch in my Friedrich Strasse hotel I walked towards Unter den Linden. The sound of martial music grew louder as I joined the crowd on the pavement. Row upon row of jackbooted fascists marched by, cries of 'Heil Hitler' produced the automatic response of outstretched arms. With tightly clenched hands I stood very straight to stop my rising panic. Filthy strutting swine, so young and so menacing.

When the last section had passed I hurried back to my hotel, locked the room door and leaned against it. My fear subsided and

I took myself to task. I must not react in this way or I'd be no good in my job. Yet I understood more clearly why the little old woman in the cobbler's shop had been so uneasy this morning.

The amiable shopkeeper's expression had changed to one of nervous alarm as she realised the reason for my visit. Her voice had dropped almost to a whisper, 'Bitte, warten sie', please wait. She led me into a small black room. Behind the counter she watched the entrance as she made a phone call.

In the doorway of the little room, her eyes still on the shop, the old woman said quickly, "Alexander Café, Kurfurstendam, eight o'clock." "Wer kommt – who will come?" I asked. "Ach ja, diese Zeitschrift," she handed me a magazine. "Hans kommt. Hans, blond, young, you will know. Now please go." So anxious to get rid of me that her instructions were far from explicit.

That evening I found my way to the café, ordered a drink, the magazine prominently displayed. Presently a young man came over. "Erlauben sie – may I?" He was blond, stocky, but then so were a lot of Germans. I took a chance. "You are Hans?" Startled, he sat down quickly. In a scarcely audible voice he answered, "But I was supposed to say, do you like this magazine." "She didn't tell me that, she was terrified."

He shook his head. "We mustn't use that shop again. Fine people but the woman is getting old. It's difficult to find first contact places."

I nodded, thinking of the march that afternoon. "Yet there were so many of you. Nearly half a million in the Party, close to five million communist votes, that's what they say over there." "That was eighteen months ago. It's hard to explain this to those who knew only the past." Then with a smile, "That's not your problem. While you're here behave like an ordinary tourist. We will show you Berlin."

Though Hitler's thugs were terrorising and hunting down Jews and communists, the powerful efficient Nazi machine of 1937, portrayed in the film 'Julia' based on Lilian Helman's book, had not yet been perfected, nor had most anti-fascists been eliminated. Hans still felt confident enough to go about with me.

After we'd made arrangements for the next day when I was to hand over the case I had brought he said, "Tomorrow evening we will go to the Tiergarten. I want you to know Erich. He will be your contact when I am not here. Walk slowly along this street, look into the shops and we will, so to speak, pick you up."

We smiled at each other, I liked him. The Tiergarten was an enormous pleasure park. On this warm spring evening throngs of people strolled about, sat outside cafes, listened to open air concerts. Hans introduced me to Erich who was his physical opposite, tall, thin with dark brown hair and eyes.

At an outdoor restaurant a gypsy violinist came to play at our table. We ate pork sausages, drank beer, whirled round in the waltz and polka. It was a wonderful evening as we put aside all our cares, joked and laughed. For we were young and full of hope. The black shadows were there but the enormity of the violence and destruction Hitler would bring, not only to Germany but to humanity, was still ahead.

Speaking quietly I asked if they could explain an incident that afternoon as I was walking along a shopping street off the Kurfurstendam. Suddenly leaflets cascaded down and though I didn't pick one up I saw the words – gegen Hitler, against Hitler. There had been a flurry of excitement, a blowing of whistles, as police rushed into the building. They emerged empty handed.

Erich and Hans chuckled. "So it worked again. We'll tell you what happens. A plank is balanced on a roof. On one end, near the roof's edge, a weighted down bundle of leaflets is placed, on the other end a pail of water. The pail has a small hole in it. As the water drips away the plank slowly falls, the weight is released and leaflets fly into the street. When the police come there is no-one to arrest."

We lifted our glasses and drank ' to our brave comrades'. Though I travelled to other cities during that spring and summer I was most often in Berlin, warmly welcomed by Hans or Erich, sometimes both.

In late August I was again on my way there but not by the straight forward Nord Express from Moscow through Warsaw. Instead a very involved route had been mapped out for me. From Leningrad I went to Helsinki by rail, then by boat to Stockholm. After an overnight stay a long train journey took me across Sweden to Malmo where I boarded a ferry to a port on the Pomeranian Bay. From there I travelled to Berlin. By now I had thoroughly entered into the role of sophisticated traveller (or so

I thought). I swept out of the station clutching my Baedeker and a few magazines followed by a porter who quickly found me a taxi. My knowledge of German was certainly a help.

There was always a first port of call, just to say I'd arrived. This person informed my contact, gave me details of the meeting place. On this occasion I felt apprehension on the part of the shopkeeper and just as on my first visit was quickly bundled off the premises.

In a small park we'd used once before I sat on a bench, an open book on my lap. Erich did not come over but glanced at me and walked on. I rose slowly, made a business of putting away my book, brushed down my dress, then strolled in the same direction. Around the corner in a more wooded area he dropped into step beside me.

"Have you brought it with you?" I nodded. A large sum of money covered the false bottom holding documents in the vanity case I carried. "Thank God. Then we needn't meet again." He slipped it into a bulky briefcase. "What's happened?" I asked. "They've got Hans." I stopped, turned towards him. "Keep walking." He took my arm. "Yes, my good friend Hans." All his sadness and grief were in those words.

His voice became brisk. "Things have become worse. They're cracking down harder. Paris for you tomorrow, too risky now for you to take anything. Tell them about Hans." Gentle again he said softly, "I do not think you will return to Berlin. All who worked with him must be replaced. So, this is goodbye, Frieda."

This young man with whom I had laughed and twirled in the Tiergarten had changed, his face grave and set. Squeezing my hand tightly he leaned over, kissed my cheek and was gone.

Desolate, alone now in this hostile city, I walked on. Hans, jolly friendly Hans, so young and lively. Once the Nazi's got hold of a communist he'd be better dead. Again, as on my first arrival I felt a violent hatred for this place with loud mouthed fascists lording it everywhere. At the station I booked my ticket then returned to the hotel.

In the privacy of my locked room I lay on my bed and wept for Hans, for Erich, for the little old shopkeeper. And for all these poor bloody communists who only a few short years ago had been stronger than the Nazis in numbers and votes. How had it happened? What had gone wrong?

Early next morning I left for Paris where I met Lois, told her what I knew.

She nodded, "It's getting more difficult for them. The papers write about a Plebiscite on 19th August. There were spoilt ballots, votes of 'no' but Hitler won and now claims a kind of popular consent for the concentration of power in his hands."

Lois was as political as I, a child too of a communist family. She was probably the best friend I made during my time as a Comintern courier.

From Paris I travelled to Basle then on to Moscow. Kurt said, "Take time off, relax, we'll be in touch." "Any news of Hans?" He shrugged. "No. Great pity. I knew him well. He was a fine lad."

Past tense. Of course there'd be no news. His work is so dangerous. Hope Erich's gone to ground. Hard for them. Easier for me, I come and go. Hans. I'd never know what happened. Maybe better not to. Slowly I walked back to the Luxe. From these vivid, dangerous days of tragedy and despair I was plunged again into the petty gossip and intrigue of life in the hotel.

Pat was away. In the quiet of our room I sorted and washed some of my clothes. Then to the Valuta shop where I spent dollars on thin sliced ham, butter, cheese, white bread, the kind of provisions not on sale in other stores. Some I put aside for Millie. She'd soon visit.

Millie eagerly poured out the latest happenings in the Luxe. "Jack's left Anna and taken up with a Russian woman who's moved into their room." "Where's Anna then?" "Got a small room of her own. She's very bitter. Talks about forming a union for wives." I laughed, "What a strange idea." "Maybe you'll want to join." "Why?" "Elsie's more in your room than hers when you're away. Says Pat needs looking after. She stays the night, sneaks out early in the morning. I've seen her."

Millie waited for my reaction. I said nothing. Disappointed she went on, "Sam told me Pat had an affair with her in

New York before he was sent to Pittsburgh. Of course, he didn't know you then. Elsie was upset when he married you."

Sam, a New Yorker working with the Young Communist International in Moscow, made it his business to know most things about people. I had no reason to doubt him.

After Millie left I propped up my pillows, leaned back and considered what I'd heard. I wasn't surprised, had seen it coming. As on previous occasions when Pat and I were apart for a time I didn't miss him, often looked forward to my next trip. Again, I realised that what kept us together was familiarity, the Party but primarily the bond of a legal marriage.

Elsie'd like a divorce followed by marriage to Pat. But I thought this unlikely though there would be no objection from me. She'd had other men before him and his narrow bigoted upbringing, of which I'd had a glimpse in Scotland, ruled that out. I smiled, remembering how important it had been to him that I was still a virgin when we married. Yet he'd be wise to take on Elsie for from her he received the adoration he seemed to need and which I had long since lost.

Strange this life. My courier work was now the most important thing. Maybe someday I'd return to the States. I shrugged, put it behind me, thought again of Berlin. Why had the Nazis been able to succeed in the one country which, as the Comintern Germans so often boasted, had the most powerful Party in Europe? With a gift of coffee beans and chocolate, like gold in Moscow, I sought out Lenchen, a well built, attractive German woman living alone in the Luxe.

As we greeted each other I became aware yet again of how short bobbed hair suited her wide face and generous mouth. Pleased with my gift she insisted on making a cup of 'real' coffee while we gossiped about mutual friends.

As she sat down I asked, "Tell me, Lenchen, with the German Party so large and powerful, how was it possible for Hitler to take over?" She looked at me in surprise. "You must understand that the struggle of the working class was betrayed by the Social-Democrats. They are the mainstay of the bourgeoisie." I'd heard that before but what did it mean?

"You were so strong ...." Lenchen interrupted. "Not all German workers are revolutionaries. Some are finished with the social-democrats but not yet ready to vote for us so they voted for Hitler." "What good was that?" I felt indignant after what I'd seen. Quickly she came back at me. "They are no longer voting for the social-democrats, the main enemy. Hitler will fail, he will not keep his promises then they'll come to us."

I could not understand this reasoning. Hitler was getting stronger and it was this I wanted to talk about. So I persisted, "Surely Hitler is the main enemy. You must be aware of how his thugs are intimidating people. You could appeal to the left-wing social-democrats, the workers not the leaders …….." Sharply she again cut me off. "Never to the social-fascists. Comrade, you are off the line."

This phrase 'the line' was common jargon for whatever policy the Communist International propounded at a given time. I was myself a loyal adherent to official Party positions. Yet I felt puzzled by this strange interpretation of events in Germany. I found it hard to accept that Hitler would fail, so overwhelming was his presence. I'd felt physically sick on my first arrival in Berlin. But I'd got used to it. Maybe that's what happens to people.

So I mused at that time but reassured myself. Surely those in charge 'must know best', those words, that sentiment which had lulled us to acquiescence many times when we were troubled by what was happening in our ranks and in our name.

Now, as I write these memoirs, I can 'revert critically to a self I no longer am', look back at that acceptance which stifled thought, defended the indefensible. We, the foot soldiers, did not discuss meaning but how policy decided by the Comintern could be applied. And I can understand this must also have been for Hans and Erich.

As the German Party followed its suicidal path of hostility to the social-democrats, they justified it on the grounds that a revolutionary situation was developing. They believed once people's minds were free of 'social-democratic' illusions they would swing behind the communists and defeat the Nazis. And to achieve this the paramount task was to win the majority of the working class to accept the communist position. Despite the growth of the Nazi vote and rising intimidation the communists doggedly persisted, over-estimated their own strength. The desire for a 'German 1917 appeared to be the important factor in this reasoning.On 30th January 1933 the formation of Hitler's Government seemed to have taken the communists by surprise. The response to what they feared would be their immediate banning was to call for a General Strike, issued in leaflet form, to all workers, Trades Unions and Social-Democrats. But the Communist Party was not immediately banned and continued to hold meetings, publish its paper, campaign in the general election called by Hitler for 5th March.

However, on 4th February Hitler moved. Communist meetings and press were banned and police interference rapidly increased. In spite of this the left-wing parties continued activity. But on 27th February the Reichstag Fire changed everything. Though it has been widely recognised throughout the world as an act of provocation by the Nazis, at the time it was enough to create wide-spread anti-communist hysteria. Nevertheless six days after the fire, on 5th March, the communists polled nearly five million votes.

This could well have been a turning point. Hitler's rise might have been checked by an alliance of the German Communist Party and the left-wing Social Democrats. It didn't happen and it seems reasonable to say that a great opportunity was thrown away.

Any compromise with 'social-democratic reformism' was considered wrong. The Communist Party wished to keep its organisation going, ready for what they believed would be the seizure of power in the coming offensive against the unstable Nazi regime.

This position of the Germans was reaffirmed by the Communist International Executive in two 'Statements on the German Situation' on 5th March and 1st April, 1933, the gist of which was that a Soviet Germany was still within reach and to say the Party had suffered a defeat was cowardly and defeatist.

As late as December 1933, after nearly a year of Hitler, the 13th Plenum of the Comintern Executive again endorsed this leftist line and it was still the German Party's view in the late summer of 1934 when I was there.

One might feel justified in saying that this communist concept of the social-democrats as 'social-fascists' assisted rather than obstructed the Nazi takeover of Germany.

Future events were to show how wrong the communists had been as the Nazis strengthened their position and the mass basis for open rebellion disappeared. Not till the Seventh World Congress of the Communist International, led by Dimitrov, a year after my talk with Lenchen, did the united front against fascism become the very centre of Comintern concern.

But for Germany it was too late.

During the war not even a coherent resistance or partisan movement, as those terms were used for France, Greece, Yugoslavia, Italy and Russia, could be established in Germany. For too many, like Hans, had died bravely far too early in the struggle against fascism which, with a different policy, they might have defeated in their own country.

Vienna

In Vienna I always looked forward to meeting Karl, my contact. Young, tall with grey-blue eyes, dark hair. From the beginning I had found him 'sympathisch'. He was a good companion, relaxed, considerate, with a ready wit. This time Karl said he'd show me Schonbrunn in its autumn colours. We walked through the gardens, sat on a bench then unthinkingly I shattered this peace.

"Karl, you've never told me about the February rising and why it failed." "Are you really interested?" I nodded. "There was a great deal of talk in the Luxe which I found hard to understand. I was only a year out of America before we went to Moscow, haven't yet fully grasped what's happening in Europe. Why didn't the German Party openly resist the rise of Hitler?" "So, you are not just a charming little courier but also a political person." The bantering tone was gone. Indignantly I replied, "And went to jail for it too. Why do you think I'm here?"

"You'd be surprised at some of the people they send. It's a great relief when they leave, they're dangerous." "They must have been 'once only' people. I'm trained and that's different." He smiled. "You always have been different but more so now." I lowered my eyes. So he did like me.

Karl went very quiet then spoke slowly. "February 1934 was lost a year earlier in March 1933." "That's a funny thing to say. Explain." He looked at me, less grim now. "In March of last year we were all geared up, the Schutzbund, the trade unions, the local Socialist Party branches, ready to go. We could have stopped Dollfuss and his Heimwher as well as the pro-Germans in Austria."

I knew about the Schutzbund, a socialist organisation with club houses everywhere, rifles stored for shooting practice and hunting. But the Heimwher? I asked Kar. "They're native fascists, Dollfuss supporters, mostly from the Alpine regions, and much smaller in size than our Schutzbund was. He paused. "It's complicated, Frieda, for there were also the Austrian pro-Germans, Hitler men. After Hitler took power they became threatening. But Dollfuss had no wish to become a German satellite. He took action against them." "So that's why they assassinated him in July. I was here in Vienna at the time." He nodded. "They denied it but it's true."

Karl seemed reluctant to go on. We sat quietly as I tried to get straight, this tangled web he had described. A woman and child went by, greetings were exchanged. His arm slipped around my shoulder, he pulled me closer, looked down at me. I raised my face. His kiss was long, sought my response and I gave it. "Frieda, Frieda, look what you've done to me. I wish we could be quite alone somewhere, in a small room." I looked up at him, knew I wished that too.

He heaved a sigh, leaned back. "But what would the comrades say? We're already breaking the rules." At this we laughed, for strict instructions prohibited emotional involvement between courier and contact. "All right, let's change the subject. Why didn't you go ahead last March when everyone was ready?"

His arm remained around me as we rose and walked on. "Because our Social-Democratic leadership was deceived by the actions of Dollfuss against the Nazi supporters. They saw him as a possible ally against the Pan-Germans. The ordinary membership knew differently but the 'top people' didn't listen."

"No, I read how Dollfuss closed Parliament and turned against you, ransacked offices, making arrests." "And that's when he could have been stopped." Karl's voice was emphatic. "We were ready, waiting for the call that never came. Our leaders still wanted a peaceful solution, afraid of a 'civil war' as they called it."

His arm came away when we sat down again on a nearby bench. "The momentum for action evaporated. People were angry with their leadership, tore up membership cards, handed back rifles, bitter and disillusioned." "And you got weaker as the fascists grew stronger."

"That sums it up. In February 1934 arrests began again and those who had loyally remained in the Social-Democratic Party asked their leaders to call for resistance. But they seemed incapable of doing so, some even fled the country. There was chaos. Sporadic, uneven uprisings took place. Without the base which had existed a year previously, this resistance was doomed." He sat still, didn't look at me. At last I said, "I'm sorry, this has been painful for you." "Forgive me. It was more than six months ago but seems like yesterday."

He told me then how on the command of Dollfuss bombs and mortars shook the working class districts, especially Karl Marx Hof, pride of Red Vienna, stronghold of the Schutzbund.

"I was part of it, I lived there. We had rifles, held out for three days. Then white flags flew from our windows as we escaped through the sewers. We were the lucky ones."

A pause. "There were executions. An old comrade, Karl Munichreiter, though severely wounded, was hanged. Can you read this?" He pulled a clipping from his inside pocket. The Neues Wiener Journal described how this man, when hanged, took seven minutes to die but managed to shout 'lone live socialism, freedom'. Sadness as Karl spoke again. "I'll never forget him, he was my friend."

"I'm sorry my questions have raked all this up. You communists were very brave." "We were not communists but Schutzbund men. The communists gave out leaflets, called for a general strike." I stared at him. "But you were a communist?"

He shook his head. "I'm a very recent recruit. I joined because of Dimitrov, not the Austrian Communist Party. His courage at the Reichstag Trial gave me renewed hope at that time. As he was a communist it seemed to me the only answer after the Rising was defeated."

"And they trust you now, to do this kind of work?" He grinned. "I've known some of them since childhood. We were friends until they got this same stupid idea as the Germans, that even left-wing Social Democrats were their enemies. But they started to change after Hitler. In February some of them stood beside me in the Hof, so you see a few communists did fight."

He laughed. "They know I'm reliable so don't worry." "Worry? Oh no. You're a strange but rather wonderful man, Karl." It came out before I realised what I was saying. A startled look and again that smile. "I can't lay claim to that. There were many like me. Let's move, it's getting late."

Among the trees Karl pulled me to him, his body hard against mine. My arms held him even tighter. I'd never been kissed like this before. "Oh liebling, liebling" he murmured as we drew apart, both shaken. "A strange world, isn't it? You find someone you could love but it's not possible. Come, we'll find a little restaurant and you can tell me all about America."

As we sat opposite each other we joked and laughed about the most trivial incidents. Then arms linked, walked slowly to my hotel. Near the entrance we stopped, wished each other well, shook hands for a long time. It was not only goodnight but goodbye for tomorrow I'd be gone.

In bed I leaned back on my pillows, relived the day. My thoughts were all of Karl, his look, his touch, his kisses. A knock. Panic. The police? I slipped into a robe and went to the door, "Karl", he locked the door behind him. Half laughing we hugged each other.

During that long wonderful night I experienced the deep fulfilment sex can give. Passion but also tenderness, concern for me, my satisfaction. It was a new amazing revelation which filled me with delight. Next morning, leave taking was prolonged. We comforted each other with the belief that surely I'd come to Vienna again. "Make it soon," Karl smiled, kissed me again then, looking to either side of the narrow corridor, he left the room.

In the first class compartment I stared out of the window, seeing nothing. Karl. So young, strong. His hands guiding mine. His mouth on mine to stop my outcry. We lay back. Laughed quietly. Both exhausted. Not for long. I kissed him again and again. A thank you. Didn't tell him that. And this morning. Gentle, different. Was it love? What is love? For him too? Twenty three. Five years with Pat. Nothing for me. Didn't know it could be like this. They'll send me to Vienna again. They must.

The distant cry of 'passports please' broke into my reverie. I quickly powdered my nose. The box of swiss chocolates lay beside me and I was reading a magazine when the passport official entered.

"Passport, madam." "Bitte" I answered in German, held it out to him. All was in order. A glance at my suitcases as I made to get up. The man waved me back with a smile, closed the door. Not the time now to dream of love. Wait till he leaves the train.

Fifteen minutes later he was back. "Sprechen sie Deutsch?" I nodded. "A little. "Perhaps you will be kind enough to help me. An Englishman has no Polish visa and I can't make him understand." I followed him through several carriages. He flung open the door of a second class compartment.

"Now we can settle this." It was a face from the Lenin school, I didn't remember the name. I gave no sign of recognition. "The officer has asked me to translate. Wants to know why you have no visa. He can issue one now but it'll cost more."

The man took his cue from me. In rapid English he replied, "I've no money. Spent it all on presents. What can I do?" "Leave it to me." I turned to the officer. "It seems he didn't understand about the return visa. And he has no money. Says it was stolen. He appears to be a simple working man."

"What is he doing in Russia?" "He wants to know why you're going there. Better tell me what work you do." "Engineer," came the answer which in fact was his trade. "I'm installing machinery." He turned to the other man, motioned with his big workman-like hands as I quickly explained.

The officer relaxed. This he could understand for many foreigners were doing such jobs in the Soviet Union. "But the visa?" he asked. I shrugged. "I'll pay it. He is a countryman and seems honest. He'll repay me." "I am greatly obliged to you. Shall I wait while he writes a receipt?" "That won't be a problem. I needn't retain you from your duties." A smile, a click of the heels, a slight bow and the man left the compartment and the train.

As it gathered speed we collapsed in nervous laughter. "I know your face but not your name." "Jack, they call me at the school. First and last bloody time for me on this job. I hate to think what might have happened if you hadn't been on this train." "Not your fault. They should have made sure you had a return visa. Carrying anything?" He nodded, glanced up at his luggage.

"My God. Some of their stupid mistakes will one day make real trouble." We chatted a bit longer before I returned to my carriage.

The customs man's request had been fortunate, sobered me, made me realise what job I was doing. There was no way Karl and I could be permanently together. Future occasional contacts would be heaven, to be treasured. Last night would forever remain with me, Karl always remembered.

And so it has proved though I was never to see him again. From him I had learned that with the man's understanding and active involvement a woman too could greatly enjoy that act so much desired by men and too often patiently endured by women.

It is sad to learn that well over fifty years later, Shere Hite in her recent book 'Women and Love' can write that still most women get very little satisfaction from their men, that the emotional support so necessary for a woman is lacking.

I felt fortunate to have met Karl. I knew what was possible though many years were to pass before I found it again.

Shanghai

Not long after my return I had a summons from Kurt. His approach on this occasion puzzled me for usually he was clear and concise. "You've been doing this work for six months.

How do you feel about it?" "Why do you ask?" "We've found for some that is the limit. They cannot continue the strain of travel, isolation, the need for constant caution. And you?"

"If anything I've enjoyed it, especially my last trip." "Yes, Vienna is lovely at this time of year. The Paris people think you've adapted well, learned to cope with the unexpected. So we're sending you to China."

"China?" I repeated. He looked at me sharply, "You don't feel up to it?" "It's not that …….. How could I tell him that more than anything I wanted to be with Karl again. "It's a bit of a shock, that's all." "I understand but you'll be all right. It's war there. You'll take money to help our people and, with luck, bring back accurate reports of what is happening." "Why with luck?" I seized on those words.

For a long moment he looked at me. "You're one of those who needs to know. All right. Shanghai is not like a European city. It will be dangerous, more so than even Berlin. But the Chinese Red Army needs money." He paused. "It is not an easy assignment." I smiled, "Are any? When do I go?" There was nothing else to say.

"Paris first, they'll see to everything. Tomorrow morning?" I nodded. In a daze I left the Comintern building, walked slowly to the Luxe. It would be months before I'd see Karl. But then there was no guarantee that I'd ever be sent to Vienna again. In any case I had no choice.

My mind raced ahead. I was young, didn't worry much about the danger. To go to China at any time would be a great adventure, to go for the 'cause', that was something. My excitement grew.

I parted with Pat on easy terms. He didn't seem to mind and I was glad to get away. But to what was I going?

In late 1926 Chiang-Kai-Shek, in alliance with the communists against the war lords and foreign occupiers, led the revolutionary armies of the Kuomintang across China towards Shanghai. During March 1927 a general strike, organised by Shanghai communists, closed down the entire city outside the International Settlement. By the time Chiang arrived the workers were in complete control.

Without warning, aided by business world and underworld, with full foreign approval, Chiang treacherously turned on the workers, disarmed them, executed the leaders. Communist organisations were smashed, its members hunted down, not only in Shanghai but in the larger cities of China. Thousands were slaughtered, many beheaded.

Despite this wreckage of the revolution in the cities, successful peasant uprisings led to the first beginnings of the Red Army and the setting up of Soviets in rural districts.

By 1929 there were ten thousand men in the Red Army whose most important single quality was its ability to fight a kind of guerrilla war, concentrating its main forces in the attack, swiftly dividing and separating afterwards. Positional warfare was avoided. In the territories gained, deep consolidation followed before another move forward was made.

But it was a basic tenet of communist theory that the working class would make the revolution with the peasantry as allies. Events in rural China were standing this on its head. Under pressure from Moscow the Chinese Red Army was ordered to make conventional warfare in assaults on cities. Though opposed by Mae Tse-Tung this was tried and failed. The Red Army was considerably weakened. Despite these failures there were further such demands on Chu-The and Mao Tse-Tung, the army commanders.

However, at the end of 1930 Chiang Kai-Shek launched his first 'extermination' campaign against the Soviets. The Red Army resumed its original guerrilla tactics and defeated this and four subsequent attacks.

In 1933 Chiang returned to the assault with over a million men, new equipment, new methods including blockades of wide areas. The fighting was still going on. Little news came from the battle zones.

This was the position in the autumn of 1934 and even as I prepared for my trip, a military conference in Kiangsi decided to withdraw to a new base. 80,000 men and women had been marching for several days before the enemy knew what was taking place.

The Long March of 8,000 miles had begun!

A LONG JOURNEY

In a Paris hotel room I waited for Lois. She was late, flustered, upset. "Sit down, get your breath back, what's happened?" "Andre's wife killed herself last night. She was one of us, couldn't take any more. He's bitterly reproaching himself. Says he should have seen it coming." "Poor man. Are you all right now?" She drank the glass of water I held out.

"Sorry about this. I only heard late this morning." We sat quiet as she became calmer. With a shake of her head she turned to me. "London first for a clean passport. No meeting with friends, no hotels. Can you suggest a place?" "My sister-in-law lives in the suburbs. They're not political."

Lois approved, gave me money, details of my London contact. "Fly to London, quickest and safest." The flight passed quickly as I was leisurely served with a three course dinner.

At a small café near St Pauls I found my contact, Alison, a middle-aged, upper class woman I'd met and didn't like. She didn't care for me either, made it quite plain. "Why they chose someone like you I'll never understand. I'll have to get you into shape."

"I'm not a novice. I've been doing such work for six months." Alison ignored this. "New passport first. Here's the form. You lost your old one, give it to me." I handed it over. "Now get photographs at this address. Be here again at twelve tomorrow."

Horrible woman, so different from Lois. But we were stuck with each other. As the week progressed my protests grew louder. "You're spending too much on clothes. It's Comintern money."

She was scathing. "You know nothing about it. You'll be on that ship for thirty days and must look the part. The right kind of clothes are necessary. And for God's sake get your hair styled and your nails manicured."

Evening dresses for dances and balls, fine cottons for the equator, silk dresses with matching jackets, pleated skirts to be worn with plain shirts and soft woollen cardigans, matching shoes, all this we bought. Smart luggage, a new hand bag and last of all a corset, the long kind that came well above my tummy and over my bottom. "I don't wear those." "Pack it, you'll need it." And with this enigmatic statement I had to be content.

When my new passport came I left for Paris. There I was taken to headquarters, a large gloomy house down a side street. Andre handed me a wide money belt. "It's lined so the bills won't crackle, a hundred thousand dollars." "So much?" This was an enormous sum in those days.

"Wear it near the waist, the top part of your corset. You'll forget you've got it on." Lois smiled encouragingly. It did frighten me to have such a large amount of money in my care. Andre explained, "Before Hitler the money went through a Berlin Bank to The International Red Help Society in Shanghai. The Knomintang smashed that. Now we need people like you."

I nodded, "It's just …… He smiled, "Here is money for your expenses, emergencies." The small well fitted vanity case had a clever false bottom.

"Be glad, my girl, that it's only money, not documents you're carrying, "King Alexander of Yugoslavia assassinated. Barthou shot."

Andre bought a paper. "My God, it must mean Minister Barthou's dead too. In Marseilles. They think Croat nationalists are responsible." He turned to me. "And you a Yugoslav. Thank God you're on your way. We'll have to lie low. They'll turn Paris upside down now." It was 9th October 1934.

I had no worries in Venice. Paris had arranged it all. Travelling to my hotel in a gondola was a novelty I enjoyed. Within a few days I boarded the Italian S S Conte Rossi. A sigh of relief and a silent thank you to Andre when I found I had a small stateroom to myself.

From the beginning I needed to make rapid decisions. It was not long before the few young women near my age became friendly with Italian officers. Parties in cabins, evening assignations on deck followed and pressure was put on me to become part of this. But I pleaded ill health and remained with the middle-aged group who gazed enviously and judged harshly.

I soon realised Alison had worried too much about my wardrobe. Perhaps some romantic cruise in her past had brought memories. Not all the women wore my kind of clothes, some were quite shabby. But I did need my evening dresses. Everyone was going to a Gala ball, a celebration of Mussolini's take over of Italy.

Carefully I picked a low cut long blue sequined gown, reminiscent of the twenties, loose yet outlining the breasts. From the waist down panels swung out as I danced the evening away with one uniformed fascist after another. I'd convinced myself this was the right thing to do to allay suspicion and smiled at the thought of my money belt, snug under my strong corset, which I didn't feel and neither could they. If only they'd known.

Belatedly remembering my ill health, I spent the next day in bed.

A lonely little Swiss woman sought me out to walk the deck with her. "It will do you good," she'd say as she talked on and on. "I'm returning from leave, have quite an important job in the Swiss Bank. We have our problems. The red bandits are bold and some even work in Shanghai." Fortunately we were leaning on the rail for her next bit of gossip shook me. "You know, people from Europe bring money to those Chinese communists, mostly Dutch guilders. We stop everyone who brings them in."

"Not lira, pounds, francs, dollars?" I asked lightly. "Everyone has dollars, many Americans visit Shanghai. No, it's been mostly guilders." I tucked this information away to pass on, thankful my money was in dollars.

As we neared the equator I felt almost grateful to Alison for the fine loose cotton dresses. The poor nuns on board sweated in their white woollen habits. Some young colonising German men too were unprepared for such weather and a whiff led to evasive action.

Though I raided the ship's library, time passed slowly and I was pleased when the Swiss woman told me, "You'll have to start packing. Only a few more days now."

In mid-November the S S Rossie arrived in Shanghai.

Apprehension, fear of what might happen during entry was quickly dispelled as I was waved through. Returning Chinese were still being questioned when my taxi moved off to the hotel in Bubbling Well Road where I was to make contact. It was a rambling old structure with high-ceilinged public rooms, long narrow corridors, the furniture and hangings a strong Victorian and Chinese mixture. My room was large and comfortable. But why not a busier, modern hotel?

That night I locked my door and propped a chair under the knob. Tomorrow I'd be free of this hundred thousand dollar burden. The next afternoon, promptly at four o'clock, I made my way to the large lounge where tea was served. It was here I'd be recognised by the magazine on my table.

The trio played Strauss waltzes, arias from the Mikado. The tea was good, the scones well buttered. It might have been Lyons Corner House. When the musicians put aside their instruments at half-past five the room slowly emptied. I sat grimly on for another half hour but no-one came.

Now I was in a quandary, already conspicuous in this largely residential hotel. To remain in all day might arouse suspicion, enquiries. Yet this was not a European city where I could freely wander. I knew nothing of Shanghai but remembered that the little Swiss woman on the ship had said Nanking Road and the Bund were its heart where shops and banks could be found. The next morning I watched the coming and going. Everyone hired a rickshaw. The sweating 'coolies', barefoot with trousers rolled to the knee, muscles taut, backs bent, like pack animals between the shafts, strained with their burdens. A wave of revulsion that human beings should be so employed. But I was playing a part and must do as others did. I left the hotel, got into a rickshaw and asked to be taken to Nanjing Road.

The shops were luxurious. I found an American restaurant, a cinema, a bookshop where I replenished my supply. By four o'clock I was back in the hotel. Again no-one came. I tried not to worry, spent the evening reading a detective story. Tomorrow I'd lunch again in that American restaurant.

Tall fine structures, granite, marble, as though made to last forever, lined the Bund. The colonisers had built well, their banks and business premises proudly proclaimed functions and titles. Here were shipping companies, finance houses, new big hotels, the Bank of England, the Bank of America.

A continuous stream of people flowed through. On the Wangpu River a teeming traffic of ships loaded and unloaded.

And in complete contrast, huddled against this grand background, were the stevedores, the down and outs and unemployed, beggars clothed in rags.

During the tea interval that afternoon two old English gentlemen happily and loudly discussed Chiang Kai-Shek's victories over the 'red bandits' who were on the run. With great satisfaction they pronounced, 'He's done it this time'. In the abandoned areas there was still fighting but he'd soon have them under control and the retreating 'communist scum' had no chance.

What had happened since I'd left Venice? Was it true that the Red Army had been defeated? The men had spoken with such confidence. And again, no-one had approached my table.

Full of foreboding, I lay on the bed. My contact might be involved, perhaps in prison or even dead. I'd have to return to Europe. What a waste it would be, the preparation, expense, the long journey. And this money must be badly needed. Was there an alternative? I sat up. If they couldn't come to me, might I reach them? Through Moscow? Ridiculous. Paris? Yes, that dentist who always informed them of my arrival.

A chance, it might work. To his address I sent a cablegram: "Happy Birthday. Missing you and Uncle. Wish you were here."

Three days later a tall, burly middle-aged European walked to my table during four o'clock tea. "May I?" He went on to say the right words, sat down. My relief was so great I blazed with anger, "Where the hell have you been?"

His voice was low, soothing. "All right, all right, it's over now. I know it's been hard for you, eight days. That cable was smart thinking. We'd no idea you were here." I regained control. "You've come, that's all that matters. What went wrong?" He shrugged. "At times our communication system breaks down. It's difficult." Then with a smile, "Dinner at 7.30. I'll call for you and you can hand it over."

For the first time I smiled back.

That evening I said to Otto, "Before I return will you show me something of Shanghai?" He didn't answer, just looked at me. Then, "We don't want you to go back. We need you here." "Why?"

He sighed, "I see I'll have to tell you but the less talk the better. Recently a number of American comrades had to leave hurriedly, barely escaping arrest. They broke rules, drank too much, held parties to which they brought women. One of those was a police agent." His voice was bitter.

I found it hard to credit. The stock plot of the spy novel. But it explained one thing which had puzzled me. "Is that why I was sent to that old fashioned place on the Bubbling Well Road? It isn't suitable."

"I know. Our people had been going to the Palace but the police are keeping close watch on all the big hotels." Then, his manner more genial, he went on, "We want you to take over a flat in the French Quarter."

"Where people meet?" "No. In this flat there's a small room equipped with a radio transmitter." "I don't know anything about radios," I protested. "Your job is to live there. One of our trained men will handle that side."

This was far removed from the courier work I had been doing. We sat silent. "I'm sure your chief would agree. I know Kurt well. It's urgent. Someone must move in as soon as possible." The furnished flat was in a small modern building reached by outside stairs. Otto had said, "Your boy is reliable. He will look after you but must always be treated as a servant." "Why do you call him 'boy'? Do we have to speak like these arrogant Europeans?"

His reply had been swift, "Yes or our guard may slip at the wrong time. If we don't keep up appearances we're no use here." The 'boy' turned out to be a plump, cheerful grandfather in his fifties. It seems incongruous that I, a young woman, should address him in this way so I called him by his name, Ho Lee.

On the second evening of my move to the flat Otto came with Nick, the radio operator. He was a miner from Scranton, Pennsylvania. After the usual exchange of greetings Nick went into the small room to examine the transmitter. Otto explained. "Nick's got his own key and will be here every evening except Sunday. He starts at eleven and leaves early in the morning."

I groaned loudly. This was more than I had bargained for. In the excitement of the changeover I hadn't given a thought to how this side of the work was carried on. Otto laughed "It'll be alright. You'll see."

As Otto left Nick came out, asked for the lavatory. I showed him the bathroom which could be reached only through my bedroom.

Nick was a most unprepossessing man, scrawny with arms too long for his body. Untidy lank hair hung above a pale face with a sharp pointed nose and receding chin. He didn't return to his room but sat down in an armchair. At his first words I regarded him with amazement. "You must realise I'm doing the important work. You're here to serve me." Before I could reply he stood up making himself as tall as possible and in a condescending voice went on, "Oh yes, I expect you to have my sandwiches and coffee ready, good hot coffee." My answer was sharp. "I wouldn't count on that."

At this he put his hands behind his back and rocked on toes and heels. "You have to understand that you are here for my convenience." A pause, then coming towards me he leered as he said softly, "In every way."

I couldn't believe it. What role did this self-important little man think he was playing? "Why you stupid son of a bitch. Where do you get these ideas? You're here to operate the radio, I'm here to occupy the flat." He glowered, moved towards me again. "You're a God damn stuck up bourgeois like the rest of the women in this outfit. Because I'm a minor you look down on me."

I was furious. "You're a pig-ignorant fool. I've been among miners all my life. This job's gone to your head. Think yourself another Valentino – wave your hand and the women come running." Nick looked dangerous. I went into my bedroom, turned the key behind me. Sometime later he banged on the door. "I need the bathroom. Let me in."

"I don't give a damn where you pee, in a bucket or on the floor but you're not coming in here." His knocks became louder. I opened the door. "If you go on like this the neighbours will call the police. Is that what you want?" He glared angrily, turned and went back into his room.

I complained to Otto and so had Nick. "It's intolerable. The police might have been called. What on earth put it into his head that I'd been provided especially for his personal pleasure?" Otto whistled. "So that's what it was about. He claimed you wouldn't let him use the bathroom. I thought there was more to it." "Nick can't be relied on, I won't stay." I was fuming.

Otto's voice was sharp. "You lost your temper, did your share of the shouting. So, it's difficult but I'll talk to Nick and can assure you it won't happen again." He continued more quietly, "I'm going to trust you, tell you why you must stay. That flat holds the radio link between the Shanghai Comintern Committee and Moscow."

What he said to Nick I never learned but there was no more trouble. One afternoon Otto took me on the promised tour of Shanghai. The French Concession and the International Settlement formed a vast square in the heart of the city. Here were elegant shops, hotels, night clubs, the race course built by the British. The opulence of the Bund. He pointed out the brothels of Love Lane, to many that it was probably the largest bordello in the world, and the opium dens of Bubbling Well.

Then he took me to a different Shanghai where on the fringes of the foreign concessions, in wretched ramshackle huts, lived tens upon thousands of Chinese. Many more who were homeless filled squalid streets and alleyways. Ragged women clutching small children sheltered in doorways or huddled in corners around tiny fires. As we drove back to the centre I was silent, asked no questions. In Glasgow slums, company towns, even Hoovervilles there had not been such misery and poverty. I learned from Ho Lee that during the winter months collecting dead Chinese, men, women and children who had died overnight from exposure or starvation was a daily early morning routine task on the streets of Shanghai.

At my next meeting with Otto he said, "An old friend wants to see you." So I again met Rudi Bloom, Party name Baker. We came from the same town, Pittsburgh and I'd known him since early childhood. His wife Lily laughed as we reminisced. After dinner I asked Rudi, "What's happening? The papers say the 'red bandits' have been wiped out. What is the truth?"

He shook his head. "I don't know. There has been heavy fighting in Kiangsi. The Red Army has left." "Abandoned the Soviet areas?" "It seems so. The newspapers mention battles in

Hunan and Kwangsi – that means the Red Army is still fighting back. But we can only surmise, we have no hard facts." "No contact?" "None. Some of our people are trying to get through but Chiang's soldiers are everywhere."

Rudi leaned forward, very serious as he addressed me directly. "Take extra care. We've had word there is a special drive against communists in Shanghai, Chinese and foreign. The underworld is working with Chiang's secret police. It is a dangerous time to be here."

That night I couldn't sleep, picked up a detective story, my form of bromide. But the words seemed empty and meaningless, the dangers more real in this life I lived.

Chinese gangs Rudi had said worked with police. A whisper from the neighbours, a traitor in our ranks and they'd come in the night and take me away. Maybe even torture before they murdered me. So alone and vulnerable in this apartment. Nick wouldn't know. Of course, they'd take him too. Our people dare not enquire. A dangerous time to be here he had said.

I tried to shake off this mood but my thoughts remained sombre. Rudi's friends might never get through, never get the money I brought, the whole trip useless. The door banged as Nick left the flat. It must be dawn. Were there ways of locating radio transmitters? Too exhausted to sort that one out, I burrowed further into the blankets and fell asleep.

A week before Christmas I bought a small tree and decorations, presents for Ho Lee, his wife and the small grandson who often came with her. Word came from Rudi and Lily. I was to spend Christmas day with them. Wonderful invitation. I was very lonely and for days had spoken to scarcely anyone but Ho Lee. I spent hours choosing gifts, chocolates and wine.

Both Rudi and I had Yugoslav parents and I was delighted when the traditional suckling pig was put on the table. As we talked, laughed and drank a great deal of wine, we managed for one day to forget this strange world in which we now found ourselves.

January 1935 was a cold miserable month. Despite daily newspaper announcements that the Red Army was finished it had reached Kweichow Province, crossed the Wu River and taken the town of Tsunyi. But they couldn't hold out much longer, thundered the papers. Chiang Kai-Shek with his huge army had built road blocks, fortified all the Yangtse River crossings to prevent the reds from getting into the North. His air force was pounding the areas around Tsunyi.

Yet each day as I carefully read the news I pinned my hope to the fact that despite all prophecies of its demise, the Red Army was still fighting back.

Time dragged. I was bored with this life, forced myself to go out through cold winds swept through the streets of Shanghai. In mid-February Otto unexpectedly came to the flat. "You're leaving" were his first words. My joy at this announcement was short lived as he went on, "Your name is on a British list for investigation. We'll need to move fast."

I stared at him not wanting to believe this. "How do you know that?"

"Oh it's right enough. Someone sympathetic to us types the lists." He laughed but stopped when he saw my face. "Look, try not to worry. We'll get you away in time but you'll have to help. Listen carefully. First thing tomorrow you must see the Soviet Consul. He won't like it. The last thing they want is to get mixed up with us. But don't go away till he agrees."

"Agrees to what?" "To get you a quick passage on a Soviet cargo ship to Vladivostok. Make it clear there is no time to lose, you must leave Shanghai within the next few days. Once you've seen him sit tight until you get a decision."

As Otto had warned I was not welcome at the Soviet Consulate. My request was coldly received. The tall, stout, blue-eyed consul, impatient and angry burst out, "You Comintern people get into trouble and expect us to bail you out. What is it this time?" "I don't know except that my name is on a police list and I need to leave before they find me."

In the inner office I sat silent while he strode up and down. Then abruptly, "I'll go into it. Come back tomorrow."

Half rising I remembered Otto's words and sank back into the armchair. "I'll wait, I've nothing else to do." He stood looking down at me. "Your instructions, I suppose?" I nodded. To my surprise he laughed, "It's that German isn't it? He's a tough man, knows his business." There was respect in his voice. The Consul smiled and walked out of the room.

I sat and worried. There won't be a boat. They'll get me, bound to. Must have got the list from London. I'm here on my own passport. Never thought I'd stay. Can I stand up to questioning? I don't know anything important. They won't believe that. It might be the Chinese, not the British. Do they pull out fingernails? I shivered, hugged myself, rocked in the chair.

The Consul returned. "You're in luck. A ship is leaving day after tomorrow but you'll have to board tomorrow evening after dark. The captain knows you are coming." He gave me details of the steamer and dock. I wanted to hug this big man, dance around the room with him. As I stood up and stammered my thanks I think he knew how relieved I felt. We shook hands, he smiled down at me. "My regards to your chief but tell him I'd prefer not to see any more of his colleagues."

That evening Otto came to the flat. Skilfully he inserted documents into suitcase linings, cutting, taping, pasting. I'd never seen it done before. Then over coffee I received my final instructions.

"Pay off Ho Lee in the morning. Be ready for six o'clock tomorrow evening. It's dark by then."

Otto came in a car which he drove himself to an isolated part of the harbour where a motor boat was waiting. A Chinese man was in the bow. The wind whipped up the sea as I clambered into the boat. My cases were lifted in. Otto waved and was gone.

Exhilaration, fear as we sped through the dark cold February night. The police patrol boat might stop and challenge us. But very soon the ship loomed ahead. A rope ladder was flung over the side, my boatman grabbed it, beckoned and helped me onto the first rung. Clinging tightly I took one step up then stopped. Voices called 'quickly' but I couldn't move as the towering side of the ship yawed on the heavy sea. A seaman's legs descended. With this arm around my shoulder and a push from the elbow I reached the deck. My luggage followed.

Then I was in the captain's cabin. He was not pleased to see me, not even a handshake as he said, "For now you will be absolutely silent. We are sailing at dawn and port officers will soon be aboard to give us clearance. Unless they are suspicious it is a cursory examination. You should be all right."

And so it proved. Sometime later from my cubbyhole I heard voices, laughter, the clink of glasses. Then they were gone. The captain called me out. "Tonight you will sleep in the sick room. Tomorrow we will find you a cabin."

He paused, looked at me. I stared back. For a time there was silence. He's been lumbered and thinking what a nuisance I am, I reflected. Can't blame him. Not his job to have passengers like me. But oh my God how glad I am to be here.

Less curt now he confirmed my thoughts. "It is not easy to explain you. We have eight passengers on board, Russians who left after the revolution and now wish to return. You must make up some plausible story as to why you embarked so late. Be very discreet." Exhausted, slumped in my chair, I nodded. "I am very grateful to you. You've probably saved my life."

The captain's expression changed. Clearly he'd not thought of that side of things. His voice was kindly as he said, "It has been an ordeal for you. I will send food and drink to the hospital room." Though the bed was like a board, I slept long and well. When I awoke we were at sea.

Only now as I write this am I more fully aware of the dangers which faced Nick and me at that time.

In a most informative book, 'The Long March', published in 1985, Harrison E Salisbury, one time New York Times correspondent, writes of those early days of the thirties. He tells his readers that in the spring of 1934 wireless communication of the underground bureau of the Chinese Communist Party Central Committee was in the hands of two Chinese, Li Zhusheng and Sheng Zhougliang.

Chiang Kai-Shek's secret police arrested Li in June and threatened him with death. He gave away the location of the wireless transmitter and the identity of Sheng. The transmitter and Sheng were seized. That, writes Salisbury, for the time being ended communication between Moscow and the Chinese communists.

That was in June 1934. Were Nick and I the first replacements when I moved from my hotel in November 1934? Might something like that have happened to Nick and me in that flat in the French Quarter where I lived, which housed a wireless transmitter? Did anything take place after I left? I'll never know.

But I can't help feeling now that my name on that British list which made an abrupt departure so necessary was perhaps a bit of luck rather than the opposite.

☙

My narrow dark cabin with an upper and lower berth and two lockers was cold and damp, clearly not intended for a passenger. In my euphoric state such Spartan quarters didn't matter. The elderly passengers were curious but spoke little English. There was no need for explanations. We smiled and nodded, sat around a large table eating plain Russian fare, schi (thick meat and cabbage soup), golubtsy (cabbage leaves stuffed with meat), minced meat cutlets. A pot of jam stood beside a large samovar. Tea was available at all times.

During the bright cold days I stayed on deck as long as possible for there was no comfort in my cabin or in the always crowded small public room. From the East China Sea we passed through the Korean Strait into the Sea of Japan. Then suddenly the weather changed. The captain called us together, spoke calmly. "No one is to go on deck. There is a gale ahead, seas will be high. Keep your lifebelts by you."

"Is there danger?" asked a high nervous voice. "We'll ride out the gale, there should be no danger." His voice was quiet, reassuring. He came over and in a low voice repeated these instructions to me in English. I nodded, half-smiled sympathetically at the others.

That night the gale hit the ship with such ferocity that I thought it would keel over. Now I knew what 'the fury of the sea' meant as great waves pounded us. The ship plunged and turned as the violent tempest shrieked around us. Lying in the lower birth smothered in blankets I rolled with the ship, held tight. My suitcases slid from side to side.

Somehow a seaman got to me with cold rations. "Stay put," he said in Russian, gesturing with his hands. The waves slapped as they swept over the lower deck. I shivered, afraid this might be the end of the ship and me. But on the third day this nightmare of wind and water was over. Later in Vladivostok we were told it had been one of the worst storms for years. Ships had foundered and we were lucky to have come through.

The voyage was near its end. Tomorrow a passage would be cut through the frozen sea to the ice bound ports. "It will be a beautiful sight if you can rise early," the now friendly Captain explained with a smile.

Shortly after dawn a crash shook the ship. Though I wore several sweaters under my black woollen coat, thick shoes and stockings, they were little protection as I stood on deck in the intense cold. I knew I might never again see such dazzling beauty. Our freighter followed in the wake of the ice cutter as thick ice crunched and churned under its impact and was pushed aside. The sea glistened as our ship plunged on but behind us the ice again closed in. As the sun shone this vast expanse glittered and sparkled. Strange that a ship could pass through such thick whiteness.

Soon we docked. Passport and customs officials clambered aboard. There was no-one to meet me and they asked question after question. Not until the captain intervened and explained did they allow me and my luggage ashore. The one available hotel was adequate and warm. Glad to be out of the biting wind I smiled at the receptionist. A long look but no comment as I was assigned a room.

Otto had warned me. "We haven't been able to reach them. They won't know who you are and few foreigners use that route. Sort it out when you get there." Just like that. But I was so glad to be on Russian soil that nothing seemed too difficult.

Lunch time. I was tired, hungry. It could wait. As I sat down in the dining room a by no means sober man lurched over and sank heavily on a chair at my table. "Fellow American?" he held out his hand. "Could say that. What are you doing here anyway?"

"Trying to teach these stupid bastards to put fish in cans. They just don't know how to work machines. But I'll show 'em then I can get back to God's country."

He was homesick, lonely and wanted to stick with me. After I finished my meal I excused myself. "See you around." I smiled and quickly walked out.

The directions given by the curious receptionist were accurate and soon I found myself at the police station. In my pidgin Russian I asked to see the chief. "You can talk to me," said the man at the desk. You've just arrived from Shanghai." So they knew that.

"I must see the chief." I repeated. He turned to the other officer in the room. "Kostya, she won't talk to me, wants the chief." They laughed uproariously. Seeing my expression he said, still smiling, "Sorry if I disappoint you but I am the chief."

At this I tried an apology but he waved it away and led me to an inner room. I told him I had to make contact with the Comintern representative in Vladivostok. "I know the man you need. But first the ship's captain has to verify your story. All being well, your colleague will call for you at the hotel this evening."

Still embarrassed, I tried to thank him but again he smiled, walked to the door with me. That evening Bernie from Brooklyn, New York arrived at the hotel. Greetings, explanations, then down to business. Tickets for the trans-Siberian Express were at a premium. I might have to wait.

He was back early the next morning with a ticket for the train which left that day. "I was on to Moscow last night. They were delighted, must have got going right away to get you this so quickly. So what's cooking over there?" "Can't tell you, can I? You know that. Anyway, thanks very much."

He saw me off, stowed my luggage in the compartment where I had the bottom berth. A middle-aged man was already above us arranging his things. I remembered then that no distinction was made when tickets were issued. So for ten days I'd be sharing this space with a man I didn't know.

"Looks ok. Just hope he doesn't snore," Bernie laughed.

Sergei was polite but distant, went out each morning to shave and dress. It was Misha, tall, broad, expansive, who took me under his wing. Though plainly dressed in a beige Russian-style shirt and tight trousers tucked into leather boots, he had the authority and bearing of a military man. He insisted I join him and his friends for breakfast, produced a large tin of red caviar and a loaf of bread. From the samovar at the end of the carriage came hot tea. "Eat, it is better than the dining car and a nip of vodka is essential."

So this was to be my morning routine. Misha spoke English and became my interpreter. We played cards and when someone produced a gramophone hooted with laughter as we tried to foxtrot in the corridor while the speeding train swayed.

Distances between towns and settlements were great. At every station we stopped for an hour or more and Misha insisted I wear his 'valenki', special pressed wool boots, to keep my feet warm. In these I tramped up and down, glad to be in the cold air. Once Misha reappeared from the station restaurant, with a bow handed me a box of chocolates.

Now and then in my role of foreign traveller I'd find something to criticise. I complained about the lack of fresh fruit, vegetables, realised I was pushing it a bit as this was February in Siberia. At the next intersection when our train going west met the one going east Sergei entered our compartment and dropped a dozen apples on my lap. Misha who had come to interpret said, "He wants to tell you that his job is to oversee catering arrangements in dining cars. The fruit is from the other train and he hopes you will now stop your criticism."

Red faced. I kept saying, "Sorry, I'm sorry to Sergei. He nodded stiffly again and again. Misha enjoyed it, a mischievous gleam in his eyes.

Outside was the vast frozen landscape, mile after mile of empty stillness, sometimes beautiful, often desolate. I stared for hours, glad to be in the warmth of the train.

A few days from Moscow, Misha entered my compartment, closed the door, sat down beside me. I put down my book as he spoke, "I've a confession to make. Bernie told me to keep an eye on you." Misha was startled at my reaction. "Who are you, why didn't you tell me?" "How could I?" he protested. "You had to play your part and my knowing wouldn't have helped you." It was true, I simmered down. He moved closer," Little golubchik, I've become very fond of you."

I made to move but he put his arm around me, held me tight. "We've got a few more nights when we can be together. I promise, you'll enjoy it." He kissed me ardently. I pulled away, stood up. I liked him well enough but not in that way. "We'll stay friends, that's enough Misha." He threw up his arms, "Why are you making me suffer, my little dove? What have I done that you should treat me so?" "That's very good, many women must have heard those words." He looked up at me sheepishly. I couldn't help laughing and soon he laughed with me.

When the train pulled into Moscow, Volodya was waiting, greeted me with a broad smile, picked up the precious suitcases. My reception by Kurt surprised me. High praise, congratulations, clever of me to have sent the cablegram, a bonus of 500 rubles, the only recognition one could give in this work.

"Do all your couriers to China get this treatment," I asked. "Certainly not those who return without having made contact." His disparaging tone annoyed me. "Have you any idea what it's like to be alone in Shanghai day after day, waiting for someone who never comes?" He shrugged, "You managed." And that was that.

Chapter 20

Goodbye to Moscow – Dublin

As I was leaving the Comintern building with Volodya and my now document-free cases, Bob Mcilhone, who had replaced Bill Rust, told me Pat was in Ireland. "Let me know when you're ready to join him and I'll arrange it." "I need time to think about that," I smiled, amused at his puzzled expression.

Our former quarters at the Luxe were occupied and I was given a small, pleasant room on the fourth floor in the new annex. Fortunately, I'd been too tired to unpack, for in the night I woke covered with lice, large, white, fat. Shuddering I brushed them off, jumped out of bed and ran down to the foyer.

"Voshi. Lice. My bed if full of them." The startled man on duty shook his head, "Nothing can be done till morning." Loudly I shouted at him, "None of your 'zaftra budet', something has to be done now. Call the Commandant." He stared at me, shook his head, repeated, 'zaftra', tomorrow. "Now. Call the Commandant immediately, do you hear." He came of his own accord, roused by the noise. I was barefoot, in pyjamas, very cold and very angry.

Apologies. A comrade on the run, ragged, exhausted, ill, had occupied the room immediately on arrival. He'd been transferred to hospital. Orders had been given that the room be fumigated, cleaned. Someone had slipped up. A woman now appeared. The commandant, long acquainted with me, gave her instructions. A hot bath, a new room to be prepared, my infested luggage to be taken away and treated.

Lying in bed after a thorough scrubbing I could not sleep. Perhaps the man had typhus. I might die here like Effie Geddes who had taken English children to a Pioneer camp and caught that fatal illness.

In the morning I insisted on seeing the Luxe doctor whom I knew of old and did not like. "There's nothing to worry about. You can't possibly get what he has." His tone was superior. "What was it?" Why wouldn't he tell me? "Well, if you must know, he had acute inflammation of the testicles." The doctor smiled, maliciously I thought, at the expression on my face. What could I say? The joke was on me or at least that's how he saw it. I'm sure the story made the round of his friends.

During my absence many people I'd known had left. Millie's gossip didn't interest me. I was delighted when my cousin Sophie walked in. "Heard you were back. A bit lonely here, isn't it?" I agreed, didn't ask when she'd arrived. We never spoke of her work, much more important than mine.

"I've been to Tagil, seen your folks. They're all right but very isolated. It's a hard life there. Your mom has only one friend, a Volga German woman. They sent a lot of them to Siberia, remember?" I nodded. Kulaks they were called, displaced from their fertile lands when collectivisation was introduced.

"How is mama? She never wanted to come here." "She was right. For her there's nothing. You going soon?" "Kurt's getting me a ticket. What can I take them?" "Food, from the valuta shop. Lots of it. Books, your mother was always a great reader." "But mom's not ill, is she?" "In good health. The air there is marvellous. No, it's loneliness. Get some magazines and papers from the Americans, they always bring plenty. She keeps asking what's going on in the outside world for the papers here give little information."

My cousin smiled. "Did you hear about Leila? Someone tipped her off and she brought a suitcase full of Kotex." We burst out laughing. It was a perennial problem for foreign communist women.

"Come to Mira's tonight. There's a party. Volodya will be there and Felix. You like him." Mira was Sophie's Russian friend who had a room not far from the Luxe. Volodya, her husband and Felix were both N.K.V.D lieutenants. "I'll be glad to. It's so empty here, no one to talk to but Millie and all she does is gossip."

Sophie looked at me. "Don't trust her. Never criticise anything or anybody when you're with her." "You mean ....." I asked wide-eyed. She nodded. "An informer. Don't let on. Be relaxed, but mind what you say." Older and wider than I and, though I didn't know it at that time, already disillusioned and worried about how things were going. This was the spring of 1935, just two years before the Trials were to begin.

When I arrived at Mira's party a very serious discussion centred on how best Felix should approach Nina with whom he was desperately in love. Though my Russian was not up to much I understood they were telling him to woo her more ardently, passionately, win her soul. When Nina, a tall, beautiful actress with snow white hair walked into the room all talk stopped for a moment. I felt that blue-eyed Felix, short, sandy haired and freckled, had little chance.

These people were strangers and I listened, smiled at their polite acknowledgement of me but took little part in the conversation which dealt with work, sex, children, birth, death, which shops had what. Not once was politics mentioned, strange for foreign communists whose talk at a party would have been of little else.

With hindsight, I wonder whether the withdrawal of these Russian communists from talk of the 'current situation' was deliberate, had to do with Stalin's near dismissal at the January 1934 Russian Party Congress when he received fewer votes than any other candidate. 274 were cast against him and only 3 against Kirov. By December 1934 Kirov had been assassinated 'under mysterious circumstances and Stalin had raised his hands in mock horror.

Had I known it then, this was the beginning of those events which culminated in the climate of fear which led to the notorious 1937 Treason Trials.

My leave was long, I had ample time to consider my future. Bob took it for granted I'd soon be off to Dublin. Kurt, though he knew it might be time for me to leave this work, asked me to stay. I considered a return to my home town in the States.

First a visit to my parents as I retraced part of the journey I'd so recently made and for three days travelled through a snowy landscape to Tagil which lies just inside Siberia. From there it was some miles by sleigh through pine forests to Tagilstroi, the virgin town my father was helping to build. Brilliant sunshine in no way lessened the extreme cold. The drab, barrack-like buildings stood out sharply against white hills and blue sky.

Mama hugged me. "So you're safe, Frieda, you're safe." She knew little of my work except that it was dangerous. Starved of conversation, mama talked about the lonely life, cut off from friends, deprived of all amenities formerly taken for granted, always coping with scant supplies of food and goods. Bitterly she lamented they had ever left the States.

"We'd have survived. But papa won't go back. Things will get better he says." "And you don't agree?" "Someday, maybe, not in our time. Except for the specialists, engineers and craftsmen, the workers here are still peasants, ignorant, slow, lazy." "But mother ...." I protested. She interrupted me sharply, "You know only Comintern, educated Russians. I come from the peasantry but these people are more backward than the worst in our village."

Mama had always been the realist in our family. She went on speaking, slowly. "You were too little to remember but when the revolution came we were so happy, believed straightaway things would be different. That was stupid. People don't change overnight. These peasants don't even understand what socialism means. It's not their fault. Maybe the next generation if they get schooling."

I didn't know what to say, had accepted the slogan glorifying 'the mighty heroic workers and peasants' who were successfully completing the Five-Year Plan. But as my mother pointed out few resembled the shining, eager, dedicated figures on the posters.

Footsteps made her hurriedly say, "I don't talk like this in front of your father. It's hard enough for him working in such weather." Then, with a wry smile, "Like you, he is utterly devoted to the Soviet Union."

My father embraced me, strange and bulky in his thick outer garments. From then emerged the spare figure, the lean face with its blue eyes which could flash like lightening.

During one whole evening I listened to him. "Rusting in Tagil goods yard are machines and tools we need. I say to the men, 'get them to the building site, how can you let this stuff lie here in the open, it belongs to you, you're the bosses now' but they look at me as if I was crazy."

"Why don't you take it higher?" "I did. They listened, made notes, nothing happened. Some of these people wouldn't last ten minutes back home. Too much vodka around." "So things aren't going too well." "Don't get me wrong. You should see the new Palace of Culture going up. Factories, schools, hospitals. Houses come last."

He went on with enthusiasm about methods which enabled them to get below the frozen earth, the permafrost, and so carry on work in the coldest weather.

Papa belonged to that band of Russian and foreign pioneers whose conviction, spirit and selflessness combated the inertia around them as they carried on under extremely difficult conditions. Many were to become victims of Stalin's terror, denounced as 'enemies of the people' or in the case of most foreigners, spies for the countries from which they came.

Mama asked about my work and I told her some of it. "Best say nothing to your father. He'd want to boast, couldn't keep quiet. He's very proud of you." She knew him so well.

I spoke to her about my doubts for the future. Her reaction surprised me. "There's nothing for you in Russia, nor in the States." You say Pat wants you to join him. Then do it. A marriage is a marriage. Give it another chance." "I'll think about it. You know I'm not happy with him." "You'll survive, you'll manage, look at me." "Mama you've changed. This place is bad for you."

She was nearly in tears then. "You're right, do what you think best. But I fear for you, wandering alone in a hostile world. Better the devil you know." "Not always, mother. I'm nearly twenty-four now, not eighteen." "Not for six more months," she protested and we both laughed, leaving it at that as I hugged and kissed her.

Back in Moscow I had another session with Kurt. "Go on a few more assignments. They make up your mind. We'll talk again." So reluctantly to Berlin with its sad memories of Hans. My contact with a stranger was short, charged with tension and danger.

I went to Vienna gladly. In the café I sat, eyes on the entrance, wishing it to be Karl. But it was a short, tubby man who came to my table, said the right words but looked at me strangely for my disappointment must have been apparent. Hesitantly I asked about Karl. He shook his head, didn't know anyone with that name.

Spring had not yet come to Vienna. Snow flurries were driven by gusts of wind. Heads bent, people hurried through the streets. I scanned the crowds for that tall figure with the grey-blue eyes. I didn't find him.

During that long train ride to Moscow scarcely articulated, impossible hopes were painfully put aside. It was time for a decision. Still uncertain, I left Moscow for London where I had friends and possibly a job. The Nord Express sped across the German countryside, fields still covered in snow, dark pine forests. In the half darkness a deer raced the train. So close, antlered head, large eyes, straining body. Then it was gone.

I burrowed in my corner. Did it know where it was going? Did I? If I returned to Pat could I convince him that a new and different relationship between us was possible? It is said that 'hope is eternal' and now I entered the world of fantasy, set out a scenario in which Pat became like Karl, a good companion with whom I could laugh, joke, share experiences on equal terms. And of course our sex life must change. Why couldn't we enjoy that delight I'd had with Karl? Why hadn't he ever been like that? We'd talk about it, I could explain. After all there had been Elsie and other women in his life so he shouldn't mind about Karl. Surely he would enjoy it more than the mechanical act I'd put up with, not knowing it could be so different. Slowly the idea, the belief that I'd be able to win him over, make him understand, took hold. After my courier work he'd see me in a different light, a capable woman, an equal.

A brief stop in Paris then London and straight to King Street. Harry Pollitt rose from his desk as I entered his office. In his usual jovial way he greeted me, "You look better than ever. Very smart too." "You can blame Alison for that. Dressed me like a right, middle-class lady." He laughed then said, "I've heard from them that you've done a fine job, especially in China." We spoke about Shanghai and The Long March. I told him what I'd heard from Rudi. It all seemed so far away.

"Glad you're back?" "How can one tell so soon? It's been a strange life." "Dublin now for you?" "I think so." He gave me a long look as we shook hands. "You know there's always a job here for you."

Pat was waiting as the Liverpool boat edged towards the Quay. The familiarity of years together made conversation easy on our way to his lodgings. The landlady brought a tray with tea and buttered scones.

Then there was silence. Feeling my way I said, "Pat, let's talk about ourselves, how we see each other after five years of marriage. You know I nearly went to the States instead of coming here." "Why on earth did they want to send you there?" "They didn't. I wasn't at all sure I wanted to come back to you." There, it was out, what would he say now.

That false laugh. Just so had he reacted when I arrived from the States. "Well you're here now, so what's it matter? There's nothing to talk about." "But there is. Feelings matter," I had to get through to him. "Frieda, all that really matters is the Party and the movement. Anything else is secondary." "It wasn't when you thought your mother was dying. Feelings mattered to you then, didn't they, and the Party didn't come first." "That was different."

"Was it? She was your mother. I am your wife. Don't you feel anything about that? I want to know what you think. Aren't you at all interested in what's happened to me these past months? I know about Elsie. You should know about Karl. I was very fond of him, learned from him. That's one of the things I want to talk about. I'm not eighteen any more Pat." He'd risen as if to go but now sat down with a thump. "You mean you .... with another man?" "Yes and I found it wonderful. Why was it never like that with you?"

Pat couldn't face this. I should have understood that such things weren't spoken of in his private world. Despite his socialism his long Catholic conditioning was deep and clearly he still equated sex with sin but had worked out his own approach to this. Somehow, he seemed to have convinced himself that within marriage a quick emotionless act, which yet gave him the relief he so much needed, was different.

I was to learn that he 'sinned' in a much less inhibited way with other women. When a close Party friend told me she'd had a torrid affair with him I was surprised. "I hope you don't mind too much," she'd said. "I didn't think he had it in him," I answered, which in turn surprised her. When I told him I knew about it but continued my friendship with her Pat couldn't understand it. He denounced her as a 'whore', forgave himself because of that. A typical Victorian man's outlook.

But such understanding came much later. Now as he slammed out of the room I sat very still, tears of anger streamed down my cheeks. The fantasy was over. Finally, I rose, powdered my face. My luggage remained unpacked. Money? Enough. I peered into the small spotted mirror, adjusted my hat, put on my coat.

Pat came in. The false smile was there. He was going to pretend all this had never happened. "You've not unpacked, then?" "I'm returning to London." The heartiness slipped away from him. He looked older, uncertain, weary. A long silence. He spoke first. "Don't go Frieda. Please. Let's give it another try." Never had I seen him like this before. It was the first time he'd admitted that things were not as he pretended. I remained silent. "We can make a go of it, you'll see, it'll be better." "That's what you always say and it doesn't happen."

It was one of those moments in my life when two paths opened before me and I had the opportunity to freely choose one or the other. Behind me were successful months which had demanded self-reliance, the ability to face danger, make judgements and quick decisions. Sure of a job in London I knew I could look after myself.

Pat's appeal had surprised me. Only an hour before he had walked away from my pleas for a better kind of life between us. He had not suddenly become kind, tolerant, understanding of my needs, willing to meet me halfway.

Aware of this, though not perhaps as clearly as I here have stated, why did I stay? Why for more than twenty years did I live a life which despite pleasant intervals, was in the main one of accommodation, adjustment and frustration which ended only when I at last walked away from it?

It was the kind of life many women of my generation experienced but it need not have been mine. Some women did travel the other path but they were mostly middle-class and educated. Though she had changed in recent years my mother had never held up marriage as a goal. For me she had wanted education, the economic independence that could bring.

Why then? Not till I read Kate Millet's 'Sexual Politics' did I begin to understand the more than two thousand years of oppression which had shaped me in spite of all my illusions of emancipation. I was part of my times, though resentful I subscribed to the mores of that period.

Four years at high school, a term at university had still left me basically an ignorant, uneducated young woman with no cultural background, no understanding of so much that went on in the world. Even the names of pioneering women of early days both in America and England who fought for women's rights were only vaguely known to me. This kind of knowledge was unimportant, considered outside our Party politics where the main thrust was towards achieving socialism in our time. Once that came, women would get the equality our men preached but few practised.

When after the Russian revolution the humane socialism of my childhood changed into the controlled communism of later years it was a progression I accepted without thought or doubt.

Paramount in my life was the Communist Party as the movement which fought for workers' interests, for the transformation of society to socialism. Paradoxically it was so structured that creative Marxist thinking about the problems in one's own land had been subordinated to a set of dogmas, imposed equally on every country, based solely on the experiences of Russia in which the only successful workers' revolution had taken place. Decisions of the Comintern were not questioned. Discipline in the Party was strong, 'the line' strictly adhered to. One's desires and personal life were secondary.

That was Pat's view and mine yet my resentment and at times rage at the way I was regarded by him was also a part of me. My mother had never taught me to be submissive to men, the contrary was the case. Her belief in equal rights had been very much a part of her but the definition of those rights was different from today. I see her now as a feminist, not in the modern sense, but as one of those strong, working class women who fiercely fought their men for the right to be consulted and considered, who felt their opinions as to how their joint lives should be conducted were as valid as those of the men.

Yet she never questioned that it was her role to run the home, see to the children, do all the things that was expected of mothers and wives, nor did she expect my father to share these tasks. This revolutionary concept, so central a part of present day feminism, was not of her time. She did not question the institution of marriage itself which was a part of her world. As it was of mine. I was not strong enough to defy the conventions of those times both inside and outside the Party. Of course, there were sometimes affairs between men and women in the Party but rarely was the marriage bond broken as a result.

Does this explain my behaviour, my reason for staying with Pat? An apologia? Perhaps. I'd like to see it rather as a need to understand and come to terms with that young woman of twenty-three who did not seize the opportunity to become independent but despite stirrings and inclinations, accepted the old role which the society of the time imposed.

I did not take to Dublin. The Party was small, public activity at a minimum. When we did emerge, the experience was unpleasant as in the Easter Rising procession. We turned out in force, were allotted a place at the very end of the march. Our red rosettes identified us.

An old woman wrapped in a shawl shouted, "The antiChrist, it's the antiChrist." Men holding short sticks threatened us, women dashed from the crowd and spat at us. Stumbling, hands raised, we walked backwards. As we rounded a corner they did not follow. Our rosettes disappeared, we melted into the crowd at

College Green. Angry, shaken, I didn't understand it. After all, the Irish Party was legal. These were ordinary people not fascist mobs who roamed London's East End.

Later that year we tried to hold a public meeting under a street lamp on a quay near O'Connell bridge. We gathered around a platform from which Pat was speaking. With an air of confidence he declared, "The Communist Party has come to Dublin and it has come to stay ....." when from the back came a rush of people. Over went the platform and Pat with it.

"Into the Liffey, into the water with him." With a few well aimed kicks Pat free himself. Our attackers had been from the mission in Dominick Street Church where priests were fervently preaching about the 'antiChrist of communism'. This same group had tried to attack Madam Despard's Workers' College in 1932.

In Belfast when our United Irish Party tried to get a hearing it was the Protestant loyalists who gave us a bad time. Pat stood on the Custom House steps above a large crowd. "God Save The King" was sung over and over again. Though he shouted his loudest, the meeting had to be abandoned.

In late October we were asked to help in Willie Gallacher's election campaign in West Fife. The comradeship, excitement, hard work was a welcome change. When the result was announced we danced in the streets of Lumphinnans. Scotland had a Communist Member of Parliament.

I hated going back to Dublin and soon left for a job at King Street. Pat was to follow.

Chapter 21

King Street – 'Olga Petrova the Beautiful Spy' – Cable Street – Birth of my Son

Beattie Marks greeted me in her usual gruff way. "Look what the cat dragged in" but her smile was warm. Soon I was seated with the typists Mac and Una in front of the large open fire at one end of the cluttered general office where Beattie ruled. Hot cups of tea were passed around. I'd missed this easy friendliness.

"How long are you staying this time?" "For good. Anyone know where I can sleep tonight?" Beattie laughed. "Don't worry, we'll find you somewhere. Your job's with Johnnie. The girls have to fit him in and he's always grumbling."

From the first I liked Johnnie Campbell, then industrial organiser of the Party. As I entered his small room at the rear of the building he got up and leaned across the desk holding out his hand. "So you're the new ger-r-l. Welcome comrade." His accent was broad Scots.

Johnnie was a slight man with a sallow complexion and straight plastered down dark hair. He'd been wounded at Gallipoli and exposed to such severe frostbite that he was awarded a one hundred per cent pension. He also got a Military Cross for bravery. On his feet were heavy built up shoes and he walked with a limp. In slanting, sprawling wide-spaced lines Johnnie wrote his letters and articles. He rarely dictated.

Flitting in and out of the general office was a woman I'd not met before. She was blond, blue-eyes with an 'English rose' complexion but not the delicacy which most often went with it, rather a 'jolly hockey sticks' girl with a somewhat horsey face.

"Who's that?" I asked? Beattie's face hardened. "That's Olga. She's a spy." Mac protested, "How can you keep saying that? You've no proof of any kind." Beattie turned on her in anger. "But that's what she is and one day you'll all know it's true."

She held firmly to this belief and didn't laugh when we jokingly referred to 'Olga Petrova the beautiful spy', the name of a song popular at that time which we sometimes sang after Olga had left the room.

Olga had been a voluntary worker with the League Against Imperialism. Nothing was too much for her. As I understood it, Percy Glading, who'd been in India in 1925 and worked with the League, recommended her to Harry as a most efficient secretary. During my time at King Street Beattie never changed her opinion about Olga and later nearly had a breakdown because no one would believe her view of this woman.

But Beattie had been right all this time, for in 1938 Olga emerged as an informer for British Intelligence during the trial of a well known communist for espionage. He may well have been framed as many of us believed at the time, but the testimony of Olga, the chief prosecution witness, was crucial because of her years at King Street. Harry attended the trial each day. When it was over he sought out Beattie.

"His back was to the fireplace, he always stood like that." Beattie told me. "Then he went on, 'Go on, say it, say I told you so. You were right and I was wrong and I'm sorry for the pain it caused you'."

Many years later Charlie brought me a cutting from the 'Mail on Sunday' dated 29th July 1984. Angus Macpherson had interviewed 'Olga Petrova'.

> "The old lady held the green leather-tooled scrap book on her knee and smiled as she gazed at the title – The Mysterious Blond, Miss X ---. I could make out the date, 1938, and the headlines – Miss X's evidence. Spy ring smashed by Blond.

'Oh yes, that was me.' …….. She is now 77, married to a Canadian and a grandmother."

There was much more. And our Beattie, then also an old woman, was referred to.

"Something in her look told the MI5 girl that this woman suspected her ……. Fortunately the song 'Olga the Beautiful Spy' wasn't popular for very long."

Another vindication for Beattie, if one was needed, after so many years.

Pat arrived to take up a job with the London District where Ted Bramley was secretary. I found an unfurnished cold-water flat at the top of an old house in Petherton Road near Clissold Park. There was a large living room, a sizeable kitchen and up a steep flight of stairs two attic bedrooms. The rent was twenty shillings a week. Our furniture was minimal, tables, chairs, bookshelves, divan beds. Coconut matting in the living room, lino in the kitchen. A stove and wash boiler were hired from the Gas Company.

It was enough. We were both busy in the Party, out much of the time. Pat was deeply involved in East London, in anti-fascist work and the tenants' battles against slum landlords.

I was in Highbury Branch where I met Hetty and Reg Bower who gave support when I needed it and became life-long friends. Selling Daily Workers, speaking at street corner meetings, we were working towards a united front against fascism. For by the summer of 1936 Mussolini was in Abyssinia, Hitler in the Rhineland, Franco had invaded the Spanish Republic.

In Stepney, Bethnal Green, Shoreditch groups of black-shirted youths roamed the streets attacking Jewish children and old people, creating tension and fear. The fascists boasted of their growing numbers in the London boroughs, four thousand in Shoreditch alone.

And to prove this point Oswald Mosley announced that an anniversary rally on 4th October 1936 would start with a march through the heart of the Jewish east end, up Leman Street, past Gardeners' Corner and along the Commercial Road.

On that famous day I was among the tens of thousands at Gardeners' Corner determined to stop him. The crowd grew by the minute, a solid wall of people. We cheered for the driver who left his tram standing at the corner of Commercial Road and Leman Street. Mosley wouldn't get through this way.

Now and then the police tried to push their horses into the crowd and there were scuffles and fights. But for the best part we waited, singing, chanting, 'Stop Mosley', 'Stop the Fascists', 'They Shall Not Pass', the battle cry against Franco's fascists in Spain.

A triumphant roar went up as we learned that the blackshirts had turned tail and were marching through deserted streets back to the Embankment. People hugged and kissed each other. Some were in tears.

Pat had been in the thick of it at Cable Street to which the fascists had been diverted. Here a fierce battle raged against police and fascists as barricades were raised with the help of the local people. Mosley and his thugs met their Waterloo.

Police surrendered to our lads who didn't know what to do with them. Finally, they locked them in empty shops, first solemnly removing their batons.

It was a glorious day. We celebrated our victory in Victoria Park where Mosley was to have spoken.

In the late autumn of 1936 Harry Pollitt called me to his office. "They want you back. Said you were one of their best." "Moscow?" "Yes, back to your trips, travelling, seeing the world. He became serious. "They say they need experienced people who can cope when emergencies arise."

I stood looking at him, not answering. Puzzled he went on, "It's getting a lot tougher. Our people are having one hell of a time in Germany." Then I told him. "I'm pregnant." Harry beamed. "I'll be damned. Well, look after yourself now. Don't do anything silly." As I was leaving the room he called after me, "And see he grows up a good communist."

But I was not so happy. Forgetting the loneliness and boredom, I remembered only the excitement, danger and glamour of courier work. It attracted me more than having a baby. And yet .... I thought of that first one I'd lost. It would be good to have a child. When I told Pat he was silent, then said, "Don't go.

You've done your share of that work." It was not the reply I'd expected. Again the Party did not come first. For the next few days I thought of little else. Finally, I decided to have the baby, I was twenty-five, Pat was thirty-eight.

Six weeks before the baby was due I left work. My new friend, Ynys, an attractive Welsh woman who had joined our Highbury branch, was also pregnant and we were constantly together. May Day was near and I said to her, "It's always been a special time for me. When I was little mama tied a red bow in my hair because it was the day when workers all over the world would be marching with red flags. Let's go early, watch them pass."

"But we're not far off our time. Look at us." We laughed but I insisted. "I'll go alone if you won't come." As Ynys and I left for the Embankment I could not then have known that this year's march was to become the historic May Day of 1937 which identified the menace and threat of world war at a time when our boys were fighting in Spain.

At the front led by Bert Papworth and Bill Jones were the busmen in their white coats. Behind them thousands of people carrying a vast assortment of posters calling for peace, and an end to fascism, against Mosley and for Government aid to Spain. Some wanted an end to unemployment, others a shorter working week. Prominent were the red and gold and blue tasselled emblems of the trade unions. Co-operative Guild, Labour Party, Communist Party, Trade Council banners passed us. Bands played. Children waved from gaily decorated floats.

I started to sing an old Wobbly song – "If the workers take a notion – They can stop all speeding trains – Every ship upon the ocean – They can tie with mighty chains." Ynys laughed. "You don't know how funny you look standing, singing. Come on, let's go there. You'll have plenty of time later for your old songs."

Joking about our size we hurried to the underground. At Marble Arch we fell in behind our branch banner for the march into the park. I was enormous and so was Ynys though she was taller. As we neared the platform on which Harry Pollit was standing he gave a loud laugh and waved to us. The waiting crowd turned, cheered us on.

My son Pat was born at six in the morning on 5th June, 1937 at the Royal Free Hospital where Yny's David was born a week later. Now my world centred around this little creature whom I hadn't been sure I wanted. Cuddling him tightly I smoothed the down on his head, caressed gently the small face. A fierce surge of love for this tiny helpless thing.

The girls from the office came with a satin chemise for me and a woollie for the baby. I was touched. No one else had thought of giving me a present. "It's you who did all the work," said Wyn Brooks who some forty years later came to be known as 'the battling grandma of Charing Cross' during a NUPE strike.

They admired young Pat, agreed with me that he was beautiful. "There's never been such a wonderful boy, has there Frieda," laughed Beattie. I didn't mind the ribbing, they were good friends.

But then the talk turned to the outside world, Spain and our men over there, the Basque children refugees, the blackshirts who were continuing their forays into the east end. As they left Beattie said, "There's several jobs going when you're ready."

In the autumn I talked to Ynys of going back to work. She thought I was mad. "Why on earth do you want to do that? You're managing on Pat's money. It's much more comfortable being at home." I explained to her that I wanted to work so that to some extent at least I could be economically independent. Ynys nodded. "I agree it's nice to have money of one's own. But you can always get 'round a man and have what you want from him. You just need to go about it in the right way."

"That's not for me. I can't bend that way. It'd be demeaning to have to wheedle and coax a man to get enough money to keep the home going." "You won't be any better off working," Ynys retorted. "Knowing Pat, he'll give you less and keep more for booze and cigarettes. He won't help you at home either. You'll be doing two jobs and the responsibility for the baby will be all yours."

There was much truth in what she said. Coming from a home where the girls carried the coal scuttles while the lads sat with their feet up, Pat at no time even thought of taking on any of the housework or the care of the child. But I was too much immersed in the Party to be content with my present life. I had never contemplated staying at home and leading a housewife's existence. That I should work was part of my background and experience. The job I'd been offered with the International Brigade fulfilled both my need to earn money and to work for the movement.

And from my mother had come the strong belief that a woman must learn to stand on her own. "Get an education," she'd said, "So you can earn your living. If a woman works, can keep herself and her children, she can tell the man to go to hell." It sounded even better in Serbo-Croat.

I never did convince Ynys but when he was five months old I weaned Pat, found a day nursery for him. Later Marie, an unemployed Dutch communist girl came to live with us and looked after him. She had board and part of my salary. Young Pat became so fond of her I became jealous. Not till years later did I free myself of such possessiveness and acquire my daughter's viewpoint – 'the more people who love your child the better.'

Chapter 22

International Brigade

Blackstock Road on a Saturday afternoon. Through the crowded North Islington shopping street we pushed our way, offering leaflets, calling out 'Help buy medical supplies for Spain', 'Give a tin of milk for a Spanish child'. Posters on our handcart announced that we were the Aid Spain Committee. People stopped, asked questions. Small crowds gathered as we explained.

An older woman, handing over a tin of condensed milk, said, "Give me some leaflets. I'll collect from women at the Co-op. Where shall I bring the stuff?" We gave her the address of the local Labour Party near St Paul's road which was our base. "Soap too, we told her, "bars of soap if tins of milk cost too much." For these were the depression days.

There was indifference, abuse. We were told 'Go back to Russia'. Mosley blackshirts called us 'dirty Jews' and sometimes it nearly came to a punch-up.

On week-day evenings we knocked on doors but every Saturday afternoon it was into the streets, a mixed group of Labour supporters, communists, trade unionists, Co-op Guild members – the local committee.

When in July 1936 the Spanish generals, led by Franco, rose against the elected government, we had hoped the democracies would help the Spanish Republic. It didn't happen that way. Britain and France refused to sell them arms, adopted a policy of 'non-intervention'. The fascists had no such inhibitions. From Berlin, Rome and Lisbon, tanks and planes, small arms, flowed to their friends, the Franco rebels.

Among the first volunteers had been two members from our local Communist Party Branch. Impetuous, young, black-eyed Johnnie Stevens, anxious to have a first-hand go at the 'fascist bastards' and Ken Stalker, serious, determined and fully aware of what lay ahead.

A letter described days of training as they learned to handle machine-guns and rifles. Johnnie, tired of mutton or goat with beans, longed for fish and chips. They'd met local people, volunteers from many other countries, with whom they'd toasted the Republic in strong red wine. The letter ended, "These are our last days here. Soon we will be off to the front. Salud!"

In their first battle at Jarama in February 1937, Ken was killed. Johnnie was taken prisoner and shot. A Labour man wounded in the same battle, told us bitterly, "We were on the hills, fighting with old weapons while the enemy advanced with their new automatic rifles, machine-guns and artillery. We couldn't use our machine-guns, the ammunition didn't fit."

His first came down on the table. "Non-intervention – if only we'd had the right bullets that day." 600 British Volunteers went to the front on that raw February morning in 1937. By nightfall there were not more than 300 left in the ranks.

From the very beginning there had been Britons fighting the fascists in Spain, first singly, then in groups and finally as the British Battalion of the International Brigade. Here at home the recruitment of volunteers and the arranging of their passage to Spain was carried out by the Communist Party. It was to assist in this that I joined the staff at the offices of the Brigade in London, in an old house in Lichfield Street not far from the King Street Party headquarters.

For many months I was to work closely with R W Robson, former secretary of the London Communist Party, a tall, spare, north-country man with smooth iron-grey hair, a thin, lined face, thick spectacles. To me he had always seemed forbidding and aloof. How wrong I was.

This dedicated, tough former British Army sergeant kept beside him, for half a day, a lad in a suicidal mood who had wanted desperately to go to Spain but had been rejected on medical grounds. With deep pity Robbie talked to him and a less despondent young man finally left with the address of his local Aid Spain Committee.

On the reverse side Robbie had many times to deal with bereaved, sometimes hysterical relatives, especially mothers of those killed in Spain. Compassion, sympathy with their grief, he'd try to tell them how their sons had felt. He'd come out of these sessions tired and deeply unhappy. I found him easy to work with, considerate, competent. His quick, dry humour often defused difficult situations. He left the Party many years later, for personal reasons.

In the hands of Robbie, as we all came to call him, lay the responsibility for organising the recruitment for the International Brigade. The 'Scotland Yard volunteers' were only too obvious. Criminals also seemed fascinated by the prospect of escape abroad.

Half the men who went to fight in Spain were Communist Party members but here too Robbie had to be firm. He told us about two miners who, while being interviewed, kept their hands firmly in their pockets. Reluctantly, at his request, they drew them out. Each man had fingers missing from his right hand but both protested they could shoot just as easily with their left. A man of 63, veteran of two wars, bitterly claimed he was as good as any young fellow of twenty.

Frequently I travelled to Paris, taking and bringing back lists of names, funds and information needed for the smooth despatch of our volunteers to France.

Recruiting had been carried on openly until on 9th January 1937, the Cabinet decided to make the Foreign Enlistment Act of 1870 applicable to the war in Spain. People guilty of an offence under this Act were threatened with imprisonment of up to two years or a fine or both.

More difficulties came when the British and French Governments decided on a policy of 'non-intervention' and announced a system of control. For these reasons the previously open contact with Paris became clandestine.

Nevertheless, I continued my journeys, enjoyed this bit of excitement and escape, the railway trip, the channel steamer, being met in Paris. My first visit to French Party headquarters startled me. With its large, marbled foyer and elegant staircase leading to upper, carpeted rooms, it was very different from our narrow little building in King Street with its lino-floored rooms and stairs where two people could scarcely pass each other.

My small hotel was on the Left Bank and I retraced the steps of earlier days, found again the little restaurant where I ate veal escalope and drank rough red wine.

On my return a feeling of apprehension as I neared Dover but not once was I challenged. Outside our offices in Lichfield Street Scotland Yard detectives hovered conspicuously, threatened and followed the men as they came out. But it was difficult to stop British subjects from leaving for Paris on a week-end ticket for which no passport was needed.

On some Friday nights Victoria Station became a scene of excitement and merriment as busloads of men, haversacks on shoulders, greeted one another. The cry of 'comrade' could be heard from end to end along the continental platform. The frustrated plain clothes men, always an intimidating presence on these occasions, were unable to detain the 'trippers'.

Because the Spanish frontier was closed the men had a difficult and dangerous night climb over the Pyrenees before, exhausted, bruised and foot sore, they arrived in Spain.

The other side of our work was often harrowing. In February 1937, at the battle of Jarama, the British dead numbered nearly 150, with many wounded. More than 50 had been killed at Brunete in July of that year. Casualties occurred in old skirmishes.

When I joined Robbie in the autumn of 1937 these battles were past. But deaths still were reported and I became involved in the hard task of notifying relatives, dealing with the shocked and bereaved who came to the office, explaining about the Dependants' Aid Committee.

The outer office was often full of people, new recruits, returned Brigaders, worried relatives who hadn't had letters but most often wives and mothers of the dead. Some were hysterical, abusive, others quiet, numbed by grief. A few, reserved, calm, wanted their allowances from the Dependant's Aid increased.

In January 1938, at the battle of Teruel some 20 of our men died. During March and April, on the Aragon, at Calaceite and

Boadilla, another 20. Then suddenly in August 1938 the casualty lists increased day by day.

The International Brigades, now incorporated in the Republican forces, were to play an important part in the crossing of the Ebro River, going on the offensive into Franco territory. In this action nearly 70 of our men were killed. The letters started going out as each new list came in.

Phone calls without respite. Relatives, friends, crowded into the office. A young woman with a crying child in her arms waved a letter at me. "Check your list again. This came last week. He said he'd be home soon. Here, see for yourself." An old man grabbed my arm. "My grandson Joe, is he all right? We haven't heard for a long time."

More questions as people crowded round. I was near to tears when Robbie came from the outer office. He spoke loudly, above the din, "Please listen. I will see everyone. Try to be patient. I know how hard it is." The clamour stopped. People sat where they could, some on the floor. The phone went on ringing.

By early September the lists of casualties had almost stopped. People still came, though fewer than in the first hectic days of August.

One morning the outer door swung open. In strode a tall, erect, beautifully dressed woman, well over fifty. Before I could rise from my desk she asked in an imperious voice, "Who is in charge here?" I walked towards her. Looking down at me she said, "I want to know how my son, Lewis Clive, died." For a moment I was silent then answered, "Mr Robson has someone with him. If you would like to sit down I will ….."

My sentence remained unfinished as she replied, "I shall stand." And there she stood, elegant, haughty, as though holding her skirts away from the slightest contact with any of us. Her quick contemptuous glance around the bar, drab office rested briefly on the other occupants.

Four women sat in a row against the wall, quiet, subdued. Facing away from them, alone in a corner, sat a short, plump woman. She had been here yesterday and the day before. Her son too was dead but she refused to believe this. Convinced that new information, saying it was all a mistake, was on its way, she sat waiting. But already she grieved. Hugging herself, gently rocking, she repeated over and over again, almost as a sigh, 'aiya, aiya, aiya'.

Robbie appeared with a young woman, composed though her eyes showed she had been crying, "You understand, Comrade Robson, I had to come." He gently reassured her and she left.

I spoke to him quietly as he looked questioningly at the seated woman then at Lady Clive. He gestured to her and showed her into his room. Lieutenant Lewis Clive had been killed in August on the Ebro front. After the Republican forces had crossed the River Ebro, all the fighting centred around hill-top positions. It was in the battle for possession of the key hill, protecting Gandesa, that the British engaged in their toughest action.

And it was here, at Hill 481, that Lewis Clive's life had ended. He'd gone straight from hospital to resume command of No. 2 Company after learning that one acting commander had been killed and three others wounded. Oxford Blue, author, sportsman, Labour councillor, a tall cheerful courageous man, he had died bravely.

Except for the woman in the corner, the room was quiet. A lorry rumbled by. The excited voice of a newspaper-seller reached us, "Chamberlain to visit Hitler". I felt sad and angry. The government was making a deal with the Nazis while on the Ebro some of its citizens were fighting the fascists, and dying, as had Lewis Clive.

Lady Clive emerged from the inner office, walked towards the door, then turned and spoke. "I wouldn't have minded so much if he had died for the Empire. But for such a rabble ….." She swept out of the room.

My immediate resentment passed quickly. She was a mother, just like the little East End woman rocking in the corner. My own very new son had made me more aware of what they must be suffering.

Although continuing at the front during part of September the Ebro was the last battle of the British Battalion. The Republican Government had decided to withdraw the International Brigades. Our men would soon be on their way home. But both French and British Governments made their return as difficult as possible, so the Battalion did not reach England until 7th December 1938.

What a welcome they got at Victoria Station. A vast crowd had come to meet them. We shouted ourselves hoarse and as I cheered the tears were coursing down my face. There were short speeches of welcome from Clement Attlee, Stafford Cripps, Tom Mann, Willie Gallagher and Will Lawther, Miners' Union President, whose brother had died in Spain.

Commander Sam Wild replied to the speeches. A sharp order rang out. The soldiers lined up on the narrow platform. Banner bearers raised the flags of all countries who'd fought the fascists. The Battalion, led by three wounded men, was played out of the station by the drum and bugle bands, which were almost drowned in the tremendous cheer which went up from the crowd.

I remained at Lichfield Street until the office was finally closed.

By March 1939, the Spanish Republic had fallen.

Chapter 23

A Welcome Visit

As the boat train steamed into Victoria the passengers spilled out of the carriages. There she stood, a short sturdy figure still wearing that old black coat and upturned felt hat. She looked older, the face more lined, her hair nearly white, but under the thick arched eyebrows the same big brown eyes.

She saw me, waved. Above the hissing trains, the clamour of people, her voice called. I ran towards her. Three years since I had seen my mother. "I had to come to London to see you and the little one. I may never have the chance again once I get back to America."

That evening my mother played with her grandson, talked to him, made him laugh. The child crawled around the room, stood upright, holding on the lower bookshelves. As Lenin's 'State and Revolution' tumbled out she laughed. "Starting early, isn't he?" When we tucked Pat in after his bath mama leaned over and kissed him. "He's a lovely boy, take good care of him."

After supper we sat contentedly before the open fire. "So, you're leaving Russia for good. Why mother?" She looked away from me clearly reluctant to say anything which might upset the warmth between us. "Frieda, you've always been such a dedicated communist. It is so incredible what is happening over there that I know you won't believe me." "Believe what?"

Her head moved slowly from side to side. The large work hardened hand smoothed down her skirt over and over again, a familiar gesture when she was sad. She looked at me with pity. "People are frightened. Hundreds have been arrested in Tagil. A man is jailed on the orders of a high party official who the next day might be in the cell beside him."

"But they must be traitors," I burst out. "Look at the Trials. Zinoviev, Radek, trusted communists who betrayed the Soviet Union."

I had read the findings of D N Pritt and Dudley Collard, respected lawyers who had attended some of the trials and upheld them. That little sceptical smile of my mother's made me uncomfortable but she must be wrong. "Do you remember Matt Batic from East Pittsburgh? He liked you. Gave you rides on his shoulders, made you fly around the room. And always brought candy bars." I did remember him, a burly giant we ran to meet as he climbed the road to our house on the Hill. "What about him?"

"He went to the Soviet Union before we did. Wanted to help as he was a skilled engineer. A foundation member of our American Party, he joined the Russian Party straight away. Well, he was arrested early on, charged with conspiracy. They said he only came to Russia to spy. Do you believe that?"

"No, of course not. It must have been a mistake. They took him for someone else. Where is he now?" "God knows. We never saw him again. I'm very much afraid for your father." "Papa?" I was startled. "They'd never touch him. He's been a communist since the beginning." "So was Matt. I tell you Frieda, no foreigner is safe now. And the poor Russians. The N.K.V.D. seem to pick up communists before anyone else."

Mama explained to me that she was able to return to the States as she'd kept her American nationality, travelled regularly to Finland to renew her passport. But my father had taken Soviet citizenship and could not leave. "I hope I can do something for him when I get home. He took American citizen papers before you were born." "You mean papa wants to leave?" That couldn't be true, not from 'the land of socialism' where working people ruled. Such things did not happen there. "Yes." My mother's voice was hard. "He wants to leave, difficult as it may be for you to accept that."

Then she relented, took my hand in hers, patted it. "I'm not surprised at how you feel. I suppose I'd be the same if I hadn't seen it for myself. Sophie is doing what she can to get papa out."

Eagerly I asked, "But she doesn't think like you?" "She's seen a lot more than I have of what is happening. Some of her closest friends, Felik, Volodya – you knew them – were arrested. Felik either jumped or was thrown out of a window at N.K.V.D. headquarters. He's dead."

My mother was tired. Her shoulders drooped as she closed her eyes.

I was shaken by what she had told me. It must be a ghastly mistake. Only a few nights ago our Highbury branch secretary had spoken of the need for vigilance as the mighty Soviet Union was besieged from all sides by capitalist countries who hoped for its downfall. My mother did not understand this. Innocent people did get caught up when spies, traitors and 'enemies of the people' were being rooted out.

So in this Party jargon, these clichés in which we spoke at the time, I rationalised, recovered myself, swept aside what I could not understand. Yet I remained troubled by the horror of Felik's death. Nothing our secretary had said could justify that.

But it was not till 1956 after Khruschev's speech to the 20th Congress of the Soviet Party that I remembered with bitterness and shame how I had rejected the truths my mother tried to tell me.

During the rest of her visit neither of us spoke of this again. One evening we were still up when Pat came in full of drink. He clutched the door, gave us a broad foolish smile, mumbled 'enjoying yourselves that's good', then turned and stumbled up the narrow stairs to the bedroom. The door above slammed, a chair fell over, a thump as he landed on the bed.

"Is he often like this? It's hard for you, isn't it?" The acute humiliation I felt spilled over. Near tears I answered, "Tonight he's worse than usual. But till I saw you looking at him ……." I stopped and my mother said, "You've got used to it, haven't you?" "I scarcely notice. He's out such a lot, meetings all the time. And our friends are different, mine from around here, his from other parts of London. Yet we rub along somehow."

"That's because you don't care for him, which is just as well. You seem able to shrug it off. He was always a drinking man." This and the difference in our ages had been mama's main reason for opposing the marriage. But there was no 'I told you so' as she leaned over and smoothed my hair. "Maybe when we get settled in Pittsburgh you can come over. Tony's there and papa might be too, if we're lucky. All together again, like it used to be."

I shook my head. "I've my own life over here mother, an interesting job, lots of friends. In his own way Pat's fond of the boy. Don't worry about me, I can look after myself."

"But there might be a war. I think that devil Hitler wants all Europe. You and the child would be safer in the States." It was July 1938. As always mama was following events closely, deep in the Daily Worker and News Chronicle each day during her stay with me.

Despite my brave talk, my mother's departure left a great emptiness. It had been a long time since anyone had shown such love and concern for me. I turned to my small son, cuddled him, held him close.

Chapter 24

War

The sun shone, the sea sparkled as war came to Britain on 3rd September 1939. On Hastings beach my two year old son squatted at the water's edge, busy with pail and spade, chortled happily each time waves flowed over his feet.

From the promenade a man shouted, "We're at war with Germany. Chamberlain's been on the radio." Families gathered belongings, called children, left for the streets. I sat alone, watching my absorbed child spooning sand into his pail. What might happen to him now, to all of us?

Pat had returned to London two days earlier after the Germans had crossed the Polish border. We'd agreed I stay on for if it meant war London might be bombed.

The beach was nearly empty when I wiped down the tired toddler, tucked him into his pram. Slowly I walked along the front. A clergyman came up to me, very earnestly said, "Try not to worry. Trust to God that all will come right." I smiled up at him.

At last appeasement was over. Could Hitler be stopped from just marching in, taking what he wanted? How did the German-Soviet Non-Aggression Pact signed only a few weeks ago fit in now?

I'd had an argument with Pat about it. "It can't be true, not with that swine Hitler. They wouldn't do such a thing." "Calm down. It's clear they had to do that." "You must be mad. With the Nazis? How many communists have they murdered? How many Jews? That pogrom last November, did you see Picture

Post?" "As usual your feelings cloud your judgement. No matter how hard they tried they couldn't get a Pact with France or our government against Hitler." "But that didn't mean they had to do a deal with them. All these years we've put our guts into fighting the fascists, here, in Spain, all over and now ………."

Pat had interrupted, "Are you saying Stalin doesn't know what he's doing?" That had pulled me up. Angry, confused I'd said no more. I hated and feared the Nazis whom I'd seen in action in Berlin. Because of friendships made during my courier work I somehow felt personally involved.

The promenade was quiet as I sat on a bench, rocking the pram. No one to talk to, nowhere to go except the lodgings.

Yesterday's Daily Worker had written of 'a struggle defeat of two fronts', the military defeat of Hitler and the political defeat of Chamberlain. Then it went on, 'We are in support of all necessary measures to secure the victory of democracy over fascism'. Surely that meant we must go all out against Hitler and the Nazis.

On the Tuesday Pat made a flying visit, advised me to stay put. J.B.S. Haldane's book about German air attacks had scared us all. The child had to come first. I found new digs, got in touch with the small local Branch, none of whom I knew.

Harry Pollitt's pamphlet 'How to Win the War' was just out. Then on 12th October the Daily Worker announced that the war was 'unjust and imperialist'. A hurriedly convened branch meeting, a speaker from London. No baby-sitter but I couldn't stay away. My son slept soundly in his pram at the back of the large room.

I listened to the new 'line' straight from the Comintern in Moscow. The speaker, a stranger to me, waved a copy of the Manifesto which our Central Committee had issued on 7th October and spent most of his time quoting from it.

> 'The truth about this war must be told. This war is not a war for democracy against fascism…. It is not a war for the defence of peace against aggression… it is a fight between imperialist powers over profits, colonies and world domination.'

Young Pat woke and started to cry. I picked him up, cuddled him. As the speaker read out another bit from the Manifesto I sat up, incredulous.

> 'Nazi aggression has been checked and limited by the power of the Soviet Union and today Hitler sues for peace. It is the rulers of Britain and France who demand the continuation of war.'

The speaker finished. There was an uneasy silence, certainly no applause. The shock to others must have been as great as mine.

A man behind me jumped to his feet, anger on his face, in his voice, "What you've read out is nonsense. I fought in Spain where Hitler's weapons helped Franco kill some of the best people I ever met. They were communists, because of them I joined the Communist Party. And now you're taking Hitler's side, saying he wants peace. That's rubbish. Maybe from what you said the Russians for their own reasons wanted a pact with him. That's their business. Ours is to wipe Hitler and his Nazis off the face of the earth."

A few cries of 'hear, hear'. Questions to the speaker received evasive answers, many quotations from the Manifesto. At last it became clear that behind this abrupt 'turn around' of our Party was the German-Soviet Pact. The Manifesto was not to be the new 'line'.

The angry man strode to the platform, threw his membership card on the table and walked out of the room.

Depressed by it all, I sat still, my son now quiet in my arms. In this moment of crisis I felt unable to grasp this, let alone get up and challenge it. Again that phrase, which had been dinned into us, surfaced. Awful as it seemed to me, 'they must know best'.

But two comrades, Harry Pollitt, Secretary of the Party and Johnnie Campbell, then editor of the Daily Worker, to their credit, did challenge it, described fascism as the main enemy of the British people. Six months later it emerged that others of the Central Committee had also been opposed to the Comintern 'line'. On 8th May 1940, Palme Dutt, leading theoretician of the Party wrote in the Daily Worker,

> 'The debate in the Central Committee on this vital issue lasted over a period of nine days (with interruptions); it was the sharpest and most intense debate in the history of the Party; the viewpoint which was finally adopted in the October Manifesto was at first put forward by only a small minority and became a majority in the course of the debate.'

Pollitt and Campbell, who had for a time refused to accept the Communist International's interpretation of the war, were removed from the leadership of the Party and sent into the wilderness.

By late spring in 1940 I was back in London. My son was with my sister-in-law, Bella in Chesterfield. Pat and I moved into the two top rooms of a terrace house in Myddleton Square, Finsbury, just behind Sadlers Wells.

When news came that Hitler had taken Paris I wept. Where were Lois and Andre now? Communists would be hunted down, wiped out. Though I obeyed Party discipline my hatred of the Nazis was as deep as ever.

For whatever reason the Nazis had held off bombing Britain but now the 'phony war' ended as in July and August of that beautiful summer the Battle of Britain was fought out over the English Channel and the South coast. By late August a few bombs had fallen uncomfortably close in Stepney and Bethnal Green. On Saturday, 7th September 1940 East London burned. From the flat roof of our house we watched the distant flames in dockland. Over two hundred planes had come by daylight and the bombing continued till dawn.

"We'd better try somewhere safer, we're on the fourth floor," I said to Pat.

Most people in our square were making for the basement of a large unfinished building nearby which had been cemented over when war broke out. We followed. In this enormous space people put themselves down anywhere, seeking corners and walls to lean on. It was still daylight when the Air Raid Warden popped in. "Everything all right?" he called cheerfully. "You'll need to put a blanket over the entrance. We'll fix up a door later."

When the 'all clear' sounded we stumbled off to bed. The next day, Sunday, the sirens screamed again. This time we took food, books, blankets to the shelter. There was pandemonium inside. A nervous young mother tried to hush a crying baby while a snivelling toddler clung to her skirts. On the floor lay a groaning old 'grannie'. "I can't stand it, haven't slept a wink, shouldn't have come back."

Beside her knelt a much younger, attractive woman. "I've a drop of brandy here. Will you hold her up?" The old woman drank eagerly. Together we made her comfortable away from the noisy entrance. "She's from the bottom of the Square. Lives alone. They evacuated her but she couldn't stand all these green fields." I laughed then said, "Let's see what we can do for that young mum."

"She came back from somewhere in Suffolk. Said the landlady was so la-di-da she was afraid to move." "You seem to know a lot of these folks." "I've time on my hands. You're not long here are you. I'm in the same house, on the ground floor of number twelve." "Well, that's nice. I'm glad to meet you."

I liked her so it was something of a shock when Mrs Milligan, the baker's wife on our second floor said, "You shouldn't have been so friendly with her. She's one of them women." "What women?" I wasn't sure what she was talking about. "You know, what has men in for money and right in our house too."

I didn't reply immediately. Finally, I said, "But she's kind you know, helps people." Mrs Milligan sniffed. "That's as may be." The baker's wife knew all about her. "Regulars she's got mostly. Toffs by the look of them, come back every week." I saw the handsome woman watching this exchange. She smiled and I smiled back.

Pat, with some of the other men, had walked the length of the basement, examined the small rooms at the back. When they returned Mr Morgan, who knew them all, asked for quiet. "This'll make a good shelter. Electricity and water are laid on.

We can have toilets at the back. Mr Devine here has some good ideas. He suggests the small rooms be kept for older people and children when this main part gets too noisy. We'll all join as firewatchers, try and get other things a bit organised." "That's fine but what about a tea trolley?" a voice called. There was laughter, tension eased. The ack-ack guns pounded and bombs crumped in the distance.

For the next ten days the bombers came both by day and night. The shelter was never empty. A rota was drawn up for keeping the place clean, the tea problem solved with a primus stove and a large tea urn. The men got pails, sand, shovels, helmets from the authorities.

One night as we sat chatting a man shyly offered to 'give us a tune'. He turned out to be a professional singer. So began our evening entertainment with more volunteers and sometimes a sing-song in which everyone joined.

Nell Vyse, the potter, had a medical student son, John, who offered help if it should be needed. A shelter committee was set up and I became secretary, regularly keeping minutes.

The builder, Mr Morgan, agreed with Pat that the roof of the basement should be reinforced. Professor J B S Haldane, an expert on shelters, came to inspect it. Yes, another layer of concrete would be an improvement. A deputation went to the Town Hall but nothing came of it. Some people, alarmed that a direct him might destroy the basement, went off to other shelters.

After the first few days those of us in jobs somehow found our way to work. I was in Kuperstein's clothing factory in Soho at this time and often walked all the way for after a night of heavy bombing transport wasn't available. Many left work early, rushed home before the evening blitz.

In the shelter the talk was all of damage, where the bombs had fallen, what had been destroyed. It was all by word of mouth for the papers carried nothing. One could believe only what one saw though that was more than enough as in the mornings we picked our way among broken glass and tangled hosepipes.

Fire watchers from our shelter patrolled our square, dealt with small incendiary bombs. One night when a large batch fell many of us dashed out of the shelter to help. It wasn't only the danger of fire. We might become a well-lit target for a bomb.

Myddelton Square was bombed one night, the flats opposite sliced diagonally. The church in the middle protected us from the full blast though our windows were blown out. We were away for the evening but Idris Cox who was staying at our place got the full strength of it. Sadly, some of our shelter friends were killed.

In mid-November the blitz on London eased as the bombers made for the provinces. People drifted away from the shelter though a bad raid might bring them back. But for some the initial alarm and fear gave way to a kind of fatalism. "If it's got your number it'll find you," they'd say and go home for a good night's sleep. We also stopped going as fewer sirens sounded during the nights.

Chapter 25

Manchester – Birth of my Daughter

In late November Pat was given a new job in the Party. "Lancashire this time, they want me to go there as the new District Secretary."

Pat was very pleased. 'They' were Bill Rust and Palme Dutt who from the beginning had been solidly behind the Comintern position on the war. To them Pat had given every support.

Since his deportation he had often felt himself undervalued by the British Party, confined to minor positions. In the United States he'd led impressive strikes, been a national leader of the unemployed, co-ordinated and directed the work of the Party in the tough coal and steel area from which I came. His new assignment was more in line with this American experience, would give him wider scope and more authority.

Pat went on ahead while I stayed behind to tie up ends and supervise the removal, not easy in war time. The plan to pick up my son in Chesterfield had to be abandoned for in late December Hitler's Luftwaffe heavily bombed Merseyside, followed by blitz-scale raids on Manchester a few days before Christmas. However, by mid-January we were together in temporary accommodation in the council house of a comrade on the Wythenshawe estate, a good way from the centre.

The Party was calling for a People's Government and peace. Herbert Morrison ordered the suppression of the Daily Worker for allegedly sabotaging the war effort. But for a time I ignored the outside world, concentrated on my three and a half year old son. I realised how much I'd missed him and listened with delight to his endless chatter. I found a house in Longton Avenue and we moved to West Didsbury.

At night if the siren sounded I'd find my son standing in his cot, arms outstretched, eyes still closed, waiting to be lifted into the Morrison shelter which had been installed in our living room.

When Hitler invaded the Soviet Union on 21st June 1941, everything changed. "It's a shock but at least now we'll both be on the same side," I said to Pat with some elation. His reaction was confused. "You forget it's the Soviet Union that's being attacked." Then more hesitation. "But of course this changes the character of the war. When a socialist state is involved it can no longer be considered an imperialist war. It becomes a just war." Convoluted reasoning, I thought but answered, "Call it what you like, we can go back to where we were before that Pact, get stuck into the war effort, help defeat those strutting Nazi swine."

Churchill promptly declared support for the Soviet Union and on 12th July an Anglo-Soviet Mutual Aid Pact was signed. A passage in a letter dated 8th July 1941 which Harry Pollitt, once again General Secretary of the Party, had sent to every member read: 'In supporting the Churchill Government we do it whole-heartedly without any reservations.

From this point on there was a change of mood, a release, as we plunged into full support of the war. Paramount in the thinking of some of our leadership must have been the need to support the 'land of socialism'. But as Pollitt and Campbell had shown earlier, hostility against the Nazis was still very strong as they faced us across the narrow English Channel.

I could no longer stay at home, needed now to be of use in what had become my war against those mindless brownshirted bastards who had killed Hans, murdered so many communists and Jews.

When I spoke to Pat he nodded. "What about full time for the Party? We're losing people all the time to the forces and industry." This was something new for him. I waited, what had he in mind? He went on, "We need people who can speak, organise. You've had some experience of that. I think you'd be alright."

Was the position so desperate, for never before had he regarded me in this way. "How about it? The boy can go back to Bella or to my mother. The girls can look after him." I shook my head. "I've a better idea. What will I earn?" "She's got three kids of her own. Did us a favour. It's not fair to ask her again. He can go to Fortis Green School. They charge around three pounds a week so my salary will cover that. And far better for him if he's at school with children his own age and good teachers."

I didn't tell him my other reason. Pat's mother was bent on getting the lad christened in the Catholic church and had tried to get Bella to do this without consulting us. Though my sister-in-law had resisted, if he were to go back the pressure would continue.

A progressive school like Fortis Green, run by the educationalist Beatrice Tudor Hart was ideal. It had been evacuated to Aspley Guise, near Bletchley, far from large cities or bombs. My friend Hetty Bower's child was there as was Ynys's David. Housed in an old mansion, bare but comfortable, with extensive grounds, it had a staff of kindly people, Quakers, pacifists, teachers who had brought their own children.

An old stable had been converted by parents into sleeping quarters, rough but adequate. Here once a month I stayed, arriving late on Friday for a long weekend. It was a precious few days when my son and I played together, roamed the nearby woods and fields. As a special treat we'd have tea in the village. Parting was always a wrench as Pat cried, clung to me. I'd walk away from the gate blinded by tears. On one occasion I went back for a forgotten umbrella. Pat, a huge apple in his hand, was happily chasing after the other children. "The little monkey, and me thinking he's as miserable as I am." I laughed and was also reassured.

Later I learned there had been gossip about me among some of the Party women in Manchester, 'only too anxious to get rid of her kid, can't be bothered to look after him like we do'. Bessie Wild too got some of the flak as did others with young children who nevertheless took part in the public work of the Party. The 'Sisterhood' was still years ahead though in many ways we worked together and helped each other.

During these months there was excitement, tension, urgency in the Party. Our desire to help the war effort made us allies in the Ministry of Information campaigns to increase production. With Jessie Coughlin, Mollie Mandell, Bessie Wild and others, I toured in the Ministry vans, spoke in factory canteens, through loud hailers in the streets, urging more production and, as the war developed, the opening of a second front.

Much of this was done through the National Assembly of women which the Party had started nationally. We worked with well-known Labour and Co-operative Guilds women, Mrs Knight, Mrs Bamber, Mrs Page. Housewives, women from the factories, joined the Assembly.

Twenty of us went to London to the Soviet Embassy taking greetings and pledges from factories for the embattled Red Army. When Mrs Churchill came to Manchester a deputation visited her, a textile worker stepped forward, asked her to tell Mr Churchill we wanted a second front now. She smiled, made no reply. Sir Hartley Shawcross, then Area Regional Co-ordinator for the North West, politely received an Assembly deputation, explained the difficulties. We told him this did not satisfy us, a second front was needed. It was during this time I became a member of the Party District Committee and later the Lancashire Women's Organiser.

Much to our delight the ban on the Daily Worker was lifted and publication began again on 7th September 1942. The fiercely fought battle at Stalingrad, where Hitler's advance was halted, made the Russian Army popular among the British people. That hard tenacious struggle went on for months until the German Field Marshall Paulas surrendered with all his remaining troops on 1st February 1943. This victory rubbed off on British communists and we suddenly became so well liked that it didn't seem real. The membership of the Party in our area increased three-fold.

At this time the authorities were having a hard time finding billets for the many Americans who flooded into Lancashire. They came to our street and a large beefy man, a mess sergeant in charge of stores, moved in with us. Large lumps of butter, chickens, hams were dropped by him on the kitchen table. "You mustn't do this," I said, "It's not right." "Look lady," was his answer, "what's good enough for the officers is good enough for me. You should see the size of the parcels they take to their billets. So why can't you have some too?" I thanked him, said no more. We ate well during his short stay.

Things were now better between me and Pat as we worked together, sometimes spoke from the same platform. So I was not upset when in the spring of 1943 I became pregnant. Pat whistled when I told him. "That's a bit of a facer. Are you sure?" I nodded. "The Doctor confirmed it today." I waited for his reaction though I'd already made my decision. "It's up to you really, isn't it. You'll have to look after it." Lightly I answered, "Well it'll be yours too you know."

He shrugged. Not for a moment did he see himself in any way responsible for the upbringing or care of the child. He called himself a 'good provider' but children were a woman's job. I knew well how his mind worked. It was useless to have a row about it. "I'm going to have the baby and I hope it's a girl. I've never wanted Pat to be an only child." Unfortunately, in the third month of pregnancy I was rushed to hospital where I had a miscarriage. When they told me I didn't cry or sob, just sat there with tears streaming down my face.

"What's the matter, luv?" from the woman in the next bed. Wiping my face I answered, "I've lost the baby."

Her eyes opened wide as she looked at me almost with disbelief. "You must be the only one in the ward that's sorry. Most of us are here after we tried to get rid of them. Four I've got. It's enough." She spoke bitterly. Hollow-eyed, drawn, she looked more than her thirty years.

When I was fit again I returned to work but decided that as soon as I was stronger I'd have another child. Young Pat came home to stay. He was past six, could read well but his writing was illegible. I panicked, felt guilty, accused myself of neglect. He'd be miles behind the others at the local school. I need not have worried, he quickly adapted and did well.

An older comrade, Mrs Huyton, came in to help on a paid basis. She took over some of the house-keeping too. Friendly, cheerful, she was so reliable that I had no worries about the boy, though I did try to spend time with him, kept weekends free.

On 6th June 1944 came D-Day, the Second Front was opened. In the east the Russian armies were advancing. It had come at last, the joint action which was to end the war.

Pregnant again in August 1944, I was determined that this time nothing must go wrong. After a few months I went on half-time and eight weeks before the child was due I stopped work altogether. When I knew the baby was on its way, I phoned Mrs Huyton who had agreed to look after little Pat. Enid, a good friend came quickly at my call.

"Shall I get a taxi?" she asked. "We'll walk. Withington Hospital isn't far. It'll help the birth." Enid confessed later that she had been very anxious during that walk and as it transpired, with some reason. The nurse who examined me said, "You've cut it pretty fine, haven't you?"

Two hours later, at five o'clock in the afternoon of 30th April 1945, I watched as the little thing popped out, mottled, wrinkled, lean. "It's a girl," the nurse said and I beamed with satisfaction. Within a few minutes my daughter was in my arms. I'd been conscious all the time, helped the midwife.

Pat came that evening, admired and went. I was tired, glad to be alone, to sleep, full of delight with my girl child. Margaret was no trouble, took to the breast, sucked, slept, paid no attention to me. The nurses were lenient, the cot by my side. I picked her up, cuddled her, played with the tiny fingers. Ten days later I was allowed home and Pat was introduced to his sister.

In the interval, on 8th May 1945, the war in Europe had ended.

❦

The 1945 election in July was the culmination of our political work. From the time the election was announced in May, Pat had tirelessly nursed the constituency of Preston, where he was Party candidate. He was very popular among the 'rank and file'.

Pat enjoyed people, he enjoyed being liked. Charming, witty, a quick pat, a friendly laugh, this had always been his way. At the same time he had this enormous capacity for encouraging others.

When things became really tough his tremendous courage at times almost justified the old slogan at which we now laugh, 'there is no obstacle which a Bolshevik cannot overcome'. It might have been written with him in mind.

As a platform speaker he ranked with Pollitt and Gallagher in the old time oratory which touched the emotions and quickened the pulse. Hecklers were positively encouraged, for he was always ready with a witty or stinging reply which brought laughter, cheers or jeers from the crowd. 'The best agitator in the Party' was how Johnnie Campbell years later described him to my son Pat.

As the election drew near the children and I joined Pat in Preston. An elderly couple, long time communist Jimmie Steward and Mrs Stewart were our hosts. Jimmie was also Pat's election agent and put his small open-topped Austin 7 at his disposal. Labelled by Pat 'the people's car' it became a familiar sight in Preston with the upper half of him sticking through the roll-back roof and young Pat's head just above the opening. Julian Amery, the Conservative candidate, went around in a large sleek car and this Pat exploited to the full.

At this time the Party was seen as a new force in British politics well outside the ranks of its traditional working-class supporters. The Preston committee rooms were packed with volunteers and helpers of all kinds.

Nevertheless, I was taken aback when one day a well-dressed woman approached me, cooed at Margaret in the pram, then asked, "Tell me Mrs Devine, how could my husband become a parliamentary candidate for your party? He's a very able man, he'd make a good politician." Politely I tried to explain that our candidates weren't simply people who wanted a career in politics, but I'm afraid I left her somewhat confused.

On the hoardings large posters showed a smiling, handsome younger Pat. At a factory meeting a woman said, "That can't be him, not a bit like his pictures." But as they listened, they warmed towards him, clapped with the rest.

Margaret, two months old and breast fed, limited what I could do though most evenings I was able to leave her with Mrs Stewart. A reasonable speaker, I attracted considerable, often curious attention. Young Pat, eight years old now, sat in the front row. He went everywhere with me or his father and so got an early introduction to practical politics.

And what a campaign it was. A 'tour de force' one comrade described it.

Harry Pollitt came down for a brief tour of Lancs constituencies. He was billed with Pat and a large hall booked. The crowd was enormous. But to my amazement they did not respond to Harry in the way I'd expected. These were not the Lancashire 'old faithful' but people new to our movement, most of whom knew us only in our war time role, whose friendship for the Russians dated from the Battle of Stalingrad. There was polite applause for Harry. Then enthusiastic clapping, cheers, with some people rising from their seats as Pat got up to speak. It was him they wanted, him they'd come to hear.

It is a small wonder then that a kind of unreality developed, a firm conviction grew among some of our own people that we'd win this election. How could we lose with such a campaign?

So voting day came but the results could not be announced till the forces' votes came in. In late July we learned that Pat had polled ten thousand votes yet lost his deposit. Though a much smaller vote in the constituency of Stepney made Phil Piratin a Member of Parliament, he was the only one of our candidates, except for Willie Gallagher who retained his seat, to be elected. Our vote was good but not good enough as Labour was returned with a resounding majority.

The results were a shock to me and most communists. We had expected more victories. Clearly the proposal put forward by our Party before the election to participate in a coalition government, including the Tories, was a complete miscalculation. So involved had we been in the war effort, we failed to see that with the ending of the war old realities would assert themselves.

The pressure for change had been building up even in the early thirties. Now after a 'people's war' the electors had decided there must be a 'people's peace'. By the end of the war five and a half million men were under arms, forty percent of the working population was directly involved in war production. Food and clothing rationing, British restaurants, joint production committees in the factories, air raid wardens, fire fighters, shelter leaders – all this had been carried through by ordinary people. Working people had achieved dignity and power, it was impossible now to ignore calls for 'fair shares'. There had been an implicit contract during the war that things would be better in peacetime, the Beveridge report in 1943 and Butler's Education Act in 1944 were part of this.

In the Forces the Army Bureau of Current Affairs made Beveridge known wherever troops were gathered. The 'Forces Parliaments' were immensely popular, with wide and free ranging exchanges of opinion. At home too in the papers, pubs, wherever men and women gathered, what Britain would be like after the war was being discussed.

And so in 1945 the people voted for profound social change and for the Party they thought would be most likely to provide this. The 1945 election was of tremendous significance as it ushered in a completely new era in British history.

We were not the only ones who had misjudged the mood of the people. A bitterly disappointed Churchill had confidently expected to again be Prime Minister. Attlee, the Labour leader, was overwhelmed by the tremendous majority of nearly one hundred and fifty seats for his Party.

In the aftermath of the election 'lessons had to be learned' and Pat was faced with a strong challenge to his methods of leadership. He was accused of diverting forces and resources to Preston at the expense of Rawtenstall, another Lancs constituency. It was asserted he lacked flexibility, had shown poor judgement and failed to create collective leadership.

In the end Harry Pollitt came to Manchester and met with the District Committee. While 'objectively' weighing the pros and cons, Harry let it be known that it was time for the Lancashire Party to have a 'native son' as its leader. This was decisive for as secretary of the Party nationally and himself a Lancs man, his prestige among the members was enormous.

I'd been aware there had never been much love lost between Pat and Harry. In retrospect it is possible that previous incidents may well have influenced Harry's advice. Some eighteen years earlier, before I knew either of the two men, Harry had been sent by the Comintern to mediate in the bitter American Party factional struggle. Pat was at this time a member of the U.S. Party's Central Committee. At some stage he fiercely challenged Pollitt as an 'outsider'. The passion prevailing at that time between the two factions was shown when, at this juncture a Yugoslav miner jumped up, pulled out a knife and said, 'shall I get him Pat'.

Also, Pat became Lancashire secretary when Harry was 'out in the cold' in 1940. This may well have rankled with him.

What later came to be called 'the cult of personality' was reflected in the style of both men.

At the meeting I spoke up for Pat, said he should be judged not only on the election but for his work during these years when the Party had greatly increased its membership and influence. But the result was a foregone conclusion as Pat lost the vote.

It was a bitter blow for Pat. But there was one high peak which reflected his capacity and popularity. At the National Congress of the Party in November 1945 the election of the new Executive was by a 'free vote' rather than for a circulated list recommended by the outgoing leadership, usually referred to as a 'panel'. I later learned that 'unofficially' the District Secretaries had been mobilised to see that certain people, including Pat, should not be considered. Though his vote was lower than before he was nevertheless elected onto the Executive Committee.

The job Pat was given in London was National Organiser of the newly formed People's Press Printing Society whose aim was to win support for the Daily Worker. District Committees of the Society were formed, but they never took off. He became National Bazaar organiser for a time then went on to other work on the paper.

This gradual 'demotion' caused frustration and anger, led to a renewal of his heavy drinking habits and a great deterioration in our personal life.

He'd never been a good husband but he certainly was a very good communist and I've always felt he got a raw deal. The Party Leadership could have used him more wisely and fruitfully. An able man, a skilled organiser and agitator, his place should have been in the mainstream of Party life not on the sidelines.

As usual Pat had gone ahead and I was left to supervise our move to London. The flat he'd found was in Hackney.

With Margaret in my arms I walked through the top floor of an old house which stood among the debris of the heavily bombed East End. The two bedrooms were small, the living area a narrow kitchen with a coal fire range. Tacked on the back was a closed porch with a butler sink and gas stove. I looked out at the tiny yard. A lean black shape ran across, disappeared into the rubble.

Rats. I shuddered, turned on Pat, "Couldn't you find anything better?" He shrugged. "It's the bombing. I was lucky to find this." Then defensively, "Downstairs is a doctor's surgery. You'll need to clean it, that was the condition. But there'll be no rent." I was speechless. Didn't I have enough on my hands with two children and the need to make this squalid place habitable. The boy looked at me imploringly, he didn't want a row.

And Margaret had to be fed. I said quietly, "That means you can give me an extra pound, pay for my work as a char. God knows we'll need it." Pat looked startled. Clearly that had not been his intention.

On Monday morning I found a school for Pat, the old forbidding three-storey kind. The still bricked up ground floor had been used as a mortuary during the war but the second and third floors, with their high ceilings, were spacious and light, cheerful with the noise of children.

Before we'd been in Hackney a week, Robin Jardine knocked at our door. Robin had been manager of Collets Bookshop in Manchester and our lodger. A Scot, son of a surgeon and an educated mother who did 'good works', he'd taken a Classics degree then gone on to theology. Though qualified for the ministry, his early social work in the slums of the Gorbals had turned him to socialism.

In his early forties, shy, quiet, Robin was a bachelor. Round shouldered, slightly balding with pale blue eyes behind thick glasses, he was one of the many thirties intellectuals who had looked to Russia and spent two years there working on the Moscow Daily News. On his return he joined the Communist Party. He was a 'loner' read a great deal, walked in the hills around Manchester, but also became part of the family, sharing our festivities. Sometime before we left Manchester he had come to London for a job on the Daily Worker.

Now he came into the small kitchen where a fire burned. Nine-month-old Margaret was in the play-pen holding on to the bars. "Sit down, Robin. Keep Margaret company. You'll have to excuse me, the nappies are on the boil. Then I'll make a cup of tea." Through the open door of the porch I watched him playing with the baby, cooing and smiling. As we drank our tea I moaned about the inconvenience of the place, the extra work, the lack of fresh air for Margaret unless I took her out in the pram. "I can do that for you. Victoria Park's not that far."

"Marvellous." Margaret loved going out, beamed as I tied on her woolly hat and strapped her into the large pram in the hall below. I watched as Robin pushed her along the dingy street. When they returned Margaret's cheeks were rosy and Robin was laughing. "She kept me busy picking up the toys she flung from the pram, though it was a great game."

I fed the baby, put her down for a nap. "Stay for lunch. Have you time? The boy'll be back soon from school." It was a happy meeting for young Pat was fond of Robin. He told him about his new teacher and of course about the mortuary. "Some of the boys say the ghosts of people who were killed by bombs are walking around down there. But I don't believe that." They smiled at each other. After lunch the lad went back to school.

Robin sat quiet then slowly, hesitantly began to talk. The recent Christmas haunted him. He had a room in a colleague's house but though they celebrated downstairs, Robin had not been asked to join them. Christmas eve, Christmas day, Boxing Day. He'd never before felt so alone. "I walked through the deserted streets, mile after mile. I didn't want to go back to that empty room."

For the first time I realised the depth of his loneliness. As he got up to go, I said, "Come again tomorrow if you've time and take the baby off my hands. She enjoyed it today." He came everyday when he was free, took Margaret to the park, waited for Pat's return from school, brought some of his rations to help out with lunch.

I asked him to look after Margaret while I went house hunting. Always I returned in despair. "To get anything half-way decent we'll have to look right out somewhere and I only know inner London."

It was then Robin suggested he buy a house in the suburbs and we'd share with him. My spirits rose. "Can you afford it?" House buying was far beyond our means. "I was left money by my father. Still have some of it." I discovered later he'd been left forty thousand pounds, a fortune in those days, most of which had been given to the Party, the paper and Labour Research.

Pat welcomed the move and, in the spring of 1946, we were settled in Ilford. After Hackney everything seemed spacious, the back garden like heaven with an arch of roses and honeysuckle just outside the door.

Before we moved Robin handed me a letter, writing what he found hard to say. He thanked me for helping him at a time when in his despair and loneliness he'd seen little point in going on living. I hadn't thought of it that way, he'd helped me enormously with Margaret.

With Robin as a real part of our family came an insight into a different world. His extensive library lined the walls of his room, it included childhood books, among them Kipling's 'Just So' stories inscribed 'To Robin Ian Jardine from his Dad. 31st October 1902'.

Robin introduced the children to tales and books I'd never heard of. Alice, the Mad Hatter, Sam Pig, Peter Rabbit, Till Eulenspiegel, became familiar to them. An Oxford Junior Encyclopaedia appeared. As Pat grew older he read the Arthur Ransome stories, Bevis, the Story of a Boy, which became a favourite and remained so for many years. Soon came an introduction to the Brontes, Jane Austen, George Elliot, Trollope, Hardy, Shaw and so many other authors of whom I'd scarcely heard and which I also avidly read.

To young Pat he spoke freely about his days as an ambulance driver in the first world war in which his brother had been killed. Robin took Pat to the boat race, cycling in the countryside. Boxing day treats, Peter Pan, Toad of Toad Hall came from him.

Robin Jardine

What he brought to our family made an impact, influenced me as well as the children. Robin, we were later to realise, was important in our lives.

But of course it worked both ways. From us Robin got companionship and certainly the love of the children. This extended even to the older grandchildren who knew him well. He lost much of his shyness in later years and became quite a loquacious man who laughed easily and seemed happy enough.

☙

My decision not to seek work at this time was because of John Bowlby's book on Child Care, emphasising the great need of a

From left to right Pat, me and Margaret in the garden at Betchworth Road, Ilford

young child to be constantly with its mother. He was just as wrong as Truby King before him, for Pat, who had been much away from me, was far bolder and more confident than Margaret in the early days. But for the next five years, till Margaret went to school, I stayed at home.

However, I was almost immediately absorbed into the Ilford Party, called on to chair or speak at factory gate meetings, ended up on both the London and later Essex District Committees.

Evictions at that time happened often and while Robin looked after Margaret, I spent one morning sitting on a mattress in the Ilford Town Hall with an evicted woman and her children. She wanted to go to the Ilford half-way house, much superior to that dreadful place in St George's Lane Hornchurch, which she'd once already experienced. Run by the Essex County Council, it was like a large warehouse with little privacy for anyone. The police couldn't shift us but a priest came and she and the children went with him.

My first, and as it turned out still my best woman friend, was Jean Dalziel who lived nearby. Together we wrote, stencilled and gave out our leaflets in the early morning to the men streaming into Howard's Chemical Factory in Ilford Lane.

I ran for Council, became, in the local papers, the 'notorious Mrs Devine'. But on one occasion, when I shared a platform with Conservative and Labour candidates, I got the best of it. Though I spoke of local issues, these were the cold war years and of course, as we did in those days, I strongly defended the Soviet Union against the stand of the United States.

The chairwoman tried to stop me. An irate Tory in the audience shouted, "How dare you attack our ally and anyway what do you know about America or Russia?" With great aplomb, or so I hoped, I answered, "I am an American and have lived for two years in Russia." These words appeared in the local paper and the chairwoman was also taken to task for her attack on me which, they wrote, was not her function.

I still savour that small triumph after all these years for at that time it was mostly hard slogging work. And the local police were certainly overzealous towards us.

On a sunny Saturday afternoon I was near the market in Ilford Lane asking passersby, men and women, to sign a peace petition. Two policemen who had been watching me for some time came over and suggested I stop bothering people.

"Has anyone complained?" "They don't have to. We just want you to stop." The voice was sharp now. "I can't see I'm doing any harm. Only those who wish to do so sign the petition." The largest of the two leaned menacingly towards me, "Lady, the next time you accost a man I shall put you in for soliciting." "Why you ..." I didn't finish. He might have arrested me for swearing at a policeman. I stood still, seething with anger at their insolence. But I stayed, spoke only to women or couples. For a time the police watched, then strolled away.

Although we were not subjected to the ferocious persecution engendered by McCarthy in the United States, it was a difficult time for communists.

Chapter 26

Back Home to Pittsburgh – The F.B.I.

Early in January 1948 my mother wrote, "Frieda you come for a long visit. We want to see our grandchildren and we'll pay your fare. Make it soon, it's been so long."

I read the letter again and with growing excitement realised there was no reason why we should not go. For the first time in many years I wasn't working. Margaret would be three at the end of April, no longer a baby. Pat's eleven plus exam was early in March.

Home. To see my parents, show off my children, be away for a time from shortages and queues. Pat was at one of his many meetings but that night I waited for him. I needed his approval for legally I could not take Margaret and Pat out of the country without his signature. Merry, full of bonhomie, he agreed it was an excellent idea.

By late March we were on the Queen Mary, economy class. A lift took us to our small air-conditioned cabin in the bowels of the ship. This enormous vessel was like a small city with its shops, bars, cinemas, and swimming pools. Though I was very seasick and a nursery coped with Margaret for part of the day, Pat roamed the ship, found first class and the crew's quarters. For a boy of eleven it was a great adventure.

As we neared shore we were all on deck straining for a first glimpse of the Statue of Liberty. From Pennsylvania Station in New York we set out on the long train journey to Pittsburgh.

My brother Tony met us, rumpled the children's hair. "Well you guys, what do you think of America?" Then holding me by the shoulders he examined my face. Never one to mince words, he told me the truth. "You look too old for your years, tired and worn. It must have been a hard war for you." He picked up little Margaret, carried her to the car. The luggage was stowed and we were off. Pat's eyes were everywhere.

Then Tony spoke of our parents and what had happened since their return from Russia. "Don't be disappointed in the house. It's nothing as big as our old place. But it's a palace to what it was when they bought it. Our father arrived from Russia without a dollar to his name. But he was working the day after he got back. With war in Europe there were plenty of jobs for skilled men. They saved every penny, bought this little neglected house with a lot of overgrown land around it real cheap. They realised what it could be like.

Dad was sixty when he returned from the Soviet Union, our mother two years younger, almost a time for retirement. But they were penniless, without home, furniture or goods. They worked real hard and after they got this place pop and I practically rebuilt the interior, so it's comfortable."

The house in which my parents lived after their return from Russia 1940/1941: Nasa Kuca

We were nearly there. Mama stood on the porch. We cried, laughed, hugged each other. Then she scooped up Margaret and put her arm around Pat. "What beautiful children. They look good in spite of that war. But you Frieda." She turned to me shaking her head. It was true. I had given little thought to my appearance during these past years. My face was pasty, my hair in plaits around my head. I'd gained weight. The suit was 'utility', the coat made from a blanket, the shoes flat and sensible.

Anton, Tony's son, came home from school. He was almost as tall as his dad. My father arrived, still the thin spare man I had known, moving quickly and purposefully though his face was grey after a day's work. He hugged and kissed us all. A drink, a change of clothing, and we were shown the garden.

He held Margaret's hand as we walked through the narrow paths. "You should have seen this place when we came. It was like a jungle, had to be cleared before we could start planting." Now it was burgeoning.

To accommodate us the front porch had been made an enclosed room just large enough for three beds. Shading our windows was a large cherry tree. I marvelled. How had they done all this at their age?

During the first week my mother served meals such as I'd not seen for many years. Large roasts, platters of fried chicken, bowls of goulash, always large helpings of vegetables. On that first evening Pat looked at me in amazement. "What a lot of food, mum." He'd never before sat at such a table. My mother smiled. When given two eggs at breakfast Margaret asked, "Both for me? Mama nodded, laughed as Margaret, tucking in, said, "Aren't I a greedy one?" The saying went around the family and my brother repeated it to me thirty years later.

On the Sunday my Uncle Louie and his wife came to dinner. There was talk of the past and much laughter. But as we became serious and political mama got up, looked out of the window. "Not so loud. Someone might be listening."

Then turning to me, "You don't understand, Frieda, what is happening in this country. Since that Churchill of yours made his speech over here things have been getting real bad for our kind of people. We have to keep very quiet."

Louie, flushed with wine and excitement, smiled at her, "Maria, you worry too much. Today we've had intelligent conversation. It's like the old days, remember, when we spoke of everything."

As I read the American papers I began to understand my mother's concern. The great witch-hunt of the House of Representatives Un-American Activities Committee, which was to reach its peak a few years later when McCarthy became chairman, was already operating.

By this summer of 1948 three government committees were conducting separate 'hearings' on Communists in the labour charges of 'conspiracy to teach and advocate the overthrow of the government by force and violence'. The battle of those who were to emerge as 'The Hollywood Ten' had begun. The Mundt-Nixon Bill, requiring registration of communists and members of 'Communist fronts' was soon to be introduced into the Senate. It was becoming dangerous not only to be a communist but through 'guilt by association' to be in any way friendly with one.

Russia, wartime ally and friend, was again as in the early twenties the main enemy. My parents' long stay in that country made them vulnerable.

When a phone call came asking me to attend at the Federal Building in Chestnut Street my mother, though worried, was not surprised. "Why should I go because of a phone call? Who are they, what do they want?" "It's the F.B.I. I've been there, and papa and Tony. Although they haven't bothered us for a long time now." "But you never wrote me about this." I was shocked by my mother's matter of fact attitude. "Such things you don't put in letters. You'll have to go or they'll come for you. It's best the neighbours don't know."

At the narrow end of a table sat my interrogator, a nondescript man, grey hair, grey suit, an easily forgettable face. He placed me on his right so that I faced him diagonally. Lying in front of him neatly arranged were files, letters, papers.

In a soft quiet voice he began, "Why have you come to the States?" I looked at him in surprise. Wasn't it obvious why I had come? "To visit my parents." "Are you sure that's why you've come?" "Well, why do you think I've come?" Sharp now, "I'm asking you." "Then I'll tell you again, to visit my parents, show them their grandchildren." "To see friends?"

"Of course, to see friends. I was born and raised here, you know." "What kind of friends?"

I turned my head to the left and stared at him. What was he getting at? "All kinds of friends, from Mt. Troy School, Allegheny High, University. From the neighbourhood where I lived. My old teachers if they're still around and remember me." He shrugged impatiently. It wasn't the answer he wanted. I was angry now. "What is it you want of me and why am I here?"

The quiet manner changed as his next question shot out at me. "Are you a communist?" "Yes." "Have you a card?" "Yes, I belong to the Communist Party in England." "What links have you with the American Communist Party?" "None." "But you know people who are communists, don't you? You go to their social evenings and picnics." "I've been away from this country for sixteen years. I don't know what might have happened to people during that time." "What about your parents?" "You must ask them, mustn't you?"

This sparring went on for some time. At length he said, "I hope you'll be more friendly on your next visit." It was a dismissal. At the door I stopped, turned around, "Who's your stool pigeon?"

His questions about social gatherings made me aware that someone was giving him information about my movements. He didn't answer. We looked at each other and I walked out. In spite of my brave front, I was shaken. He was trying to tie up my visit with the American Party, perhaps hatching some sort of frame-up.

Without knowing it I'd already met this informer, Cvetic at a fundraising picnic of the progressive Yugoslav newspaper, 'Glasnik'. Pat had run up to me holding a bottle of cherry cream soda. "The man wouldn't let me pay for it. Said I could have as many as I want." "Why should he do that. They won't make money that way. "Because I'm English, he says he likes to hear me talk. He asked a lot of questions about England."

Later, passing the soft drinks stand, I stopped to thank this stranger for treating my son. At this time the ordinary little man with an out-size beer belly made no impression on me.

Cvetic had for long been a hanger-on at all progressive functions and was a member of the Communist Party, recently joined. A few years later he was to become a star performer for the Un-American Activities Committee, chief prosecution witness in anti-communist trials, fingering people of every kind, steel workers, miners, teachers, musicians, wildly inventing hair-raising evidence where none existed.

The press and radio made him a celebrity. Ghost writer Peter Martin wrote articles for the Saturday Evening Post which were published under Cvetic's name. From these a film was made, "I Was A Communist For the FBI. In this widely circulated movie an old friend of mine, Steve Nelson, Communist Party organiser in Pittsburgh, was shown as a murderer.

Sometime later when Steve was being tried under the Smith Act, Cvetic was the chief prosecution witness. Defending himself, Steve forced Cvetic to admit in court that this accusation in the film had no basis whatever.In fact, as this quote from his book, 'The Twelfth Juror' shows.

> "Did you ever see murder committed in the Communist Party?"
>
> After much hedging Cvetic said, "No I did not ... I know of no murders in Western Pennsylvania. If I had, I would have reported them to the police authorities."
>
> To this Steve retorted, "Yet you didn't hesitate to sell a scenario to a movie company for twelve thousand dollars which inferred murder was committed by myself."

Of such were McCarthy's 'heroes' made and this was the man who informed on me in Pittsburgh.

More calls from the Federal Building came within the next weeks. On one occasion this nameless man kept me for well over three hours, returning again and again to the same question – who were my communist friends.

I could not then have known how important to my interrogator was the 'naming of names', later to become a key question in the McCarthy hearings. But my previous experiences in the movement and my courier work had made me very much aware of the need for silence, never to implicate anyone else in what was happening to me.

My mother, father and brother were called in. So that we might know what was asked and answered, we compared notes.

In what turned out to be my last session with the grey man I decided to find out why I hadn't been granted the work permit for which I'd applied. I needed a part-time job for I was completely dependent on my parents.

The man looked surprised. "You've no right to work in this country." "I was born here," I protested. "The permit was necessary only because I'm not permanent." He shook his head. "You're not an American citizen any more. You lost US nationality during the war. There was a new law and you came under it. No chance of you getting a permit." "So, you're telling me I'm British not American." For the first time he laughed. "That's right. No longer under the protection of the USA."

Ignoring his next question I sat quite still as I absorbed this startling information. If what he said was true, and it must be, what was I doing in the Federal Building? I stood up.

"Hey you, sit down. I'm not finished yet." "If, as you say, I've lost my American nationality then you've no right to question me. I won't come again. If I receive another call I'll go to the British Consul in Pittsburgh. I'm prepared to take this right up to the Ambassador. And there's always the newspaper." I walked out and he didn't try to stop me. Neither I nor my parents heard from him again during my visit. To my mother I said, "If I'd known my coming would bring you this trouble I'd have stayed at home."

She put her arm around me, "We knew it might happen. But it was more important that we see you again and our grandchildren. Forget the FBI. Let's enjoy these few months we have together."

Soon after my arrival a cousin had made a snide remark about my plumpness. It was true and it annoyed me. Angrily I'd retorted, "Maybe if you'd been through six years of war, three more of continued rationing and had two young kids to feed you might not be so free with your remarks. The children needed what protein was going and we lived on stodge."

Abashed, he apologised. In spite of all the food I made a determined effort to lose weight, eating only meat, salad and fruit, and lost more than a stone. An altered hair style, fashionable longer dresses, high heeled shoes quite changed my appearance.

The children settled in well. Margaret was claimed each morning by the little girls of the neighbourhood while Pat and his new friends explored, roamed the near-by woods, made dens.

I took Pat to the blockhouse at the junction of the Ohio, Allegheny and Monongahela rivers, the old fort which a hundred years earlier had been the gateway to the west. But I went alone to the Hill to stand once more outside the old farmhouse which for so many years had been my home.

At Allegheny I found my old English teacher, Miss Heck. "Frieda, is it really you? Come into my room. Ah those wonderful days when you were here. Children wanted to learn then. It's all changed." Perhaps it was Miss Heck who had changed for she was old now, in my eyes. It was nearly twenty years since last I'd seen her.

"I meet you brother sometimes. He tells me you're a much travelled woman, China and Europe. Will you speak to the girls in my Travel Club. We'll announce it right through the school that an old graduate will tell of her adventures. We'd get a good attendance."

Remembering my FBI interrogator and 'guilt by association, I said, "Maybe it's not such a good idea. You knew, didn't you, when I was at school here I was a communist. I still am. It would do no good at all to you if I were to speak to your club."

Her face flushed, "I know your family, fine people. If I were younger ...." She didn't finish her sentence. "Miss Heck, you were one of the best teachers I ever had, that's why I came back to see you. I've never forgotten your classes, the fun we had and the help you gave us." We talked then of the old days, laughed a great deal. She stood at the door as I left and when I looked back at the end of the corridor she was still there.

My mother put me off when I asked how my father had managed to get to the States. They'd never written about it. "Wait till Sophie comes. She got him out." Sophie told me my father had been tipped off by a friend in Tagil to clear out at once as he was on a list for arrest. A deeply disturbed man arrived at my cousin's door in Moscow. How was it possible that he, devoted to the Party, had been denounced as 'an enemy of the people'. He had not expected this. It might happen to other people but not to him.

"Your dad posed a real problem," Sophie went on. "As you know he'd given up his American passport and was a Soviet citizen. Luckily, I still had influential Russian friends who hadn't yet been touched. You met some of them at Mira's party, remember?" I nodded. Big burly men who drank Vodka like water.

"Within a few days I was given a document, very official looking, with signatures and seal. My friend said, 'Tell him to leave right away and use this as a passport. It should work. If not ......' he shrugged his shoulders. It did work and he got back to the States."

Sophie waited for my reaction. I was utterly confused. "How could they make such a stupid mistake as to suspect him?" "It wasn't a mistake, not with him or the others. It almost seemed Stalin was trying to destroy the best communists." "You can't mean that." My indignation did not surprise her.

"Listen to this then. You recall your friends from 'upstairs' in the Comintern who arranged your trips?" "Yes, Masha, Volodya, the chauffeur, a nice friendly man. What about them?" "All were arrested. And the charge? Contact with foreigners." "But that's ridiculous. They couldn't do their work if they didn't mix with foreigners or make arrangements abroad."

She nodded. "A lot of foreign communists were taken from the Luxe. Lenchen, Kurt, you know them. Czechs, Austrians, Yugoslavs, many from the section I worked with, people who couldn't go back to their countries. Most Americans and British weren't touched.

I shook my head in disbelief. I couldn't accept that such things happened in the Soviet Union. Yet it was not some stranger, but my cousin telling me this.

"I was there, Frieda. I saw it. It was unbelievable yet while it was going on it seemed almost normal. My friends kept a packed suitcase and warm clothes ready. Each day we went the rounds to see who was missing. At the same time there were more parties than ever before, every evening, a sort of 'live and be merry for tomorrow you may die'. And how true it was for many. I try but I find it very hard to forget."

I sat looking at her. I was incapable of comprehending, accepting this horrible truth she was unfolding to me. Stalinism had touched my powers of reasoning just as physically it had touched its victims in the Soviet Union. I turned on Sophie, accused her of slandering that great country. Sadly she replied, "I wanted so much to talk with someone who'd lived there, knew the people I'd known. They killed Felix, you know. But it was stupid of me to expect you to understand."

When I did understand after 1956, I shuddered at my intolerance and ignorance at that time. Though my cousin and I became friendly again, this episode still returns to haunt me.

Sometime in June came the news that Yugoslavia had broken with the Soviet Union. My father and the older Yugoslavs were shocked and dismayed. As the American Party laid down 'the line', denouncing Tito as a Trotskyite traitor, they made their choice. Though Yugoslavia was their homeland, Russia was the country of the only successful workers' revolution. But it was a bad time for them.

We were returning to England in mid-August so towards the end of July mama began planning a large farewell party to be held outside the house in the large stone area below the garden. My mother was never happier than when our extended family got together. Some of these raw young people who had come to the States before the first World War were successful business men and women living comfortable lives. Few were interested in our kind of politics. Now there were children and grandchildren, a real 'gathering of the clans'.

Friends as well as relatives came. We ate enormous amounts of food, drank red wine and slivovitz, sang, danced the Kolo. It was a real Yugoslav 'knees up'.

Then it was over. Good-byes were said, tears shed. I was never to see my father again.

In her next letter my mother wrote. "The morning you left the FBI man phoned. He wanted to make sure you had really gone."

Family portrait during America visit:
Back row John (my sister's son), me, Tony (my brother)
Paula (my sister), Anton (my brother's son).
Front row Sebastian (my father), Margaret (my daughter),
Maria (my mother), Pat (my son),
Gus (Paula's husband)

Chapter 27

A New Life

At last, I had acted to end the personal crisis in my life. Tense, somewhat apprehensive, I sat with my friend Ynys in her living room waiting for the phone to ring. It came, Pat's response to my letter saying I'd left him. There was an explosion over the wire. So you're back. I'm coming right over. That whore you're staying with has put you up to this."

I didn't repeat this to Ynys. She'd told me herself of the affair she'd had with Pat during the war while I was evacuated with my son. When Pat discovered I knew about it he could not understand my continued warm friendship with Ynys. This abusive outburst angered me, strengthened my resolve.

"He's on his way breathing fire and brimstone. You'd better leave us when he gets here." "Are you sure you'll be all right?" I nodded, "He shouts, that's all." But Pat was quiet when he arrived, spoke in an authoritative, confident way. "I know how you must feel. When you come back there'll be a change. It'll work out this time, you'll see." "I've heard that so many times, Pat. As you well know these last years have been worse than anything before." "That's just not true," he retorted and continued to put forward reasons why things would be different.

An hour dragged on in alternate bursts of talk and silence. He realised he was making no impact on me, his confidence slowly drained away. From long experience I knew that what he promised wouldn't happen and even if it had, unlikely as that was, I just didn't want to live with him anymore.

At last I stood up. "There's no point in going on with this. I'm not coming back whatever you say. We should have parted long ago." His manner changed as he shouted "We'll see about that. You'll be back all right. I'll make sure of that." The door slammed. He stormed out of the house.

Ynys came into the room. "Brandy, you need it."

It was true. Though I had remained calm throughout, my hand shook as I took the glass. "He won't leave you alone. It's only the beginning." "I'm not going back, Ynys, no matter what he does. It's been a long time coming."

My visit to the States had been a kind of catalyst. What I had seen and experienced made me again aware that there was an unnecessary frustration and tension in my life.

Pat had changed little with the years. Though I'd become a mature woman with ideas of my own he still too often saw me as the malleable young girl he'd married. At times we'd worked amicably together, as in Lancashire, but he'd never regarded me as an equal. Pat did not discuss but pronounced and in his superior way dismissed my opinions when they did not coincide with his. There was no real communication between us, just the familiarity which years of marriage brings.

All this became clearer to me soon after my return and I wondered that I had lived in this way for many years, with no affection or consideration of the kind my father still showed for my mother. Yet I had no thought of leaving at that time. The children were young, we depended on his salary as I was not working. Life continued as before. For years we'd both gone our own ways, his friends mainly in London where he worked, mine in Ilford. I again became active in the local Party and as soon as Margaret started school I got a job.

But my new awareness made me less tolerant of his drinking. While in a responsible post he'd kept it under control but in a job which gave him little personal satisfaction he was rarely sober when he came home. I tried to talk to him in the mornings but he did not accept that he drank too much and became very angry.

The care of the children, a full-time job and my absorption in political activity made it possible to muddle along. But these heavy demands began to tell on me. I tried to get Pat to do jobs around the house and in the garden which most men usually do. I also needed to go out more in the evenings. Furious rows broke out over this but Pat never gave way. I refused to share the same bed, slept on a mattress, had to fight off feelings of hopelessness and defeat. My unhappiness was apparent to young Pat, approaching seventeen. One day he burst out, "Why do you put up with it, mum? Why don't you leave?" "Yes, I've thought of that. But where can we go? How will we live?"

For months I'd worried about this. Would we be able to manage on the seven pounds ten shillings I earned? Robin, in whose house we lived, could not escape the increased conflict. When I told him I intended to end it somehow, he offered me a loan which made it possible.

I'd know I could not tell Pat I was leaving him, discuss arrangements for the children in any 'civilised' way. So, while young Pat was hitch-hiking on the continent with his mates and Margaret and I were on holiday with Ynys and her daughter Janet in the summer of 1954, I sent my letter.

As Ynys had said, Pat did not give up but told woeful tales to mutual acquaintances, leaned on women friends who I believed would be on my side. But then women didn't leave men in those days, it was usually the opposite. When the growing gossip threatened to become a public scandal, Bob Stewart, head of the Control Commission at Party centre, called us both in.

To Pat he said, "Frieda has a right to leave you if she wishes. She is not your property." Then sternly he warned us, "You are communists in the public eye, known in your locality. If either of you brings the Party into disrepute over this you will be expelled."

At that time expulsion seemed to both of us 'a fate worse than death'. I now had a breathing space in which to start my new life.

Robin's loan and a local authority mortgage made it possible for me to buy the house my son and I chose by matchlight in the late afternoon of a dark October day. It met our requirements, that it should not be in Ilford yet reasonably near to Pat's grammar school, big enough to accommodate lodgers to supplement our income.

The spacious rooms with their high ceilings were larger than any we'd ever lived in. There were other benefits which we came to appreciate in the spring. We did not face another house but a large expanse of back gardens full of greenery and blossoms.

Flowering trees were everywhere, in the street, in gardens both front and back.

A helpful Barking Council surveyor and a friendly woman estate agent made short shrift of the paperwork and even before my mortgage became final, I was handed the keys so I could assess and measure. Although newly decorated the house showed the ravages of multi-occupation when bombed out people had lived there during the war.

Now I worked as never before to make the place habitable. But for my good friends Bob and Jean Dalziel who had taken young Pat into their home, and Ynys who looked after Margaret, I don't know how I'd have managed. For I lived in Chelsea, had a full-time job in Barking and the house was in Wanstead.

The workmen were soon in, turned on electricity and water, installed a gas stove in the scullery, gas fires, meters and rings in the rooms I was to let. Carpenters replaced worm eaten wood as stipulated by the surveyor. At week-ends Ynys, the children and young Pat came to the house. We measured for curtains and floor covering, made long lists of furniture for every room, chose colours and patterns.

I had Robin's books and shelves and a few pieces he'd asked me to store but everything else had to be bought as economically as possible. Each room except the scullery and kitchen would be a kind of 'bed-sit'. At last we got it all together and almost our final job was to stain floorboards around small carpets in the larger rooms.

As young Pat and Margaret moved into their new home we celebrated with our friends. Excited, happy, we surveyed our sparsely furnished rooms. They looked good for Ynys was an artist and I'd taken her advice about colours and materials. By February I had let two rooms, one to a nurse at Wanstead Hospital and the other to an elderly woman book-keeper.

My abrupt departure to Chelsea had cut me off from the Ilford party. When I phoned the office to say I was again in the district, I had a visit from Charlie Brewster, Essex District organiser.

The months went by and I resumed work in the Party. Charlie found many reasons why he needed to consult me and came often to the house. One day I looked at him as though I'd never seen him before. He was tall, broad shouldered. Dark brown hair rapidly receding, a strong nose but it was his blue eyes under long dark lashes which drew me. Suddenly I found him very attractive.

"Frieda, you fool," I said to myself, "He's more than ten years younger than you and everyone knows he's a confirmed bachelor." But the chemistry was at work in both of us and soon we became lovers. So, in my early forties, for only the second time in my life, I again experienced how sweet sex could be when accompanied by tenderness and consideration. We were truly in love and within a year Charlie moved in with me.

Deeply involved in our different ways, Charlie and I talked about what was happening, agreed to disagree on occasions, but always as equals. We found time to paper and paint, improve the house, plant grass where potatoes had grown during the war.

Our love life was more than satisfactory. We were happy with each other, much to the annoyance of some who had decided that with such an age difference our relationship couldn't last.

In 1959 Pat decided to marry again and now wanted a divorce which he'd previously refused to consider. But it was I who must pay for it. By this time Charlie and I had been living

Charlie Brewster (my husband)

Wedding photograph:
Front row centre Charlie Brewster and me.
Front row from left second Miss Betteridge (our lodger),
third and fourth Iris and Leo (friends),
fifth and sixth Charlie's father and mother.
Front row from right first and second Joe and
Kay Ball's children, third my best friend Jean Dalziel,
fourth from right Margaret, fifth from the right (next to me)
Ann Long (Pat's ex-wife).
Back row left: first Bob Dalziel (Jean's husband),
second George Brewster (Charlie's brother), fourth Pat.
Back row right first and second Kay and Joe Ball (friends),
third – Robin Jardine, fourth Mike Long (Anne's brother)

together openly for some years and found it amusing when in the divorce petition, I became an 'adulteress' and he a 'correspondent'. But I was very glad that it was finalised, that I was at last 'free'. We were married on Boxing Day of that year and celebrated with family and friends. My son, in his last year at Oxford, had married Ann Long in that same year.

Chapter 28

Horrifying Revelations – A Watershed

When at the private session of the 1956 Easter Congress of our Party Harry Pollitt spoke of 'confessions of guilt made under pressure in the thirties' trials', of the errors made by Stalin during the war, I turned to Charlie, sitting beside me. "What is he talking about? Do you hear what I hear?"

Charlie just shook his head as Pollitt went on about the fabricated evidence against the Yugoslav Party. "We now withdraw our previous attacks on Tito and Yugoslavia including the statement by myself at the London membership meeting in 1948 and James Klugman's book 'From Trotsky to Tito'.

Harry spoke of the recent Soviet Party's 20th Congress which he, Palme Dutt and George Matthews had attended. They and Daily Worker correspondent Sam Russell were excluded from the secret session. Subsequently they were told about Khruschev's attack on Stalin.

The impact of this on the delegates to our Congress was too sudden. There was disbelief, bewilderment, horror and more questions were raised than could be answered. A resolution was passed that 'we request the Soviet Party to provide us with a full text of Khruschev's speech'.

It was only afterwards that criticism and discussion became louder as our leadership received a flood of correspondence. The Daily Worker published letters of enquiry and protest. In a note attached to a letter from Professor Hyman Levy, the editor of the Daily Worker agreed that charges of antisemitic persecution in the Soviet Union were 'essentially correct'. But there was great dissatisfaction at the lack of information. We wanted to read Khruschev's speech.

It was first published by the United States Department of State on 4th June 1956 and subsequently in the New York Times. I read it in the London Sunday Observer. Its authenticity was accepted by the Political Committee of the Party in the Daily Worker on 22nd June 1956 though that paper never published it.

The shock was enormous. Disbelief gave way to pain, grief, sleepless nights. It must have been so the world ove,r as communists everywhere were suddenly confronted with the nightmare of Khruschev's revelations, the forced confessions, torture, executions.

In October 1956 came the Hungarian uprising and with it a complete disintegration of the Party in Hungary. Soviet troops intervened. The Daily Worker refused to print Peter Fryer's dispatches from Hungary. About a third of the staff resigned, among them Gabriel the cartoonist and Malcolm McEwen, Features Editor.

I wrote to our Political Bureau saying that if the Hungarian people didn't want a Soviet type regime, then it shouldn't be forced upon them by an invitation. Droves of people now resigned from the Party, among them leading trade union officials and intellectuals. In the branches the Executive 'line' on Hungary, that the invasion was necessary, was being hotly debated. Gone were the days when what the leadership said was accepted without question. At emergency branch meetings held to endorse the Executive's position, out of the five thousand who voted more than a thousand were against and four hundred abstained.

The Suez crisis broke about the same time as Hungary. It was with relief I turned from my soul searching to join the massive Trafalgar Square protest against the actions of our own government. After the meeting, ten abreast we marched up Charing Cross Road. Ynys was on one side of me, Charlie's mother on the other as we linked arms. Each time mounted police charged us we dived into doorways, laughing at our escape.

At the Easter 1957 Congress we expected a full explanation from our leadership as well as a prospectus for the future, outlining the path our Party would now follow. But what we were offered did not satisfy me or some of the others. Despite trenchant challenges by Hyman Levy, Ford 'bell ringer' Johnnie McLaughlin and Christopher Hill, the vote for the Executive was overwhelming as the old 'discipline' prevailed. For the first time in my life, I voted against.

Christopher Hill, later to become Master of Balliol, was quoted in The Times (23.4.57). "We have been living in a world of illusions. That is why the 20th Congress came as such a shock. We had not been prepared for this by our leaders. We lived in a snug little world of our own invention."

I agreed with that. A far deeper change was needed than had been put forward at Congress. When the platform announced that more than seven thousand had resigned from the Party a voice called, "Yes, some of our best comrades are gone." The reply was, "They were not our best comrades otherwise they'd still be here with us." Among those who had left were Doris Lessing and Edward Thompson. Christopher Hill was soon to follow.

I was saddened when Willie Gallagher, against the wishes of the platform, defended Stalin, recalled his concern for our Party when he and Willie had walked in the Kremlin gardens. Labouring under great emotional stress, he appealed to us all to believe him when he said these tales of Comrade Stalin could not be true. Tears streamed down my cheeks as I realised that this fine old communist, a dear friend, seemed incapable of grasping mentally the new terrible truth that had burst upon us.

We, who'd been in the Party in the thirties, were asked by more recent members why we had so easily accepted that old honoured Bolsheviks who helped make the revolution could become the 'traitors' of the Treason trials.

How to explain that for us the world at that time had been a frightening place. The Spanish Republic was soon to be defeated by the Franco fascists, Hitler each day gained strength in Germany, Mussolini was on the rampage in Abyssinia, Oliver Mosley's uniformed black shirts appeared on London streets. It was entirely plausible that there should be traitors in the only 'socialist' country in the world, unbelievable that Stalin could be wrong. British lawyers had accepted the authenticity of the trials, the accused had confessed.

But to understand our view of the world at that time cannot exonerate our unquestioning acceptance of Soviet and Comintern pronouncements as we substituted faith for reasoning. A younger comrade had turned on me accusingly, "You were there. Why didn't you see what was going on?"

When the Luxe became a quiet place and heavy red wax seals went up on doors of empty rooms as devoted comrades, leading members of their Communist Parties, such as Copic of Yugoslavia, Popov and Tanev of Bulgaria, the Hungarian veteran, Bela Kum, Eberlein from Germany and so many more were sent to their deaths, I wasn't there for I had returned to England in the spring of 1935.

I was a very unhappy woman, remembering with guilt how my mother and cousin had tried to tell me about what was happening. I'd turned on them, refused to believe, though they were speaking of what they had experienced. And my father had been denounced as 'an enemy of the people'.

Now I had to settle accounts with myself, make a personal reckoning. My most fundamental beliefs, my whole life had been intertwined with that of the Soviet Union. Clearly, I'd been wrong. It was only another totalitarian dictatorship. Had anything of socialism remained after Stalin's brutalities and crimes against the Party and the Russian people? I disavowed this possibility, felt with anguish that I'd wasted my life.

My son Pat patiently listened for hours to my expressions of anger and disgust with myself, reasoned gently with me, slowly brought me 'round'.

"Mother, don't feel that way. Much of what you did was right and good. Free speech fights, work with strikers in the States, when you risked your life because you hated what Hitler's Nazis were doing, your work in Ilford against evictions and for decent housing, collecting signatures against the H bomb – this wasn't because of the Soviet Union but because you believed it to be right. Your parents were socialists before there was a Russian revolution, because they wanted a just society. We all believed the

Soviet Union would show the way. We were wrong. But don't be so hard on yourself."

Charlie added his views, agreed with Pat. They convinced me to stay on and work for a real change in the Party of which I'd been a member for so many years of my life.

So, I remained, joined in the battle which was raging in our Wanstead branch. On the one side were those who believed the Party should be liquidated, on the other the 'old guard' who minimised Stalin's errors. In between a group of us were highly critical of what had happened but took the middle ground, wanted to fight for drastic change and much more democracy in our own Party. In the end we won though a member of the 'liquidationists' left.

But I had changed. The happenings of these months had for me been a watershed as I turned into a new channel that energy which had for so many years been wholeheartedly devoted to the Party.

I decided to continue my education, become a teacher. But after having my application forms turned down by twelve colleges, sitting a three hour Clearing House exam on English language and usage, and hearing no more, I gave up hope.

Out of the blue in late October 1957 came a request from Goldsmiths' College that I attend for interview. Everything had to be settled within days. The Director of Education for Leyton to whom I applied for leave encouraged me. "Yes, of course you may have time off for this interview and others which will follow. We'll keep your job open."

Very different was the reaction of my immediate superiors in the Salaries Department. "You haven't a chance, especially not at Goldsmiths'. That's the best college in the country, part of London University." He was wrong and I was accepted. After a short chat with the Warden, I was handed over to a rather austere elderly woman. Among other things she questioned me about my children.

"My daughter is at Coborn Foundation for Girls," I tried to make it sound impressive. She nodded, "A good school. And your son?" "He's at Oxford, Balliol." At this she smiled at me.

"Do tell him he must visit St Hilda's, dear old St Hilda's." I've always believed that clinched my acceptance.

There were few mature applicants and at forty-six I was one of the oldest. We were regarded with some suspicion and before the English Department would accept me, I had to write a long essay on my son's reading habits. With the help of Robin and young Pat I produced a very impressive list, tracing childhood reading into adolescence, then maturity. Even so, I was put into the 'least able' group with only one instead of two main subjects. As it turned out, I got a First with a Distinction. But at the time none of this mattered as I settled happily into my studies.

Pat was accepted by Balliol and got a State Scholarship. His National Service over, he went to Oxford as I started my training.

I had given up a secure job with a reasonable salary. My grant came to one pound a week, a huge drop from the seven pounds, ten shillings I'd earned. It was essential I get my Teacher's Certificate and I worked hard.

Each day I had two hours travel. The running of the household remained in the main my responsibility though my seventy five year old mother, who'd come from the States for a

Visit to Balliol College Oxford to see Pat:
From left Robin Jardine, me, Margaret, my mother Maria, Pat

year's stay with us, was an enormous help. At the same time, she needed my company and attention.

Margaret was the one most affected by this change in our lives. Though eight years her senior, the brother she adored had been a friend. Just entering adolescence, she needed more time than I gave her. I was not sufficiently aware of this and my vague feeling of guilt was banished by sheer pressure of work and study. In my busy, hectic life I lacked the insight to grasp how difficult the past years must have been for her.

But when, many years later I told her that I'd felt guilty about her then, and when I left Pat, she laughed. "Mother, women are always made to feel guilty. It was the best thing you ever did, for both of us. If you hadn't left my father, life would have been miserable. I admired you for becoming a teacher, it made me feel I too could do that."

The years seemed to fly by. Our family was growing. In just over five years Pat and Ann had three children, Cathy, John and Michael. They were settled in Manchester where Pat was a lecturer in Economics at the University. Margaret had married Gideon Ben-Tovim and had one child, Ruth. She was teaching in Newham but they were soon to leave London when Gideon became a lecturer in Sociology at Liverpool University. Within the next years Rachael and Sarah became part of the family.

We enjoyed our grandchildren who added much to our busy and satisfying lives. Charlie was now a journalist on the Daily Worker and I was absorbed in my teaching.

When in the early seventies Charlie and I visited Margaret, Gideon and the grandchildren, the house seemed full of young women, coming and going. It had become the centre for the Women's Liberation Movement in Liverpool. On the door of a large top floor room was the women's symbol and under it a notice, 'Quiet please – children sleeping'.

Although working full time as head of the Adult Literacy Department in Liverpool, Margaret was also one of the pioneers of this new feminist movement.

I had read Betty Frieden in the fifties, was aware something new was stirring but only slowly did I awaken to this new upsurge of feminism. "How is this different?" I asked, and in long conversations with her, learned a great deal from my daughter. I was exhilarated, moved by these young women, so different from my early days. They generated hope and expectation by their outspoken condemnation of much women had hitherto tolerated and accepted as their lot. My support for this new movement was wholehearted.

In fact I found the world in the late sixties and early seventies exciting and challenging. The young generation of the left had found new heroes and causes, new examples of dedication in the liberation movements of Asia, Africa and Latin America.

Che Guevara was proudly displayed on T-shirts. Ho-Chi-Min became a shouted slogan. Not for them the 'one and only' model. Socialism was the heroic fight by exploited and starving peoples for a human existence. For many Vietnam became their cause.

The great culmination for all came as students, belatedly joined by sections of workers, a brief moment took over Paris as the government rocked. Though it was not, nor could it have been, the 'revolution' of which they spoke, it was a stimulating time.

In Czechoslovakia Novotny, the one remaining Stalin protégé in Eastern Europe, was finally toppled from his throne. The Czech Party produced its Action Programme, the intellectuals their 'Two Thousand Words', the people their 'Prague Spring'. I cheered as our Party fully supported what the Czech communists and people were doing.

That was twenty years ago. Except for the acceptance that nuclear weapons mean annihilation for both antagonists, the world today has become a less pleasant and at times frightening place as greed takes over from compassion. Though there is no certainty, hope must remain that change will come yet again, bringing a better life to all people on this planet.

Epilogue

When I started these memoirs, I did not realise it would also be an education for me. As I read widely to establish more fully the background of events in which I had participated, I learned a great deal about the world into which I was born, saw how differently history has been interpreted. I learned a great deal about myself too.

My childhood was happy, with a strong mother who gave me confidence and a caring hardworking father who so often provided pleasure and excitement. I look back on a life of continuity with my parents. We wanted a better world in which poverty, class oppression and racist bigotry would no longer exist, and for the greater part of our lives, in different ways, we worked towards this goal.

But it became clear to me that those parts of the world now described as 'socialist' fell far short of the kind of society for which we had fought. Something new was needed as the old 'role model' of socialism had so obviously failed.

My conviction grew that not just those who held our views but more and more people, in their own ways, must become involved in the struggle for a just society.

For I believe 'democratic socialism', and it is the word 'democratic' which is important, can only become a reality when people actively work together, whether in the community, the public services or the workplace. To advance in a socialist direction political and economic decisions must be made by those whom they effect.

We cannot yet know how this 'democratic socialism' with its involvement of millions of people would develop for nowhere had it been tried. But it needs to be thought about, worked out. Then perhaps sometime in the future we will have a society which we may truly call 'socialist'.

As I end this book I look back not only on 'how it was' but how it might have been. My parents were socialists and I followed their path. Their belief in education pushed me into high school. My daughter Margaret and I talked one day about how chance as well as circumstance plays a part in our lives.

Had the 1929 crisis not occurred I'd have finished University, remained in the United States. Instead, I married a Scottish communist organiser and came to live in Britain.

If my parents had married in the old country and stayed there, I might have looked like those women selling 'lavenda', lavender oil, in the Yugoslav harbour of Hvar where I was on holiday. Though my age, they dressed in black, hair in a bun under a kerchief, faces wrinkled by wind and sun. That is, if I'd survived the German occupation through which they must have lived.

In Berlin had the Nazis caught me I might have disappeared to who knows where. And this could also have happened in Shanghai.

Had I gone back to work again as a courier in 1936 when they asked for me, I might have perished in some lonely camp in Siberia as many from the Comintern did.

If I'd remained in the States and never come to Britain, I'd have been caught up in the McCarthy witch hunt.

Even in the war when bombs fell on our Square, I was elsewhere.

Why had I somehow escaped alive from the struggles of those times?

Now at seventy-seven I realise I learned from my children who kept me in touch with much that was happening in their lives so that I understood and was prepared to accept the new.

Also, I look back on a past that is already history, material for research, theses, even films such as 'Reds', 'Julia', 'The Way We Were', each of which touches on a part of my life.

But what pleases me most is that through four generations, in my two children and six grandchildren, the humane socialist values of my parents have survived in diverse ways in this very different world.

Frieda Brewster 1988

The Four Generations

My mother Maria in retirement in Florida near my sister Paula

Me

In my garden at 24 Buckingham Road, Wanstead, London: my daughter Margaret Bentovim (Marge), Maria, my son Pat Devine

In CND demonstration, London: Marge, me, Pat

Vietnam protest, London, Christmas Day, 1970: Me, and my grandchildren, Ruth, Mike, John and Cath, and my daughter Margaret

Me and my grandchildren in Marge's home in Liverpool: Back row Ruth Ben-Tovim, Sarah Ben-Tovim, Mike Devine. Front row John Devine, Cath Devine, Rachael Ben-Tovim

Afterword

Our mother, Frieda, spent the last twenty years of her life writing this book. She lived in London and went to the City Lit, (City Literary Institute). She attended classes and made friends with the people in them. Some of them got together when the classes finished and formed their own circle. They supported each other, reading and commenting on each other's writing. This was an important time for her and she thoroughly enjoyed herself.

Our mother tried to get her book published but unfortunately was unable to do so. We have two large boxes of different drafts and comments from publishers. We tried to persuade her, but she refused to self-publish. Frieda wrote a number of different versions, ending with the one we have published. The language is hers and we have tried to keep to the original as far as possible.

We are publishing this book twenty seven years after her death. We are doing this for subsequent generations so that her life will be remembered and the lives of her parents, our grandparents. The record will be in print for us, her grandchildren, great grandchildren and great-great grandchildren. And the book will be available to historians of the Communist Party and of labour history in the USA and UK.

We are very grateful to our mother for her legacy to us, particularly her example of activism- if you see something that is wrong and unjust, you must act. She was a lifelong communist, despite some later reservations. The values she taught us underpinned her whole life: truth, justice and solidarity. She remained active throughout her life and one of the photos above shows her at a CND demonstration in her seventies and the back cover of the book shows her at the first Greenham Common Demonstration in nineteen eighty one.

We are also remembering with love and gratitude the warm, supportive home we had, which we can see in the book, was reflected in her own home life in the USA.

Mum was an amazing woman and we are so very lucky she was our parent.

Pat Devine and Marge Bentovim 2024

Pat

Marge

Next Generations

Pat's family photographs

From left to right Cath Devine, Gabriella Engineer (Cath's and Jeremy's daughter), Jeremy Engineer (Cath's partner)

From left to right John Devine, Elizabeth Draper (John's partner), Sam Devine (John's and Elizabeth's son)

From left to right Janette Cunningham (Mike's partner), Mike Devine

From left to right Ann Long (Pat's ex-wife and mother of Cath, John and Mike)

From left to right Pat and Elena Lieven (Pat's partner)

Marge's family photograph 2022

Back row from left Sarah Ben-Tovim (Marge's and Gideon's daughter), David Sargeant (Sarah's husband), Eric Gill (Rachael's husband), Leah Yeger (Ruth's and Ben's daughter), Rebecca Bentovim-Gill (Rachael's and Eric's daughter), Eva Ben-Tovim Sargeant (Sarah's and David's daughter), Gideon Ben-Tovim (Marge's husband), Ethan Ben-Tovim Sargeant (Sarah's and David's son), Marge Bentovim, Roseanna Anderson (Josh's wife), Joshua Ben-Tovim (Ruth's son), Sophie Yelland Bentovim (Rachael's daughter).

Bottom row from left Rachael Bentovim-Gill (Marge's and Gideon's daughter), Solomon Anderson Bentovim (Josh's and Roseanna's son), Naomi Yeger (Ruth's and Ben's daughter), Ruth Ben-Tovim (Marge's and Gideon's daughter), Ben Yeger (Ruth's husband)

APPENDIX

Liberal Club Press Cuttings

PITT LIBERALS DEFY CAMPUS B[AN]

PITT CLUB DEFIES BAN

Youth calshed with authority at the University of Pittsburgh today, and when the [smo]ke of battle cleared honors [we]re even. Victory perched, [te]mporarily at least, on the [ban]ners of both the contending [for]ces.

[In de]fiance of the administration, [the u]ndergraduates' Liberal Club [w]ithin the classic precincts of [the uni]versity, transacted business, [a]djourned in conformity with [the ca]nons of parliamentary prac[tice].

[B]ut—the motion to adjourn was hurriedly offered and passed after [Dr.] A. H. Armbruster, dean of men, [ap]peared at the door and told the [L]iberals:" "Get out of here!"

THREAT WINS—FOR TIME

There were a few moments. The president of the club, William Albertson, wanted to make the dean put them out.

And the secretary, Frieda Truhar, shouted a vigorous "No!" when the motion to adjourn was put.

When the dean took out his notebook and pencil, and bade his assistant, William Dauffenbach, give him the names of the defiant students the majority of the latter concluded that discretion was the better part of valor.

[DE]FIES CAMPUS BAN

The meeting thus dispersed re[con]vened with depleted attendance on the campus a few minutes later and passed by a vote of 19 to 5 the motion before the club at the time of the interruption—a resolution condemning the Pitt Weekly on the ground that it suppressed news and truckled to the administration.

STUDENTS SEEK TO JOIN

The club apparently proved to its own satisfaction that it had not been dissolved but was a going concern—and not only a going but a growing concern, for after the melee a crowd of students who had been watching the fun rushed up and asked to be enrolled as members.

To the throng of earnest souls who participated in the incident it was a very serious matter. The authorities, too, as represented by Dean Armbruster and Assistant Dauffenbach, plainly regarded it as no laughing matter. Yet it was not without its lighter aspects.

HALL CROWDED

That a meeting was to be held had been advertised, and when the "Liberals" crowded into room 323 in Alumni Hall and a throng of other students choked the corridor to see what would happen, the whole university knew that the meeting was on.

Dauffenbach, who dispersed the meeting last Monday when Dr. Harry Elmer Barnes, of Smith College, was to speak, came into the room several times with whispered messages and withdrew. Then he entered again and naively asked Albertson if a meeting was being held.

MEETING DEFIANT

On being definitely and firmly told that the Liberal Club was in session, he asked the meeting to disband.

"No!" came in defiant chorus.

Dauffenbach retired. The discussion of the Pitt Weekly resolution continued. Herman Recht, a former editor of the Weekly, said that not the university authorities, but the student editor was responsible for its policy.

Harry Weiss, Miss Truhar and Arthur McDowell replied. It was said the weekly had garbled the facts about the Liberal Club and not given it a fair deal. The weekly had said the meeting would not be held on the campus.

DEAN RUFFLED

Dauffenbach returned. With him was Armbruster, flushed and nervous. He commanded the "Liberals" to disperse.

"We will discuss your suggestion," said Albertson, with dignity.

"There is no time for discussion," said the dean. "Get out of here! You get out first!"

Albertson, unperturbed, asked the club what was its pleasure.

NOTEBOOK 'THREATENS'

Elliott Finkel moved to adjourn. "We need the university more than it needs us," was his plea. Frieda Truhar, fiery, defiant, scorned surrender.

Out came the dean's notebook.

"Who are these people, Bill?" he asked Dauffenbach.

Finkel moved to adjourn. Motion carried.

"I wish to state," said President Albertson, still with dignity, "that the Liberal Club has held an official meeting."

Applause from the student onlookers.

"Will they be expelled from the university?" a reporter asked the dean.

"Oh, be sensible, be reasonable, won't you?" he replied.

Refers to meeting held on Friday, April 26, 1929

Pittsburgh Press (?)

Meeting held on April 22, 192_

BACK VISITING ON PITT CAMPUS
WILLIAM ALBERTSON   W. L. NUNN

Photo by Pittsburgh Sun-Telegraph.

TOM TIPPETT
Mr. Tippett, speaker at the liberal meeting on Pitt campus, discussing with Students Albertson and McDowell and Graduate Assistant Wolt-

FRED WOLTMAN A. G. M'DOWELL
man their expulsion from the University for Liberal Club activities. Nunn was co-author with Woltman of an American Mercury artic

"LEARNING."

Editor of The Pittsburgh Press:

PLEASE allow me to thank you for your sane and liberal treatment of the present disturbances at our local university. It is well that such attempts to run a university (a "Cathedral of Learning" forsooth) like a medieval feudal barony should be given the publicity you have provided in your columns. At least those who have been asked to contribute to its building fund know now what sort of an institution they are called upon to support. I am sure that many pledges already secured would not have been obtained if the givers knew then what they know now. I know of at least one.

Inasmuch as Chancellor Bowman and his board of trustees seem to think their students are serfs with no rights a university is bound to respect, I suggest to them in all sincerity that they borrow the tactics of their confreres in the coal business and hire Cossacks (humorously referred to some[...] as coal and iron police) to pr[...] their vested interests in the realm of ideas—and politics.

These campus and class room police should be equipped with [cl]ubs, so that any expression of an opinion contrary to the likings of the overlords may be met with the treatment it deserves—a clout on the head of the offending student. Since, furthermore, all truth is already known to the overlords, and reserved for their exclusive benefit, these police should take the next logical step, and padlock the classrooms. Obviously discussion is a sheer waste of time if all truth is forever determined and static—and, above all, forever inaccessible to any man bearing the horrible taint of "liberal."

Will you be good enough, through the columns you set aside for this purpose, to convey these humble suggestions to the proper authorities of our noble "Cathedral of Learning?"

A. H. ROSENBLOOM.

"I'M GOING HOME" MOONEY BELIEVES AFTER 13 YEARS

By The United Press.

SAN QUENTIN STATE PRISON, Cal., May 10.—Convict No. 31,921, whose imprisonment has agitated capitalists and laborers, students and professors, attorneys and judges, even a president of the United States, has ordered his first suit of civilian clothes in 13 years.

Although clemency has not been granted No. 31,921, who lost his identity as Tom Mooney in 1917, the aftermath of the San Francisco preparedness parade shambles, is confident of liberty.

In his first public utterance in years here today, given in an interview with the United Press, Mooney declared he was "going home."

* * *

TOM MOONEY, whose petition for pardon is to be reviewed by Gov. C. C. Young within the next few days, has walked within the shadow of the noose. The 46-year-old former labor leader, found guilty of the bombing which snuffed out the lives of 10 persons and injured 40 others, gave ample proof of this as he walked into the interview room.

He might easily have been mistaken for 60. There was vigor in his handclasp and gleam in his brown eyes, but bowed shoulders, graying hair and deeply furrowed features gave testimony of his confinement.

* * *

"YES, I'M GOING home," he reaffirmed with a smile long ago burned down by the biting winds that sweep across San Pablo Bay to the bleak prison farm lands.

"For 13 years I have waited for the moment I know is near. During every waking hour of that time when not assigned to prison duties, I have toiled to perfect the documents which are now in the hands of Governor Young. A 3,000-word petition, written by myself and bound here in the prison, has been presented to him by Tom Walsh.

"For several years he has failed to act. But the time for action has come. Every shred of evidence against me has been proven framed or perjured. Public sentiment has reached its highest pitch and the influence behind the movement for my pardon commands widespread respect.

* * *

"IF AWAKENED public interest doesn't suddenly die out I feel positive that I shall walk the streets of San Francisco again before the close of 1929, a free man," he concluded with somewhat of an effort, his breath coming in labored gasps.

"If public interest does die out," he said, "it'wil ltake 13 more years."

The first note of despair crept into his voice but it was gone in a moment and a smile lit his face once more.

* * *

THE PREPAREDNESS Day bombing occurred July 22, 1916, and a few days later Mooney and his wife, Warren K. Billings, a labor leader; Israel Weinburg, a taxi driver, and Edward Nolan, president of the Machinists' Union, Lodge 68, were arrested.

Mooney was convicted and sentenced to death. Billings was sentenced to life imprisonment. The others were never tried, as it was learned before their trials that the state's chief witness had perjured himself.

Upon the request of President Wilson, Mooney's sentence was commuted to life imprisonment. Since then many of those who were chiefly instrumental in his conviction have taken earnest action to secure his pardon.

* * *

AMONG THESE are the trial judge, Franklin A. Grieffin, and Freemont Older, who at the time of the outrage was editor of the San Francisco Bulletin.

That Mooney was a victim of war time hysteria is the contention of such men as Frank P. Walsh, Senator Thomas D. Schall of Minnesota and others prominent in public life.

The latest barrage laid down in favor of Mooney came from the Pi Sigma Alpha chapter at Stanford University.

Noted professors of political science including Thomas S. Barclay, G. H. Stuart and Edwin A. Cottrell signed a petition to the governor asking "unconditional pardon" of Mooney.

TOM MOONEY SPURNS PAROLE

Freedom May Be Short Lived Due to Stomach

By The United Press.

SAN QUENTIN STATE PRISON Cal., May 11.—The freedom which Tom Mooney believes at last is within his grasp, after 13 years imprisonment, may be short lived.

While the state may give back his liberty, another death sentence still hangs over him.

The man who was convicted of the San Francisco Preparedness Day bombing in 1916, which cost the lives of 10 persons, is suffering from an incurable stomach ailment. Aside from gaining his liberty, his one object in life is to regain his health.

"But I would rather rot in San Quentin than accept a parole," Mooney said. "My friends have urged again and again that I avail myself of parole privileges, but I'll stay here until the unconditional pardon which I deserve is granted."

With Governor C. C. Young expected to review his 3,000-word appeal for pardon within the next few days, Mooney confidentially expects to be liberated.

Family Photographs – Croatia

In Vucovar, Croatia, 1875: from left to right Sebastian's mother Apolonia, Sebastian's grandmother, Sebastian's aunt

*Grave of Anton and Apolonia Truhar (Sebastian's parents), died 1920, 1921, Vucovar, Croatia.
Inscription at bottom (German language):
Love from your children in America*

Anton and Apolonia Truhar (grave close up)

*Pichler gravestone in Ilca, Croatia,
(possibly Maria Truhar's father and mother).
Inscription on grave (German language):
Here rest in peace Adam Pichler 1842-1888 and his wife Maria
married again Blum 1861-1937. Mourned by their children*

www.ingramcontent.com/pod-product-compliance
Lightning Source LLC
Chambersburg PA
CBHW042146160426
43202CB00023B/2988